Deja Reviews:
Florence King
All Over Again

Selections from
National Review
and
The American Spectator
1990 to 2001

*For my friend, Jack Fowler, who has
endeared himself to a misanthrope.*

Deja Reviews: Florence King All Over Again
Selections from *National Review* and *The American Spectator*, 1990 to 2001

© 2006 by The Intercollegiate Studies Institute.

Library of Congress Cataloging-in-Publication Data:

Deja reviews : Florence King All Over Again, 2006931898

Deja reviews : Florence King All Over Again : selections from
National review and the American spectator, 1990-2001. 1st ed. --
Wilmington, DE : ISI Books, c2006.

p. ; cm.
ISBN-13: 978-1-933859-16-3
ISBN-10: 1-933859-16-4

1. King, Florence--Literary collections. I. King, Florence.
II. National Review. III. American spectator.

PS3561.I4754 A6 2007
818/.5409--dc22   0704

Jacket Design by Luba Myts

PRINTED IN THE UNITED STATES OF AMERICA

TABLE OF CONTENTS

INTRODUCTION

D on't make the same mistake I did and devour this book all at one setting, no matter how delicious each course. Restrain yourself or you'll risk a bad case of intellectual and aesthetic overload—because these essays are both an education and a delight. You're liable to have so much fun you won't realize how much you're learning.

The hallmark of a Florence King essay, book review or just general fulmination is that it includes both ends of the stylistic spectrum—rough-and-ready candor and exquisite judgment—but she doesn't mess with anything in between. The lady knows nothing of mediocrity. Which may be why any collection of her writings goes off like a fireworks display. Any attempt at transition between the blasts would be ludicrous, like playing a waltz between artillery barrages.

Yet there is a refinement about her bottle-rocket prose that lifts it beyond the polemical. Maybe that's why, though she may have plenty of imitators by now, Florence King has no equal.

What's her secret? My theory is that she keeps her rage flippant, and her humor raging. She's funny about things others treat oh-so-seriously, and serious about what others might not even notice. She's never met a superficial phrase she couldn't dissect, and is careful to point out its stupidities and dangers before dispatching it on the spot. Without getting a spot of blood on her. Like a one-woman firing squad.

Florence King may be a social critic in the spirit of a Mencken or Thorstein Veblen, but her style is her own as she slices through our media-induced coma like an Arkansas toothpick, aka a Bowie knife. These pieces are all evidence of a solitary mind at work demolishing the solemn idiocies of our time.

Reading this book is like having a maven guide you through the great bazaar that is contemporary American, so to speak, culture. It's a kind of public service.

Miss Florence may need only a phrase to polish off an idea, a personality, a style, or a widespread fallacy—even when they're combined in one insufferable package. ("A beau ideal of the New Man is columnist Richard Cohen, the *Washington Post*'s resident oh-dear, who is such a bundle of sensitivity that if he had been on the *Titanic* he would have apologized for damage to the iceberg.") Her acid wit makes her praise all the more coveted when she points out a gem of a book or idea. She's got a collector's eye for the bon mot ("Good writing is counterrevolutionary"—Ellen Willis), and an unrestrained enthusiasm for the worthy and civilized if and when she comes across it.

All of which may explain why my favorite part of this collection may be the book reviews. Florence King's specialty is the good review of a bad book. It would be hard, it might be impossible, to top this opening paragraph of one such review:

"Back in the Cold War, whenever I had to review an unreadable book, I always comforted myself with the thought, 'Maybe the Russians will drop the Bomb and I won't have to finish reading this.' Those were the days. This time, stuck with *A Pilgrim's Way: The Personal Story of the Episcopal Bishop Charged with Heresy for Ordaining a Gay Man Who Was in a Committed Relationship*, by the Rt. Rev. Walter C. Righter, author of the longest subtitle in publishing history, all I could hope for was an asteroid."

But beyond all Miss King's delicious lines—at times the whole book reads like La Rochefoucauld on a roll—there are original insights aplenty, including what may be the best summation of the Southern character this side of John Shelton Reed, the tarheel sociologist better known as the de Tocqueville of Dixie. In a just-about-perfect essay ("South Mouth: Why Liberals Hate Dixie") Miss Florence counts off the three distinguishing characteristics of the Southerner, all of which she herself has in abundance: Identity, Eccentricity, and Complexity. Only she makes complexity simple, which is the crowning achievement of any great essayist.

Somewhere in this feast for both mind and digestion (on Page 320, to be exact), our author mentions a "cryptic observation" about her writing she once received from Helen Gurley Brown of *Cosmo* fame. It came in the form of a note on one of her articles for that magazine: "Well, we never get anything pippypoo from Florence, she's always so warpy-and-woofy."

Miss Florence may have found the phrase cryptic, but her fans won't. Translation: Even her lightest remarks have behind them a craft and design, a basic structure and sure orientation, all too rare in this Age of Borax. What a rarity and refreshment. Enjoy.

—Paul Greenberg
Little Rock, Arkansas
June, 2006

National Review, July 9, 1990
Essay

"I'd Rather Smoke than Kiss"

I AM A WOMAN of 54 who started smoking at the late age of 26. I had no reason to start earlier; smoking as a gesture of teenage rebellion would have been pointless in my family. My mother started at 12. At first her preferred brands were the Fatimas and Sweet Caporals that were all the rage during World War I. Later she switched to Lucky Strike Greens and smoked four packs a day.

She made no effort to cut down while she was pregnant with me, but I was not a low-birth-weight baby. The Angel of Death saw the nicotine stains on our door and passed over; I weighed nine pounds. My smoke-filled childhood was remarkably healthy and safe except for the time Mama set fire to my Easter basket. That was all right, however, because I was not the Easter-basket type.

I probably wouldn't have started smoking if I had not been a writer. One day in the drugstore I happened to see a display of Du Maurier English cigarettes in pretty red boxes with a tray that slid out like a little drawer. I thought the boxes would be ideal for keeping my paperclips in, so I bought two.

When I got home, I emptied out the cigarettes and replaced them with paperclips, putting the loose cigarettes in the desk drawer where the loose paperclips had been scattered. Now the cigarettes were scattered. One day, spurred by two of my best traits, neatness and thrift,

I decided that the cigarettes were messing up the desk and going to waste, so I tried one.

It never would have happened if I had been able to offer the Du Mauriers to a lover who smoked, but I didn't get an addicted one until after I had become addicted myself. When he entered my life it was the beginning of a uniquely pleasurable footnote to sex: the post-coital cigarette.

Today when I see the truculent, joyless faces of anti-tobacco Puritans, I remember those easy-going smoking sessions with that man: the click of the lighter, the brief orange glow in the darkness, the ashtray between us—spilling sometimes because we laughed so much together that the bed shook.

A cigarette ad I remember from my childhood said: "One of life's great pleasures is smoking. Camels give you all of the enjoyment of choice tobaccos. Is enjoyment good for you? You just bet it is." My sentiments exactly. I believe life should be savored rather than lengthened, and I am ready to fight the misanthropes among us who are trying to make me switch.

A *misanthrope* is someone who hates people. Hatred of smokers is the most popular form of closet misanthropy in America today. Smokists don't hate the sin, they hate the sinner, and they don't care who knows it.

Their campaign never would have succeeded so well if the alleged dangers of smoking had remained a problem for smokers alone. We simply would have been allowed to invoke the Right to Die, always a favorite with democratic lovers of mankind, and that would have been that. To put a real damper on smoking and make it stick, the right of others not to die had to be invoked somehow, so "passive smoking" was invented.

The name was a stroke of genius. Just about everybody in America is passive. Passive Americans have been taking it on the chin for years, but the concept of passive smoking offered them a chance to hate in the land of compulsory love, a chance to dish it out for a change with no fear of being called a bigot. The right of self-defense, long since gone up in smoke, was back.

Smokers on the Run

THE BIG, brave Passive Americans responded with a vengeance. They began shouting at smokers in restaurants. They shuddered and grimaced and said "Ugh!" as they waved away the impure air. They put up little signs in their cars and homes: at first they said, "Thank You for Not Smoking," but now they feature a cigarette in a circle slashed with a red diagonal. Smokists even issue conditional invitations. I know—I got one. The woman said, "I'd love to have you to dinner, but I don't allow smoking in my home. Do you think you could refrain for a couple of hours?" I said, "Go ---- yourself," and she told everybody I was the rudest person she had ever met.

Smokists practice a sadistic brutality that would have done Vlad the Impaler proud. *Washington Times* columnist and smoker Jeremiah O'Leary was the target of two incredibly baleful letters to the editor after he defended the habit. The first letter said, "Smoke yourself to death, but please don't smoke me to death," but it was only a foretaste of the letter that followed:

> Jeremiah O'Leary's March 1 column, "Perilous persuaders . . . tenacious zealots," is a typical statement of a drug addict trying to defend his vice.
>
> To a cigarette smoker, all the world is an ashtray. A person who would never throw a candy wrapper or soda can will drop a lit cigarette without a thought.
>
> Mr . O'Leary is mistaken that nonsmokers are concerned about the damage smokers are inflicting on themselves. What arrogance! We care about living in a pleasant environment without the stench of tobacco smoke or the litter of smokers' trash.
>
> If Mr. O'Leary wants to kill himself, that is his choice. I ask only that he do so without imposing his drug or discarded filth on me. *It would be nice if he would die in such a way that would not increase my health-insurance rates* [my italics].

The expendability of smokers has also aroused the tender concern of the Federal Government. I was taking my first drag of the morning when I opened the *Washington Post* and found myself staring at this headline: NOT SMOKING COULD BE HAZARDOUS TO PENSION SYSTEM.

MEDICARE, SOCIAL SECURITY MAY BE PINCHED IF ANTI-TOBACCO CAM-PAIGN SUCCEEDS, REPORT SAYS. The article explained that since smokers die younger than non-smokers, the Social Security we don't live to collect is put to good use, because we subsidize the pensions of our fellow citizens like a good American should. However, this convenient arrangement could end, for if too many smokers heed the Surgeon General's warnings and stop smoking, they will live too long and break the budget.

That, of course, is not how the government economists phrased it. They said:

> The implications of our results are that smokers "save" the Social Security system hundreds of billions of dollars. Certainly this does not mean that decreased smoking would not be socially beneficial. In fact, it is probably one of the most cost-effective ways of increasing average longevity. It does indicate, however, that if people alter their behavior in a manner which extends life expectancy, then this must be recognized by our national retirement program.

At this point the reporter steps in with the soothing reminder that "the war on tobacco is more appropriately cast as a public-health crusade than as an attempt to save money." But then we hear from Health Policy Center economist Gio Gori, who says: "Prevention of disease is obviously something we should strive for. But it's not going to be cheap. We will have to pay for those who survive."

Something darkling crawls out of that last sentence. The whole article has a die-damn-you undertow that would make an honest misanthrope wonder if perhaps a cure for cancer was discovered years ago, but due to cost-effectiveness considerations . . .

But honest misanthropes are at a premium that no amount of Raleigh coupons can buy. Instead we have tinpot Torquemadas like Ahron Leichtman, president of Citizens against Tobacco Smoke, who announced after the airline smoking ban: "CATS will next launch its smoke-free airports project, which is the second phase of our smoke-free skies campaign." Representative Richard J. Durbin (D., Ill.) promised the next target will be "other forms of public transportation such as Amtrak, the inter-city bus system, and commuter lines that receive federal funding." His colleague, Senator Frank Lautenberg (D., N.J.), confessed, "We *are* gloating a little bit," and Fran Du Melle of the Coalition on Smoking OR Health, gave an ominous hint of things to come when she heralded the airline ban as "only one encouraging step on the road to a smoke-free society."

Health Nazis

THESE REMARKS manifest a sly, cowardly form of misanthropy that the Germans call *Schadenfreude*: pleasure in the unhappiness of others. It has always been the chief subconscious motivation of Puritans, but the smokists harbor several other subconscious motivations that are too egregious to bear close examination—which is precisely what I will now conduct.

Study their agitprop and you will find the same theme of pitiless revulsion running through nearly all of their so-called public-service ads. One of the earliest showed Brooke Shields toweling her wet hair and saying disgustedly, "I hate it when somebody smokes after I've just washed my hair. Yuk!" Another proclaimed, "Kissing a smoker is like licking an ashtray." The latest, a California radio spot, asks: "Why sell cigarettes? Why not just sell phlegm and cut out the middle man?"

Fear of being physically disgusting and smelling bad is the American's worst nightmare, which is why bathsoap commercials never include the controlled-force shower nozzles recommended by environmentalists in *their* public-service ads. The showering American uses oceans of hot water to get "ZESTfully clean" in a sudsy deluge that is often followed by a deodorant commercial.

"Raise your hand, raise your hand, raise your hand if you're SURE!" During this jingle we see an ecstatically happy assortment of people from all walks of life and representing every conceivable national origin, all obediently raising their hands, until the ad climaxes with a shot of the Statue of Liberty raising hers.

The New Greenhorns

THE STATUE of Liberty has become a symbol of immigration, the first aspect of American life the huddled masses experienced.

The second was being called a "dirty little" something-or-other as soon as they got off the boat. Deodorant companies see the wisdom in reminding their descendants of the dirty-little period. You can sell a lot of deodorant that way. Ethnics get the point directly; WASPs get it by default in the sublimininal reminder that, historically speaking, there is no such thing as a dirty little WASP.

Smokers have become the new greenhorns in the land of sweetness and health, scapegoats for a quintessentially American need, rooted in our fabled Great Diversity, to identify and punish the undesirables among us. Ethnic tobacco haters can get even for past slurs on their fastidiousness by refusing to inhale around dirty little smokers; WASP tobacco haters can once again savor the joys of being the "real Americans" by hurling with impunity the same dirty little insults their ancestors hurled with impunity.

The tobacco pogrom serves additionally as the basis for a class war in a nation afraid to mention the word "class" aloud. Hating smokers is an excellent way to hate the white working class without going on record as hating the white working class.

The anti-smoking campaign has enjoyed thumping success among the "data-receptive," a lovely euphemism describing the privilege of spending four years sitting in a classroom. The ubiquitous statistic that college graduates are two-and-a-half times as likely to be non-smokers as those who never went beyond high school is balm to the data-receptive, many of whom are only a generation or two removed from the lunchbucket that smokers represent. Haunted by a fear of falling back down the ladder, and half-believing that they deserve to, they soothe their anxiety by kicking a smoker as the proverbial hen-pecked husband soothed his by kicking the dog.

The earnest shock that greeted the RJR Reynolds Uptown marketing scheme aimed at blacks cramped the vituperative style of the data-receptive. Looking down on blacks as smokers might be interpreted as looking down on blacks as blacks, so they settled for aping the compassionate concern they picked up from the media.

They got their sadism-receptive bona fides back when the same company announced plans to target Dakota cigarettes at a fearsome group called "virile females."

When I first saw the headline I thought surely they meant me: what other woman writer is sent off to a book-and-author luncheon with the warning, "Watch your language and don't wear your Baltimore Orioles warm-up jacket"? But they didn't. Virile females are "Caucasian females, 18 to 24, with no education beyond high school and entry-level service or factory jobs."

Commentators could barely hide their smirks as they listed the tractor pulls, motorcycle races, and machoman contests that comprise the leisure activities of the target group. Crocodile tears flowed copiously. "It's blue-collar people without enough education to understand what is happening to them," mourned Virginia Ernster of the University of California School of Medicine. "It's pathetic that these companies would work so hard to get these women who may not feel much control over their lives." George Will, winner of the metaphorman contest, wrote: "They use sophisticated marketing like a sniper's rifle, drawing beads on the most vulnerable, manipulable Americans." (I would walk a mile to see Virginia Ernster riding on the back of George Will's motorcycle.)

Hating smokers is also a guiltless way for a youth-worshipping country to hate old people, as well as those who are merely over the hill—especially middle-aged women. Smokers predominate in both groups because we saw Bette Davis's movies the same year they were released. Now we catch *Dark Victory* whenever it comes on television just for the pleasure of watching the scene in the staff lounge at the hospital when Dr. George Brent and all the other doctors light up.

Smoking is the only thing that the politically correct can't blame on white males. Red men started it, but the cowardly cossacks of the anti-tobacco crusade don't dare say so because it would be too close for comfort. They see no difference between tobacco and hard drugs like cocaine and crack because they don't wish to see any. Never mind that you will never be mugged by someone needing a cigarette; hatred of smokers is the conformist's substitute for the hatred that dare not speak its name. Condemning "substance abuse" out of hand, without picking and choosing or practicing discrimination, produces lofty sensations of democratic purity in those who keep moving farther and farther out in the suburbs to get away from . . . smokers.

National Review, February 11, 1991
Essay

"Don't Have a Nice Day"

MANY AMERICANS are unfamiliar with the word *misanthrope*, as I discovered when I tried to discourage a persistent Southern women's club that wanted me to serve as its guide on a literary tour of Europe.

"I can't, I'm a misanthrope."

"Oh, honey, you don't have to let it cramp your style! My sister-in-law's a diabetic and she can go anywhere she wants as long as she takes her little kit with her."

Like any personality trait, misanthropy is a matter of degree. Taken in the literal sense, the obvious problem is one of logistics: hating the entire human race is hard to do, though a few flinty souls have done it. In the figurative sense, however, misanthropy is a realistic attitude toward human nature that Americans would do well to understand and adopt.

We hold dual citizenship in the Republic of Nice and the Republic of Mean. Torn between smile buttons and happy talk on the one side and Balkanization on the other, we are going as crazy as Timon of Athens, the philanthropist-turned-misanthrope of whom Shakespeare said: "The middle of humanity thou never knewest, but the extremity of both ends."

As citizens of the Republic of Nice we are so afraid of our dark side that hostile situations barely get started before somebody pops up and announces, "The healing has begun." Fear of getting mad is so widespread that nobody says *mad* any more. The word is *angry*: somehow it sounds less mad than *mad*. To make sure nobody gets *angry*, we pre-soften each other constantly in ways that are becoming more and more bizarre.

Recently I sent away to a Danish import house for a table that arrived unassembled. I didn't have too much trouble putting it together—it was a five-goddammit job—but what got me worked up was the packing label: *"Warning! This box contains confusing instructions from Denmark. Please use our friendly instructions packed outside this box."* *Friendly* has become a synonym for *clear* and *concise* because clarity and concision are cool qualities. It began with "user-friendly" computers to make cold technology warm, and now nearly every inanimate gizmo is touted as friendly.

In the Republic of Nice, the soft-spoken are king. Television anchors, who must somehow project an air of unthreatening authority, are lately solving this conundrum by swallowing the end of their sentences. Peter Jennings is the worst offender; his voice disappears into a prissy smirk and a little nod that recalls Colette Dowling's description of the speech patterns of unassertive women. In *The Cinderella Complex: Women's Hidden Fear of Independence*, Miss Dowling says that female executives afraid of losing their femininity turn orders into questions by raising their voices at the end of sentences, e.g.: "I want that report by tomorrow?" Miss Dowling calls this the "Diffident Declarative."

The Republic of Nice has a Rumpelstiltsken Complex. Living in dread of exploding in foot-stamping, purple-faced rage like the foul-tempered gnome in the fairy tale, we have devised various safeguards.

Plugging up safety valves is our favorite way of keeping everybody calm. In her horrified appraisal of my last book, *Lump It or Leave It*, Martha Peters of the *El Paso Times* insists that "satire is only funny when it is neither embittered nor mean." That would be news to several people in the pantheon of Western civilization, but Walter B. Schwab of Providence puts Jonathan Swift and Anatole France in their place in his May 14, 1990, letter to *Time*: "Disparaging humor is verbal abuse and can be as damaging as the physical kind, if not more so. It destroys self-esteem."

An obstetrics ward became a brooding ground for self-esteem when a couple sued a Nashville hospital for $4 million on learning that the nurses had nicknamed their baby daughter "Smurfette" because she was born blue from blue dye injected into her mother's womb during a prenatal test.

"Painful though these events have been, we have all learned a great deal about how sensitive and fragile our society is, how deeply people and groups can be hurt if great care is not taken in conducting public discourse." No, that has nothing to do with Smurfette. That's CBS president David Burke after suspending Andy Rooney for allegedly making cracks about people of another color, but it fits any self-esteem emergency. It also fits on a Miranda-sized card so that the five remaining spontaneous citizens of the Republic of Nice can carry it around in their wallets in case they slip up and say something interesting.

Code words are the pretty packages full of friendly instructions in which we wrap our real meanings. Some, like *inner city*, have been around for years, but the one that is all the rage lately is *dialogue*.

Not long ago a member of the Nation of Islam gave a speech at Fredericksburg's Mary Washington College. It was the usual Farrakhan farrago: up with Hitler, down with Jews and other whites, plus a locally tailored insult to George Washington's mother, for whom the college is named. The speech triggered such hysteria on campus that professors had to use class time for "tension-defusing" discussions of racial issues. Our local paper's letters-to-the-editor column divided along black-white lines and a town-gown split emerged, but how did the college administration describe it all? The banner headline read: MUSLIM SPEECH CREDITED FOR SPURRING DIALOGUE.

Another way the Republic of Nice puts the lid on its Rumpelstiltsken Complex is through "stress management," a phrase so suggestive of gritted teeth that you can almost hear the scrunch. The stress industry has cooperated by abandoning medicine's earlier claim that letting off steam is good for you, and so we have: TRUST HELPS HEARTS. BLOWING YOUR TOP COULD BE HAZARDOUS TO YOUR HEALTH, TWO STUDIES INDICATE.

One of these "wellness" studies took place at Duke University, the house that tobacco built, and involved 118 male lawyers who scored "hostile" on a personality test. The testees were described as "rude, abrasive, surly, critical, uncooperative, condescending, and disagreeable"—the law firm of choice for litigious Americans. Among the researchers was Dr. Redford B. Williams Jr., author of *The Trusting Heart*, who warns: "Having anger is bad for you, whether you express it or not. But we found that people who said they made a point of letting other people know they were angry had higher death rates."

The best way to bottle up anger is to turn men into women. After years of consensus seeking, reaching out, coming together, building bridges, linking arms, and tying yellow ribbons, the feminization of America is now complete. American men have been turned into their own secret police, under orders to kick down their own doors in the middle of the night and arrest themselves for "insensitivity."

A beau ideal of the New Man is columnist Richard Cohen, the *Washington Post*'s resident oh-dear, who is such a bundle of sensitivity that if he had been on the *Titanic* he would have apologized for damage to the iceberg. Male soul-searching is in and Cohen is its undisputed champ, having searched his own so often that he has become Butterfly Dundee, the man every woman would least like to have with her if she met a mugger.

Today's men have adopted the age-old feminine stratagem of hurt feelings and the newer feminist technique of politicized nagging to get their points across, as when a snippy Dan Rather demanded of his man in Alaska: "Did Hazelwood ever apologize for the *Valdez* oil spill?" But nothing is more infuriating than female strategy. Armed with her silken weaponry of ambivalence, circularity, and freighted silences, woman burrows into her adversary's very soul—sideways, like a tick crossed with a mole crossed with a crab. Instead of "humanizing" men, it would have been far better if women had copied men's stoic *virtus*. A nation of self-controlled people is less likely to blow than one giving off beta-consciousness waves. The hatreds we are trying to tamp down and deny have a much better chance of coming to the surface when people are "in touch with their feelings." If they do, they will be all the more violent from having been subjected to the feminized tactics of the Republic of Nice.

Republic of Mean

THE FLIP SIDE of the Republic of Nice is the Republic of Mean. Closet misanthropes lie thick on the ground.

How about some proportional misanthropy? "Beef! Real food for *real* people." George Bush in Omaha: "It's good to be away from Washington and out here with the *real* people." Rosalynn Carter's press secretary: "She's in touch with the *real* people." Take your pick and hate the rest.

Egged on by the compassion-impaired, some of the handicapped have turned into ogres hurling epithets at anyone who says "confined" to a wheelchair, or who does *not* say "differently abled." Somerset Maugham anticipated these closet misanthropes when he wrote: "It is not true that suffering ennobles the character; happiness does that sometimes, but suffering, for the most part, makes men petty and vindictive."

Our eagerness to get away from each other has made the ubiquitous "Ten Most Livable Cities" article beloved by closet misanthropes. People are desperate to escape crime, pollution, noise, rudeness, and traffic jams—i.e., people. Once they move somewhere new to get away from people, they find that they are hated by people who hate people who are trying to get away from people they hate.

The Welcome Wagon is dead. I see the handwriting on the mall, and it's a bumper sticker: Seattle: DON'T CALIFORNICATE THE STATE OF WASHINGTON. Oregon: COME SEE US BUT GO BACK HOME. Atlanta: GENERAL SHERMAN, WHERE ARE YOU NOW THAT WE NEED YOU?

Equality of Bigotry

RAINBOW misanthropy? It's a mystery to me how anyone can look at the proliferation of support groups and not see them for what they really are: a lunatic quest for birds of a feather by people so sick of our great diversity that they unconsciously reject it by joining Tone-Deaf Parents of Lefthanded Anorexic Kleptomaniacs just to be with their own kind.

A leading rainbow misanthrope is Sonny Carson, the black convicted kidnapper who worked in the campaign of New York Mayor David "Gorgeous Mosaic" Dinkins. Accused of being anti-Semitic, Carson replied: "Anti-Semitic? I'm anti-white. Don't limit my anti-ing to just being one little group of people." Spoken like a true misanthrope.

A movement toward equality of bigotry is leading to misanthropy by accretion. Karen Schwartz of the Gay and Lesbian Alliance Against Defamation (GLAAD) said of the Andy Rooney flap: "GLAAD opposes all forms of bigotry and believes that if you scratch a homophobe you'll probably find a racist." By this logic, the scratched racist, if scratched repeatedly, will prove to be anti-Semitic, will prove to be antiCatholic, will prove to be anti-Slavic, and so on down the list until we achieve raw misanthropy—literally.

The widespread hatred of television is a form of closet misanthropy of special interest to anyone who grew up in the radio era. We didn't hate radio and blame it for all sorts of ills. We didn't worry about how many hours a day our radios were on, and we didn't lie about our radio habits ("I never listen to it").

Today we have Judy Mann in the *Washington Post* on "Turning Off the TV Habit," about her family's cold-turkey withdrawal from the electronic beast.

"I don't miss it at all," she insists in the third paragraph. It's a one-sentence paragraph, standing alone for greater dramatic emphasis.

She goes on to say, "you realize how stupid the sitcoms are," "It is a terrible time-waster," and "Television is a lot like smoking: you only realize what a rotten habit it is once you've stopped." She also quotes her husband—"He thinks it destroys the mind"—and a Washington-area English teacher: "If TV is like a drug that numbs the mind, excessive viewing amounts to drug abuse."

Television rouses us to instinctive loathing because it is the only medium of entertainment in which the great do not keep their distance. In the Thirties and Forties, radio was a disembodied voice, while movies presented godlike stars who were figuratively larger than life and made them literally larger than life on giant screens. But the democratic size of the television screen and its permanent presence in our homes have deprived us of personages awesome and mysterious, damaging thereby the psychic dynamo that powers religious faith. In the primitive recesses of our minds, television is to us what Antichrists and heretics were to the Middle Ages.

The most revolting form of closet misanthropy is the "Oprah's Guest" syndrome. Masquerading as compassionate broad-mindedness but really driven by the notion that dignity is undemocratic, it demands that people strip themselves of all that is seemly and wallow in maudlin sludge.

MARYLAND COUPLE SHARES A GIFT OF LOVE: HER KIDNEY. After the area's first spousal transplant, the couple "crept together through the hospital corridors, both slightly bent with pain," while their teenage children "hung out with them, looking after mom and dad and making home videos of them."

When they left the hospital to go home, the husband wore a T-shirt inscribed: "My wife gave me her heart and all her love. Now she gave me a kidney." He went on: "I was so glad. I had my catheter and my bag of what we call liquid gold. I said, "Timmie, look at this,' indicating that the new kidney was working."

Added the *Washington Post* reporter: "The Warners are the kind of people who view obstacles as challenges—the glass half full, not half empty, as Kenneth Warner put it. And they are 'goal-oriented' people, he said. Warner decided he wanted a transplant kidney, and he set Christmas as his personal deadline."

But who would donate it? Said Mrs. Warner: "We woke up on a Saturday morning and I said, Why can't I give you a kidney?'" And so she did. And left the hospital wearing a T-shirt inscribed: "I gave my husband my heart and all my love. Now I gave him a kidney."

Everybody's Friend

M Y COFFEE CUP is half empty. While I pour myself a refill, look at this:

It's a Christmas postcard from Congressperson Patricia Schroeder, who evidently culled my name from the *Ms.* subscription list. The picture shows the whole family, including the dog, frolicking in the snow. The message reads: "Santa's back! So are Jim, Pat,

Scott, Jamie & Wolfie Schroeder! Jamie is a sophomore at Princeton studying Chinese. Scott works at ABC News in D.C. Jim works at paying bills and Pat works at passing them! Wolfie sleeps! Best Holiday Wishes for a great 1990. Pat & the gang." Of course, Pat contains a smiley face in the circle of the P.

It is not necessary to like people to respect them. The Schroeders among us miss a vital point that we of cooler temperaments instinctively understand: Familiarity doesn't breed contempt, it *is* contempt.

The suspicion that David Souter might share this view—might, in fact, be a misanthropic hermit—sent America into a tailspin when the fifty-year-old bachelor was nominated to the Supreme Court.

"Judge Souter is our Rorschach test," wrote *Washington Times* columnist Suzanne Fields, "telling us more about ourselves than about him." He certainly did. The vaunted independence that Americans cherish consists of two things: the single-issue pressure group and the automobile. We boast about our rugged individualism, yet when an avatar of it draws near to a position of power, we go nuts.

Women's groups demanded reassurance that Souter would "empathize" with women's issues. Presumably they meant "sympathize," though with feminists you never know. Alan Dershowitz seemed to hint at something really nasty: "I mean, this is a fifty-year-old bachelor who lives with sheep in Weare, N.H., out of this world."

Time called him "An Eighteenth-Century Man," forgetting that the Founding Fathers were too, and warned: "The more serious question about Souter's ascetic ways is whether a man who seems to prefer books to people can empathize [there it is again] with and understand the problems of ordinary people."

Finally, somebody dredged up a Souter date from the early Sixties, Ellanor Stengel Fink, who did her best to reassure the land of the free and the home of the brave.

"What doesn't come across in the accounts I've read is what a warm, friendly guy he can be," she rhapsodized. "He comes across as a steely intellectual. All head and no heart. He is a very bright person and very interesting, but he's not all brain. He's a friendly, warm person and extremely considerate." Not only that, his parents were very warm, friendly lovely people. A traditional, close family."

I daresay many people fully expected Souter's isolated cellar to yield up a dozen or so female corpses murdered by him over the years. And why not? Every newspaper reader in America knows what murderers are like: SLAYING SUSPECT DESCRIBED AS LONER. According to the suspect's neighbors, he always "kept himself to himself" and "had trouble at work." But the victim? Listen to his neighbors: "Everybody loved him, he got along with everybody. He didn't have an enemy in the world. He was such a happy person. I remember he always said a stranger is a friend you haven't met yet. He would give you the shirt off his back. One day a homeless came to the door and asked him for a drink of water, and he invited him in for a meal. He was always smiling, I never saw him frown, no, not once. Our kids were crazy about him."

To suggest that this hot, wet paragon might have had a fatal flaw, and that it might have had something to do with America's blackout of the maxim, "Everybody's friend is everybody's fool," is not permitted. Nonetheless, it is a truth universally unacknowledged that loners go happily through life, keeping themselves to themselves and having trouble at work until they die in their beds at the age of 96.

Unabashed misanthropy evokes a surprising response, as Robert Lewis Taylor notes in his biography of W. C. Fields: "Fields's defiance of civilization, over a period of 67 years, became an institution in which the public took pride. . . . Most persons, as a scholar has noted, harbor a secret affection for anybody with a low opinion of humanity."

This secret affection springs from a universal familiarity with the grind of daily life. The misanthrope has little to offer victims of crushing evil, but he is the nemesis of humanity's little meannesses, the ones that hurt most of the people most of the time. In his ceaseless battle against hypocrisy and pettiness, the ostensibly uncharitable misanthrope inadvertently becomes a warrior for the meek majority who never get even with the people who do them wrong.

It's not a bad life. For an American especially, it carries a priceless purity. Nobody can call you *-ist*, an *-ite*, or a *-phobe* when you have already called yourself a *-thrope*.

The American Spectator, January 1992
'Eminentoes'

"The Other Plath"

The Death and Life of Sylvia Plath
by Ronald Hayman (Birch Lane Press, 235 pages, $19.95)

Rough Magic: A Biography of Sylvia Plath
by Paul Alexander (Viking, 402 pages, $24.95)

W hen the expatriate American poet Sylvia Plath gassed herself in her London flat in February 1963, Betty Friedan was anticipating the publication of *The Feminine Mystique* later that year. The confluence of these two events was the first trickle in that river of no return known as the Women's Movement, for Plath, trying to write while saddled with two toddlers and estranged from her philandering husband, died in the name of Having It All.

She has since become feminism's foremost martyr. Feminist pilgrims to her Yorkshire grave have hacked her married name off four tombstones, and Robin Morgan, editor of *Ms.*, has devised a sacrificial rite for Plath's husband, Ted Hughes, now Poet Laureate of England. She wants to dismember him, stuff "that weapon" in his mouth, sew up his lips, and then "we women [will] blow out his brains." Bliss it is to be buried here and there in Westminster Abbey. Two excellent new biographies bring dispassionate yet sympathetic masculine points of view to this long-running passion play, but nothing can disguise the fact that Sylvia Plath was the Brat of Endor.

The compulsive erudition that destroyed her nerves seems to have run in the family. Her German-immigrant father was a forbidding Herr Doktor figure, an entomologist and an authority on bees, as well as a linguist who taught modern languages at Boston University, where he met Sylvia's mother, a first-generation German-American who so worshipped the written word that she claimed Baby Sylvia tried to talk at eight weeks.

As a child Sylvia read, wrote, drew, painted, danced, played the piano, and kept a maniacally thorough diary, using the entries as goads to remind herself to read more books, take more courses, get more A's, win more prizes and medals, write more stories and poems. The more she excelled, the more she expected of herself; the more she expected of herself, the more she had to excel.

When her father died when she was eight, she demanded her mother sign a paper promising never to remarry. Mother signed, thereafter devoting herself to her precocious daughter's education with such uncomplaining self-sacrifice that Sylvia was driven to rack up an endless array of intellectual triumphs to justify her mother's struggles and hold guilt at bay. In high school she sold a story to *Seventeen* and poems to the *Christian Science Monitor*, but she lived in dread of her free-lance writer's rejection slips, the eternal student in her seeing each one as a failing grade.

Her mother had moved to Wellesley so Sylvia could attend the prestigious girls' college on a town scholarship and live at home, but Sylvia insisted on the even more prestigious Smith. Her tuition was covered by two scholarships, one endowed by novelist Olive Higgins Prouty, author of *Now, Voyager* and *Stella Dallas*, who was to treat Plath like a mother. Meanwhile, her real mother took a second job to pay her board bill.

At Smith she sold poems to *Harper's*, won the *Mademoiselle* fiction prize, and in June 1953 received the coveted *Mademoiselle* guest editorship that triggered her first nervous breakdown. Many Plath partisans prefer to believe that her sensitive nerves were shattered by the execution of the Rosenbergs at Sing-Sing while she was in New York, but the real cause of her collapse was less flattering. A lifelong teacher's pet, she was thrust suddenly into the non-academic working world, a minion at the beck and call of tough-minded New York publishing pros concerned with getting out a magazine. Instead of being praised and pampered, she was criticized and made to rewrite one of her pieces four times. She responded like a true intellectual, making supercilious remarks about the "drudgery" and "detail" of offices and crying when asked to work overtime.

To get even, she threw all her clothes out the window of her hotel. Returning home in a borrowed dress, she learned that she had been turned down for a short-story seminar at Harvard Summer School. Devastated by this fresh diminishment and terrified that she had "lost her creativity," she plunged into a heavy reading program to re-establish her scholarly bona fides. When she found she could not finish James Joyce's *Ulysses*, she panicked. Fearing that she was losing her mind, she devoured the works of Freud and Jung and diagnosed herself as a schizophrenic with an inferiority complex, an Electra complex, and penis envy.

When she sliced at her legs with a razor blade "to see if I had the nerve," her mother took her to a public hospital where she was given electroshock treatments. Shortly thereafter she disappeared. After a three-day manhunt involving Boy Scouts, bloodhounds, American Legionnaires, and confusing headlines—SMITH GIRL MISSING FROM WELLESLEY—she was found in her own home, in the basement crawl space where she had hidden after taking forty sleeping pills that nearly killed her.

Olive Higgins Prouty paid the medical bills and found Sylvia a sympathetic female psychiatrist—just what she didn't need. With a new teacher figure to impress, she was thrust back into her frenzied mode. Now she became a shrink's pet, intent on having the best anxieties, the neatest dreams, the sharpest memories; striving for straight A's in penis envy, gold stars in schizophrenia, and the Electra Complex honor roll. The handwriting was on the wall and it said Phi Beta Kaput.

If Plath's story is ever turned into a country music song, it should be called "Mothers, Don't Let Your Daughters Grow Up to Win Fulbrights." After graduating from Smith she went to Cambridge and met Ted Hughes, an unwashed English intellectual in the fullness of his gummy socks, "a big, dark, hunky boy, the only one huge enough for me," the rangy Plath confided to her diary. She loved the "virile, deep, banging poems" he wrote (one was called "Fallgrief's Girlfriends"); he was "a breaker of things and people" with "a voice like the thunder of God." That very night they "made love like giants" even though Hughes lived in a renovated chicken coop, and Plath wrote a sickie poem about being stalked by a panther.

She boasted in a letter to Mrs. Prouty about Hughes's thrilling way of "bashing people around," but her patroness was unimpressed. "He sounds too much like Dylan Thomas for me to think he would make a satisfactory husband and father," Prouty warned, but Plath paid no heed. Hughes, a Yorkshireman, probably reminded her of Heathcliff; reading *Wuthering Heights* has destroyed more women than the cholera.

Once married, she turned her perfectionism on the housewifely arts, struggling to keep their sooty flat clean while the gamey Hughes, who did not bathe for three weeks during their honeymoon, dropped dandruff and nose-pickings along with poetic pearls. When his first book was published the following year, Plath wrote her mother: "I am more happy than if it was my book published! I am so happy *his* book is accepted *first*." She also said she wanted him to be acknowledged as the better poet. That's what distaff egomaniacs sound like when they're trying to be feminine. For all her insecurities, Plath was the kind of American woman who gets a lock on femininity by saying, in effect: "Listen, buster, I'm giving you five minutes to dominate me, and if I'm not dominated by then you're going to be in big trouble."

As further evidence of her femininity, she intended to have "a batch of brilliant healthy children." Seven, to be exact, since Ted, who dabbled in witchcraft, believed that the seventh child was significant. She had never given any evidence of even liking children, but she insisted that childbirth was "closer to the bone" than sex or marriage, and that being "mountainous-pregnant" was her favorite state. The feminist agenda can but benefit when an erudite woman says things like this. Plath's ultimate conundrum makes a perfect argument for day care, but her real reason for loving pregnancy has been overlooked by her feminist devotees as well as her two new male biographers: *the academic year runs nine months*.

She had a daughter and a son in quick succession, both home births aided by Ted, who hypnotized her to ease the pain. He also hypnotized her to cure her insomnia and relax her "razor-shaved" nerves, but her anxiety attacks and rages mounted. "A kind of macabre marathon for all concerned" was the way a hostess described a weekend with her. She burned the contents of Ted's desk in a backyard bonfire, reciting an incantation as she danced around the flames, then wrote a poem called "Burning the Letters." When his mistress called, she ripped the phone out of the wall and wrote "The Black Telephone's Off at the Root." Meanwhile, she was writing her novel, *The Bell Jar*, about her collegiate nervous breakdown. Instead of writing about what she did, she did what she wanted to write about. Truly creative people don't operate this way, and perhaps, deep down, she knew it.

Ronald Hayman and Paul Alexander tell substantially the same story and both tell it well, though Hayman's attempt to fold summaries of the poems into his ongoing narrative (Ted Hughes holds all the copyrights and refuses permission to quote) occasionally leads him into florid waters, e.g.:

> The suggestion of superhuman size—residue from the dream and the earlier poem—emerges in the idea that his toe, as big as a seal, is in San Francisco while his head is in the Atlantic, and, with a fond affectation of contempt, she compares him with the devil by saying he has a cleft in his chin instead of his foot.

Alexander's book is more evocative of time and place and more dramatically effective. His most macabre story concerns Sylvia's final gas bill, which must have been rather large. Ted's mistress forwarded it to a third party, writing on it: "She was your friend. You pay it."

He probes deeper into Ted's occultism, and proffers an ominous theory held by several of Plath's friends:

> After years of being repeatedly hypnotized by Ted and acting on his posthypnotic suggestions, Sylvia was highly sensitive to any signal—conscious or unconscious—that she perceived him to be send-

ing. Several times during the fall she had told her mother that Ted wanted her to kill herself; if she believed this, it might have propelled her on some new and purposeful path of action [that night].

Alexander also includes a highly significant 1950s cameo: the guest speaker at Plath's 1955 Smith graduation was Adlai Stevenson, who told the class that their highest goal should be a "creative marriage."

As contemporaries of Plath can attest, *creative* was the leading buzzword of the decade, used incessantly by everyone from manufacturers of Paint by the Numbers to employers advertising for female office clerks ("Seek creative miss to file architectural plans"). "Being creative" was a perfect excuse for majoring in English, an airy-fairy way of saying you liked to read, and an ideal rationale for free-floating discontent and unfocused rebellion.

Creative's twin was *intense*, a code word for superiority used by intellectual snobs who wanted to recuse themselves from American egalitarianism without doing anything illiberal. The creative 'n' intense set tended to make a fetish of being high-strung, the theory being that nerves are to aristocrats what splinters are to carpenters. Their favorite reading was pop-Freudian paperbacks like *The Fifty-Minute Hour*, and they never met a complex they didn't like.

When they gathered in their basement apartments to deplore Eisenhower conformity, there was an Oedipus on every rattan rug and an Electra in every butterfly chair. This aspect of the fifties, rather than the feminine mystique, may have produced the "unique" Sylvia Plath.

National Review, March 2, 1992
Book Review

"Gloria in Excelsis"

Revolution from Within: A Book of Self-Esteem,
by Gloria Steinem (Little, Brown, 377 pp., $22.95)

' S ELF-ESTEEM" is currently the bee in every bonnet and the fork in every tongue, so it was only to be expected that Gloria Steinem, the divine afflatus of feminism who has made a career out of leading the herd to trendy saltlicks, would decide to take a crack at it. She took two cracks. The first manuscript she wrote was read by a friend who told her it was too impersonal. "I think you have a self-esteem problem," said the friend. "You forgot to put yourself in."

Of course she forgot. She had been thinking of everyone but herself for years; hopping on planes the moment radical groups needed her, soothing fevered caucuses, tucking in fretful taskforces, living in an apartment with no furniture because she gave all her money away to worthy causes. Her friends called her a "co-dependent with the world," but we of coarser fiber recognize Dickens's Mrs. Jellyby, who made her own children go hungry so she could contribute to the African Children's Milk Fund, and then basked in the accolade, "She does so much for others."

Miss Steinem claims she rewrote the manuscript to include herself, but all we get are four discreet pages about her affair, at fifty, with a fabulously rich tycoon to whom she succumbed, she says, because her self-esteem was at an all-time low, plus a few scattered

references to her mother's mental illness that she covered thoroughly in a long essay called "Ruth's Song," published in 1984.

Several mass-circulation reviewers latched on to the 11th-hour
affair, giving the impression that the present book is a tell-all confessional about the secret life of Gloria Steinem. It isn't. They fudged,
probably to make things easy on themselves, because the book is
practically unreviewable; a rambling, monomaniacal exercise in
metaphysics à go-go about finding the "inner child" through meditation and achieving cosmic self-esteem in oneness and universality
with all things.

She begins by telling us how to say "self-esteem" in other languages. Not content to stop at the French *amour-propre*, Steinem the
compulsive list-maker plows on through Russian, Hindu, classical
Greek, Hebrew, Yiddish, Anglo-Saxon (*soelf*), and, of course,
Swahili (*kujistahi*). Next she reviews the synonyms in Roget's
Thesaurus and then drags us on a usage trip through the *OED*, until
the bloodied and beaten reader concludes that concern for self-esteem
is not only ubiquitous, but that the world has talked of little else since
time began.

Most books have an epigraph—a brief quotation stating the theme
or a line of poetry containing the title. This book has 54, drizzled over
each chapter and subchapter in clumps of two or three—one chapter
has five. The authors of these nuggets include everyone from Socrates
to Susan Sontag, with pitstops at arcana like "Sufi Wisdom, from the
Pleasantries of the Incredible Mulla Nasrudin."

Then there are the supporting quotations. "As Plato believed . . .,"
"As Margaret Mead observed . . .," "as J. Konrad Stettbacher illustrated . . .," "as Dorothy Dinnerstein explains . . .," "as Rilke wrote."
One after another; Audre Lorde followed by Christopher Isherwood
followed by Allison Stallibrass followed by Franz Kafka followed by
Patti Davis, who explains why she used to slouch: "We wear our attitudes in our bodies, and I grew up looking like a question mark."
Miss Steinem must look like a colon from the many times she skids
to a stop and quotes an ostensible authority out of what is obviously
a gnawing fear that she herself lacks the authority to speak her mind
without support.

Like the dirty-minded who can turn any topic around to sex, she finds her runic obsession everywhere. The revolt in Estonia was "fueled entirely by self-esteem." And economics? "I've noticed, too, that economists have begun to speak in terms of self-esteem . . . economic development without self-esteem is only another form of colonialism." Living under a white male-dominant society robbed the Cherokees of so much self-esteem that they abandoned their Council of Grandmothers. Women who dot their *i*'s with little hearts in obedience to "the smiling cheerful mask the patriarchy forces them to wear" eventually develop depression and eating problems, which are classic signs of low self-esteem. Saddam Hussein's brutal stepfather robbed him of his self-esteem, so he got it back by brutalizing others until George Bush, whose "aristocratic, religious father" beat him with a belt buckle, salvaged his self-esteem by destroying Saddam's.

Acknowledging congenital differences is bad for self-esteem. The belief that some are blessed with creative talent while others are not is a hierarchical concept, so never admit that you can't draw or sing. That means "I can't meet some outside standard. I'm not acceptable as I am." Go ahead and sing like Roseanne Barr Arnold. Go ahead and write like Diane Ackerman, yet another Steinem quotee: "Each night the sunset surged with purple pampas-grass plumes, and shot fuchsia rockets into the pink sky, then deepened through folded layers of peacock green to all the blues of India and a black across which clouds sometimes churned like alabaster dolls."

How to acquire self-esteem? Turn inward, journey backward in time, "reparent" yourself. To invoke the You of sandboxes past she provides a mantra—"I am valuable," "I am well," or just "I am"—and includes a Meditation Guide:

> Take some energizing breaths, inhaling more slowly than you exhale. Count to six as you breathe in, count to three as you breathe out. On the last count, open your eyes. Look at your hands and imagine that a child's hands are inside them. You are one and the same person—but different. You can protect and care for your inner child.

She also provides breathing instructions:

Just press one nostril closed while inhaling deeply through the other for one count, press both nostrils closed while holding that breath for four counts, and then press the other nostril closed while exhaling for two counts. . . . Yoga tells us this time of being full of breath, full of spirit, is a moment of feeling the true self; the soul.

Miss Steinem went to a "time-travel therapist" to find her inner child. She also talks to her hands: "So I ask them what they have to say for themselves. 'A banner held in liver-spotted hands,' they reply. I get a title for a future article, plus my first inkling that liver spots have a sense of humor."

Do enough of this and you will be a "Universal I," as one with nature and ready to help the ravaged planet salvage its self-esteem, like "the Chipko movement that began in the Himalayan foothills, when women hugged local village trees to save them from the axe." Being as one with nature is essential, because people who have "dominion" over the beasts of the field do not have self-esteem. To prove that species hierarchy destroys our inner peace she combs through nineteenth-century recipes and finds one that says—are you ready?—"Take a red cock that is not too old and beat him to death."

As a final fillip she recommends the development of Multiple Personality Disorder for positive purposes:

What if we could each gain access to the full range of human qual-ities that lie suppressed within us? . . . People in different alters can change every body movement, perfect a musical or linguistic talent that is concealed to the host personality, have two or even three menstrual cycles in the same body, and handle social and physical tasks of which they literally do not think themselves capable.

She promises to take us "in concentric circles," and she does. Like most feminist writers, her literary style consists of tossing a word into the water and letting it widen into a sentence. Start with communal, transforming, wholeness, burgeoning, nurturing, synthe-sizing, sensing, feeling, enhancing, intuiting, invoking, internalizing, seeking, or finding; and you will eventually get a sentence about circadian rhythms, hearing inner "clicks," and looking inward or out-ward—through a prism, of course—to where the paradigms are.

Much of the book reads like the contents of a 1972 time capsule. Early Women's Lib themes such as Chinese bound feet continue to haunt her, and the clitoris remains the whistlestop between maiden-head and personhood on her train of thought. Clitoridectomy among the Bantu is still happening, and Miss Steinem is still against it. It's an "excision of sexual will," which is bad for self-esteem, she says, and then quotes Adrienne Rich: "The repossession by women of our bodies will bring far more essential change to human society than the seizing of the means of production by workers."

Self-esteem takes many forms. I read this mewling, puking book, but I'm still vertical and able to quote back. When Samuel Johnson was asked to comment on the plot of *Cymbeline*, he replied: "It is impossible to criticize unresisting imbecility." My sentiments exactly.

The American Spectator, April 1992
Book Review

A Lot of Lance

The Truth of the Matter: My Life In and Out of Politics
by Bert Lance with Bill Gilbert
(Summit Books, 256 pages, $20)

Bert Lance has two problems that will never go away. The trouble he got into involved banking, a subject few people understand, especially the English majors in the media who never miss a feeding frenzy no matter how indigestible the fare. The only way an accused banker can tell his side of the story is to deliver monologues on compound interest and read aloud from balance sheets. Most people tune out immediately; the hardy few who try to follow it soon grow numb. In the end, nobody has any idea what the accused banker did—and nobody cares except the people who despise him on sight.

Being despised on sight by those with the power to ruin him is Bert Lance's other problem. He blames it on anti-Southern prejudice among the media elite, but in fact it's an American thing, and Sinclair Lewis would understand it. Bert Lance is an amiable big lug out of Central Casting: the Jack Carson part, the Sonny Tufts part, the guy who talks like the toastmaster's handbook. In short, he makes people think of Babbitt, and that's enough for the pseudo-intellectuals of the scribbling classes. He comes from the town of Calhoun in the North Georgia mountains, where introspection is probably not encouraged. The youngest of four, he was born in 1931, shortly after his seemingly healthy older brother died without warning of a cerebral hemorrhage. "My parents saw my birth as an example of the Christian belief that whenever God shuts a door in your life, He opens another one."

He met his wife, LaBelle, in elementary school and never had another girl. He was on the football and baseball teams ("I was introduced to sports, and the valuable lessons about life that you can learn from them"), she was a cheerleader. He was voted Most Likely to Succeed, she was crowned "Miss Gordon County." He went to Emory, she to Agnes Scott. He gave her his Sigma Chi pin and soon they were married.

Her grandfather gave Bert a job as teller at Calhoun First National so he could learn banking from the ground up. His greatest lesson was the difference between country and city banks. Character, not collateral, was his grandfather-in-law's rule of thumb; know a man and his family history well enough, and you know whether or not to lend him money. "Collateral never repaid a loan," said the old banker, and Bert found out how true this was when a farm woman who had borrowed money to buy a cow showed up one day and said, "Mr. Lance, I brung you your cow." Unable to make her payments, she had done the honest thing and wanted to hand over her collateral to the bank: it was tied up outside. Lance reasoned that the bank had no use for the cow—meaningless collateral—but the woman did, so he extended her loan on the strength of her demonstrated character and she eventually paid it off.

This is the kind of story Southern men tell so well that it's easy to miss the dark vein of existentialism that throbs deep down in the prayer-breakfast brain.

By the early sixties, Bert was the youngest bank president in America and a pillar of everything ("It was in high school that LaBelle and I formed our habit of becoming involved in community affairs"). He was also a born lieutenant in search of a captain, and Jimmy Carter was a state senator with his eye on the governor's mansion. Carter lost to Lester Maddox in his first try but shortly afterwards he was consoled, if you will, by the birth of daughter Amy. "I sent him a note telling him that the press was saying he looked like one of the Kennedys—and now he appeared to be acting like them," writes Bert. That sounded better in 1967 than it does now.

Carter won the governorship in 1970 and appointed Lance state highway director. Life with the man Bella Abzug called "a little fart" was not easy for a big lug:

> I knocked on the door of the governor's office and Jimmy called out to me to come in. He was reading the paper when I entered the room, and he kept right on reading it.
>
> I waited, and then I waited some more. He never did look up from that newspaper. I shuffled my feet. I coughed. Nothing got his nose out of the paper. After five minutes of that nonsense, I steamed out of my boss's office and stormed across the street to my own office.

We can bet he neither steamed nor stormed. The note he sent Little Cart trembles with the jocular masochism of water carriers and troubleshooters everywhere:

> I'm about ready to quit and go back to Calhoun, but if I stay, you're going to have to advise me as to how you want me to communicate with you. Do you want me to use personal visits, the telephone, or smoke signals? Whatever avenue you want me to take, please let me know and I won't waste your time and mine standing in front of your desk.

Little Cart instantly apologized, illustrating what Lance ingenuously calls "another great stride in our no-holds-barred relationship." That it was actually a love-hate relationship seems honestly to elude him. After a lifetime of small-town good fellowship, he's incapable of telling a revealing story without tacking on an upbeat bloviation. During the Ford administration Lance was investigated by the Justice Department on charges stemming from loans he had made as a Georgia bank president. The main charge against him was conspiracy, which was thrown out. Tried on twelve other charges, he was found not guilty of nine; the three remaining charges were dropped. He doesn't say what these three were, or go into much detail about the rest—sensible of him, since few readers would understand it and certainly not this reviewer.

He thought it was all in the past when he joined Little Cart's cabinet as director of management and budget, but *New York Times* columnist William Safire suddenly resurrected the charges in a series of columns based, Lance says, on a whispering campaign of leaks and innuendoes by Treasury Department officials.

Other than alluding to bad blood between himself and Treasury Secretary Michael Blumenthal ("Mike was never secure in his relationship with President Carter, and he felt mine was too secure"), Lance never names the leakers, but he nails Safire with a quotation from the columnist's own book, *Safire's Washington* (1980): "I hung in there. . . . encouraging some whistle blowers to do their thing." Finally, Safire's exasperated editor, A.M. Rosenthal, lost patience with the fishing expedition and demanded to know what specific law Lance had broken. By then, says Lance, Safire had a ready answer: "18 U.S. Code 656—misapplication of bank funds."

Thereafter, Safire wrote about "Broken Lanced," the "Lance Cover-Up," and—significantly—"Lancegate." The *Times*, Lance believes, resented the *Washington Post*'s Watergate coup and wanted its own gate story, while the *Post* jumped on the get-Lance bandwagon because going after a Democrat would stifle criticism of their liberal bias. *Time* joined the fray with a story on the "Lance affair." Next, Senators Ribicoff and Percy claimed to have "important new information" that Lance *might* have embezzled from Georgia banks. Their informant was a jailed embezzler whom Lance himself had exposed. He does not give the felon's name, but the man recanted and the senators apologized.

On it went. He was never found guilty of anything except the appearance of guilt, as in a *Los Angeles Times* editorial: ". . . . we find no blemishes on [his] record. But we are worried about him now. He should resign."

Little Cart vowed he would never cave in to the mounting calls for Lance's resignation, then promptly did, whereupon LaBelle phoned the Oval Office and said: "I want to tell you one thing—you can go with the rest of the jackals, and I hope you're happy." She later wrote *This, Too, Shall Pass*, and it did: she told Little Cart she would always pray for him.

Lance displays the same spirit of understanding that passeth understanding with regard to William Safire. He claims that when he confronted Safire in person, the columnist confessed, "We didn't want you to become chairman of the Fed," yet he assures us, "Over the years since, we have become good friends."

Eight federal agencies—the FBI, the Office of the Comptroller of the Currency, the SEC, the Federal Election Commission, the IRS, the FDIC, the Federal Reserve, and the U.S. Senate—conducted investigations of Lance and found nothing. "To this day," he writes, "I don't know what crime I'm accused of committing." It has the ring of truth in light of Clarence Thomas's reference to his "Kafkaesque" troubles, and makes this book, bland as most of it is, a valuable document on the media's increasing propensity for calumny.

Challenging the principle that public figures have not been libeled unless intent can be proved, Lance speaks at last with passionate conviction:

> Individuals who find themselves attacked by the media, with its growing malice and disregard for the truth, have no redress— unless you'd like to find a lawyer in the yellow pages, hope you can afford his fee, and then try to outspend and outlast *Time* magazine or "60 Minutes" in a court case. . . . It's a common practice in the media to repeat someone else's allegations and to claim, when they are bound to be false, that the reporter was only repeating what he or she had picked up from someone else's earlier story. The truth, of course, is that the tale bearer carries the same responsibility as the tale maker, or should.

Lance longs for the good old days when reporters were so circumspect that Americans didn't even know FDR was paralyzed, but America operated under a masculine ethos then. Over the last twenty years of feminist ascendancy, the surge of women into previously all-male enclaves has set in motion a kind of Gresham's Law of gender in which male values are driven out.

The growing feminization of America has turned journalism into a cat fight. The media's favorite buzzword, "mean-spirited," has a definite hiss to it and cannot be uttered without an accompanying sniff. Girlish double emphasis flies as reporters demand to know what the President *really* said and what he *really* meant. The ubiquitous figure of our time, "a highly placed administration official who spoke on condition of anonymity," suggests a beldame in britches hanging over the back fences of government whispering, "Don't you *dare* tell a *soul*!" Hysterical retractions and clarifications dominate the news, and the obsession with apologies brushes perilously close to, "If you don't take that back, I'll *never* speak to you *again* as long as I live!"

The beat goes on. You'll never guess who Lance's lawyers were during his 1977 troubles! Clark Clifford and Robert Altman. *Well*, you know what *that* means. . . .

When the BCCI scandal broke in 1991, *Time*'s casually nostalgic and unsubstantiated reference to a "Lance connection" led to the AP's "Banking Scandal Traces Roots to Georgia," which led in turn to an excited call from an *Atlanta Constitution* reporter: "My editor wants me to do a story about you and the BCCI as a result of the Time magazine article." All referred to past allegations of banking "irregularities" but none mentioned that he had been cleared of them. Lance states vigorously and unequivocally ("It's a damn lie") that he had nothing to do with the BCCI scandal, and anyone who has lived in a girls' dorm tends to believe him.

What you think of this book will depend upon how much kissyface Christianity you can stand, but despite his aversion to introspection and kneejerk good cheer, I now find that I like ol' Bert better than I used to.

National Review, June 22, 1992
Book Review

"In Bed with Mrs. Roosevelt"

Eleanor Roosevelt: Volume I, 1884–1933,
by Blanche Wiesen Cook (Viking, 587 pp., $27.50)

TO QUALIFY as a feminist heroine a woman must meet three tests. She must have a successful career "in her own right"; she must be "assertive and aggressive"; and she must have a pre-, extra-, or non-marital sex life, preferably ambidextrous.

What to do with Poor Nell, who did not even need to go through the trauma of changing her maiden name? Poor Nell, nicknamed "Granny" as a child and "Patient Griselda" as a young wife, who slept on the doormat rather than wake the servants. Poor Nell, whose sons claimed she didn't know what a lesbian was, whose daughter said she regarded marital relations as "an ordeal to be borne," and whose cousin, Alice Roosevelt Longworth present at the doormat incident, remembered her "rising like a string bean that had been raised in a cellar."

Women's Studies professor Blanche Wiesen Cook blames this politically incorrect image of ER on stereotypes, such as the one that sets the tone of this book: "White, Protestant, aristocratic, and 'unattractive' women are not supposed to flourish in the political arena, and are not presumed to have sex or independently passionate interests."

Unliberated women lock their bedroom doors and go without sex to punish straying husbands, but feminist heroines do not, so we must revise our assumptions about the aftermath of FDR's dalliance with Lucy Mercer. "Was there anything left between them? Was there love? Could there be trust? Could they start over? Might they even try?"

Yes, Miss Cook says, they did. She is sure of it, because the only evidence for a post-Lucy sexless marriage comes from daughter Anna and sons James and Elliott, who *said* their parents stopped sleeping together: "But children are unreliable sources concerning their parents' sexuality, and are particularly vulnerable to the historical stereotype that conjures up the frigid mother and the deprived father."

Age does not wither feminist heroines, so at 45 ER had an affair with 32-year-old Earl Miller, the New York State trooper who served as her bodyguard during FDR's governorship. Miss Cook can't prove it because somebody burned their letters—she knows not who, but she knows why. "There are two stereotypes at play here: frumpy older women do not have sex—because they cannot; aristocratic women do not—because they will not." She is sure ER did, however, and bolsters her contention by quoting James Roosevelt, one of those unreliable child sources she dismissed earlier, who wrote: "I believe there may have been one real romance in mother's life outside of marriage. Mother may have had an affair with Earl Miller."

ER certainly knew what a lesbian was because she had an "inevitable and undeniable" affair with AP reporter Lorena Hickok, a victim of "hateful stereotypes" due to her homeliness. Hick had already had an affair with contralto Ernestine Schumann-Heink, a victim of the fat-opera-singer stereotype, whose favorite encore was *Sapphische Ode.*

Surviving letters between ER and Hick prove they went to bed, Miss Cook insists, "although Hickok typed, edited, and then burned the originals of ER's letters between 1932 and 1933," when the alleged affair was at its height. Having said that, Miss Cook blithely ignores the possibility that the feverishly romantic Hick might have "retyped" the affair into being. Certainly a number of phrases simply don't sound like ER. The "Oh! Darling!" passages and maudlin love poems are tasteless enough, but what really rouses suspicions is a phrase that reeks of middle-class fallen archness: "So endeth my first Sunday."

Lesbianism is often on the author's mind and she goes out of her way to find it, even hinting that Elliott Roosevelt's sister—ER's Aunt Corinne—had some sort of passionate interlude with her brother's mistress, to whom she wrote overheated poems that ER kept and cherished. This is supposed to prove how worldly ER was on the subject, but in case we still don't get it, we are told that ER was the model for a character in *Olivia*, a lesbian schoolgirl novel by her old classmate, Dorothy Strachey.

Miss Cook goes positively ga-ga when she describes ER's lesbian friends, Esther Lape and Elizabeth Read. Rich liberal activists who held court in Greenwich Village, they "celebrated excellence in food and champagne, art and conversation. They were passionate about music and theater. Cut flowers in great profusion decorated their homes in the city and the country. Their candle-lit dinners were formal, splendidly served, and spiced by controversy." Less elegant were carpenter Nancy Cook and teacher Marion Dickerman, whom a jealous ER froze out when FDR demonstrated that he could turn even a lesbian into a handmaiden. As Miss Dickerman later recalled: "Never in my life have I met so utterly charming a man"; it seemed to her "only right and natural that people should devote themselves heart and soul to him and his career."

What the author doesn't know she manages to suggest without violating the rules of scholarly research. While the orphaned adolescent ER was living with her father's family, "three strong, very protective locks were installed on the door of her room. Was she ever hurt or abused? Did Uncle Vallie or Uncle Eddie ever actually get into her room? What kind of battle ensued?" Thus, Miss Cook plants the idea of rape when all she really knows is that the uncles were such reeling drunks that they easily could have entered the wrong room by mistake.

Despite Miss Cook's efforts to paint ER as a political titan, she still comes across as one of those freelance female activists, with a finger in every agenda, that *Nightline* calls on whenever Something Happens. The real towering female figure here, as in every Roosevelt book, is Sara Delano, whom even this author treats with grudging admiration. The disappearance of full-sailed *grandes dames* has left a void in democracy's heart that mere assertive feminists can never fill.

National Review, August 17, 1992
Essay

"A Wasp Looks at Lizzie Borden"

I F YOU want to understand Anglo-Saxon Americans, study the Lizzie Borden case. No ethnologist could ask for a better control group; except for Bridget Sullivan, the Bordens' maid, the zany tragedy of August 4, 1892, had an all-Wasp cast.

Lizzie was born in Fall River, Massachusetts, on July 19, 1860, and immediately given the Wasp family's favorite substitute for open affection: a nickname. Thirty-two years later at her inquest she stated her full legal name: Lizzie Andrew Borden. "You were so christened?" asked the district attorney.

"I was so christened," she replied.

Lizzie's mother died in 1862. Left with two daughters to raise, her father, Andrew Borden, soon married a chubby spinster of 38 named Abby Durfee Gray. Three-year-old Lizzie obediently called the new wife Mother, but 12-year-old Emma called her Abby.

Andrew Borden was a prosperous but miserly undertaker whose sole interest in life was money. His operations expanded to include banking, cotton mills, and real estate, but no matter how rich he became he never stopped peddling eggs from his farms to his downtown business associates; wicker basket in hand, he would set out for corporate board meetings in anticipation of yet a few more pennies. Although he was worth $500,000 in pre-IRS, gold-standard dollars, he was so tightfisted that he refused to install running water in his home. There was a latrine in the cellar and a pump in the kitchen; the bedrooms were fitted out with water pitchers, wash bowls, chamber pots, and slop pails.

Marriage with this paragon of Yankee thrift evidently drove Abby to seek compensatory emotional satisfaction in eating. Only five feet tall, she ballooned up to more than two hundred pounds and seldom left the house except to visit her half-sister, Mrs. Whitehead.

Emma Borden, Lizzie's older sister, was 42 at the time of the murders. Mouse-like in all respects, she was one of those spinsters who scurry. Other than doing the marketing, she rarely went anywhere except around the corner to visit her friend, another spinster named Alice Russell.

Compared to the rest of her family, Lizzie comes through as a prom queen. Never known to go out with men, at least she went out. A member of Central Congregational, she taught Sunday school, served as secretary-treasurer of the Christian Endeavor Society, and was a card-carrying member of the Women's Christian Temperance Union.

What did she look like? Like everyone else in that inbred Wasp town. *New York Sun* reporter Julian Ralph wrote during the trial:

> By the way, the strangers who are here begin to notice that Lizzie Borden's face is of a type quite common in New Bedford. They meet Lizzie Borden every day and everywhere about town. Some are fairer, some are younger, some are coarser, but all have the same general cast of features—heavy in the lower face, high in the cheekbones, wide at the eyes, and with heavy lips and a deep line on each side of the mouth.

Plump by our standards, she had what her self-confident era called a good figure. She also had blue eyes, and like all blue-eyed women she had a lot of blue dresses—handy for changing clothes without appearing to have done so. The case is a vortex of dark blue dresses, light blue dresses, blue summer dresses, blue winter dresses, clean blue dresses, paint-stained blue dresses, blood-stained blue dresses, and an all-male jury struggling to tell one from the other.

Five years before the murders, the Bordens had a family fight when Andrew put one of his rental houses in Abby's name. Lizzie and Emma were furious, so they said politely: "What you do for her, you must do for us." That's the Wasp version of a conniption and Andrew knew it, so he took refuge in our cure-all fair play, buying his daughters houses of identical valuation ($1,500) to the one he had given his wife.

Now they were even-steven and everything was settled—except it wasn't. Having failed to clear the air, everyone started smoldering and brooding. Emma and Lizzie stopped eating with the elder Bordens, requiring the maid to set and serve each meal twice. They never reached that pinnacle of Wasp rage called Not Speaking—"We always *spoke*," Emma emphasized at the trial—but she and Lizzie eliminated "Abby" and "Mother" from their respective vocabularies and started calling their stepmother "Mrs. Borden." What a cathartic release that must have been.

Lizzie ticked away for four years until 1891, when she committed a family robbery. Entering the master bedroom through a door in her own room (it was a "shotgun" house with no hallways), she stole her stepmother's jewelry and her father's loose cash.

Andrew and Abby knew that Lizzie was the culprit, and Lizzie knew that they knew, but rather than "have words," Andrew called in the police and let them go through an investigation to catch the person the whole family carefully referred to as "the unknown thief."

The robbery launched a field day of Silent Gestures. Everybody quietly bought lots of locks. To supplement the key locks, there were bolts, hooks, chains, and padlocks. Abby's Silent Gesture consisted of locking and bolting her side of the door that led into Lizzie's room. Lizzie responded with her Silent Gesture, putting a hook on her side of the door and shoving a huge clawfooted secretary in front of it.

The best Silent Gesture was Andrew's. He put the strongest available lock on the master bedroom, but kept the key on the sitting-room mantelpiece in full view of everyone. Lizzie knew she was being tempted to touch it; she also knew that if the key disappeared, she would be suspect. In one fell swoop, Andrew made it clear that he was simultaneously trusting her and distrusting her, and warning her without saying a word. Wasps call this war of nerves the honor system.

Since Emma *was* a Silent Gesture, there was no need for her to do anything except keep on scurrying.

The Borden house must have been a peaceful place. There is nothing on record to show that the Bordens ever raised their voices to one another. "Never a word," Bridget Sullivan testified at the trial, with obvious sincerity and not a little awe.

Bridget, 26 and pretty in a big-boned, countrified way, had been in the Bordens' service for almost three years at the time of the murders. A recent immigrant, she had a brogue so thick that she referred to the Silent Gesture on the mantelpiece as the "kay."

Bridget adored Lizzie. Victoria Lincoln, the late novelist, whose parents were neighbors of the Bordens, wrote in her study of the case: "*De haut en bas*, Lizzie was always kind." Her habit of calling Bridget "Maggie" has been attributed to laziness (Maggie was the name of a former maid), but I think it was an extremity of tact. In that time and place, the name Bridget was synonymous with "Irish maid." Like Rastus in minstrel-show jokes, it was derisory, so Lizzie substituted another.

Anyone who studies the Borden case grows to like Lizzie, or at least admire her, for her rigid sense of herself as a gentlewoman. It would have been so easy for her to cast suspicion on Bridget, or to accuse her outright. Bridget was the only other person in the house when Andrew and Abby were killed. The Irish were disliked in turn-of-the-century Massachusetts; a Yankee jury would have bought the idea of Bridget's guilt. Yet Lizzie never once tried to shift the blame, and she never named Bridget as a suspect.

Scurrying Away

A WEEK before the murders, Emma did something incredible: she went to Fairhaven. Fifteen miles is a long way to scurry but scurry she did, to visit an elderly friend and escape the heat wave that had descended on Fall River.

That same week, Lizzie shared a beach house on Buzzards Bay with five friends. At a press conference after the murders, they showered her with compliments. "She always was self-contained, self-reliant, and very composed. Her conduct since her arrest is exactly what I should have expected. Lizzie and her father were, without being demonstrative, very fond of each other."

They got so caught up in Wasp priorities that they inadvertently sowed a dangerous seed when the reporter asked them if they thought Lizzie was guilty. No, they said firmly, because she had pleaded *not* guilty: "It is more likely that Lizzie would commit a murder than that she would lie about it afterward."

The most puzzling aspect of the case has always been Lizzie's choice of weapons. Ladies don't chop up difficult relatives, but they do poison them. A few days before she was due at the beach house, Lizzie tried to buy prussic acid in her neighborhood drugstore. The druggist's testimony was excluded on a legal technicality, but it establishes her as, in the words of one of her friends, "a monument of straightforwardness."

Picture it: In broad daylight in the middle of a heat wave, she marched into the drugstore carrying a fur cape, announced that there were moths in it, and asked for ten cents' worth of prussic acid to kill them. The druggist was stunned. Even in the casual Nineties, when arsenic was sold over the counter, it was illegal to sell prussic acid. "But I've bought it many times before," Lizzie protested.

The druggist's astonishment mounted in the face of this stout-hearted lie. "Well, my good lady, it is something we don't sell except by prescription, as it is a very dangerous thing to handle."

Lizzie left, never dreaming that she might have called attention to herself.

At the beach, her friends noticed that she seemed despondent and preoccupied. They were puzzled when she suddenly cut short her vacation, giving as her excuse some church work, and returned to Fall River.

Back home in the stifling city heat, she sat in her room and brooded. Somehow she had found out that Abby was about to acquire some more real estate; Andrew was planning to put a farm in his wife's name and install his brother-in-law, John Morse, as caretaker. This last was especially infuriating, for Lizzie and Emma were Not Speaking to Uncle John. He had been involved, so they thought, in that other real-estate transfer five years before. Now he was back, plotting to do her and Emma out of their rightful inheritance.

Something had to be done, but what? Lacking lady-like poison, Lizzie did what every overcivilized, understated Wasp is entirely capable of doing once we finally admit we're mad as hell and aren't going to take it any more: She went from Anglo to Saxon in a trice.

Miss Borden Accepts

O N THE day before the murders, Lizzie joined Abby and Andrew for lunch for the first time in five years—an air-tight alibi, for who would do murder after doing lunch?

That evening, she paid a call on Alice Russell and craftily planted some red herrings. If Machiavelli had witnessed this demonstration of the fine Wasp hand he would have gone into cardiac arrest.

"I have a feeling that something is going to happen," she told Alice. "A feeling that somebody is going to do something." She hammered the point home with stories about her father's "enemies." He was such a ruthless businessman, she said, that "they" all hated him, and she would not put it past "them" to burn down the house.

When she returned home, Uncle John had arrived with plans to spend the night. Since she was Not Speaking to him, she went directly to her room.

The next day, August 4, 1892, the temperature was already in the eighties at sunrise, but that didn't change the Bordens' breakfast menu. Destined to be the most famous breakfast in America, it was printed in newspapers everywhere and discussed by aficionados of the murders for years to come: Alexander Woollcott always claimed it was the motive.

If Lizzie had only waited, Abby and Andrew probably would have died *anyway*, for their breakfast consisted of mutton soup, sliced mutton, pancakes, bananas, pears, cookies, and coffee. Here we recognize the English concept of breakfast-as-weapon designed to overwhelm French tourists and other effete types.

Bridget was the first up, followed by Andrew, who came downstairs with the connubial slop pail and emptied it on the grass in the backyard. That done, he gathered the pears that had fallen to the ground.

After breakfast, Andrew saw Uncle John out and then brushed his teeth at the kitchen sink where Bridget was washing dishes. Moments later, she rushed out to the back yard and vomited. Whether it was the mutton or the toothbrushing or something she had seen clinging to a pear we shall never know, but when she returned to the house, Abby was waiting with an uncharacteristic order. She wanted the windows washed, all of them, inside and out, *now*.

Here is one of the strangest aspects of the case. Victoria Lincoln writes of Abby: "Encased in fat and selfpity, she was the kind who make indifferent housekeepers everywhere." Additionally, the Wasp woman is too socially secure to need accolades like "You could eat off her floor." Why then would Abby order a sick Bridget to wash the windows on a blistering hot day?

Because, says Miss Lincoln, she was getting ready to go to the bank to sign the deed for the farm, and she feared a scene with Lizzie, who, knowing Abby's hermit-like ways, would immediately suspect the truth. The mere thought of "having words" in front of a servant struck horror in Abby's heart, so she invented a task that would take Bridget outside.

That left Lizzie inside.

Around nine o'clock, Abby was tomahawked in the guest room while making Uncle John's bed. Andrew was to meet the same fate around 11. Lizzie's behavior during that two-hour *entr'acte* was a model of Battle-of-Britain calm. She ironed handkerchiefs, sewed a button loop on a blouse, chatted with Bridget about a dress-goods sale, and read *Harper's Weekley*.

Andrew came home at 10:30 and took a nap on the sitting-room sofa. Shortly before 11, Bridget went up to her attic room to rest. At 11:15 she heard Lizzie cry out: "Maggie! Come down quick! Father's dead. Somebody came in and killed him."

Somebody certainly had. The entire left side of his face and head was a bloody pulp; the eye had been severed and hung down his cheek, and one of the blows had bisected a tooth.

Lizzie sent Bridget for Alice Russell and Dr. Bowen, then sat on the back steps. The Bordens' next-door neighbor, Mrs. Adelaide Churchill, called over to her and got a priceless reply: "Oh, Mrs. Churchill, do come over. Someone has killed Father."

Mrs. Churchill came over, took a quick look at Andrew, and asked, "Where is your stepmother, Lizzie?"

The safe thing to say was "I don't know," but the people who invented the honor system are sticklers for the truth. "I don't know but that she's been killed, too, for I thought I heard her come in," Lizzie blurted.

Bridget returned with Miss Russell and Dr. Bowen, who examined Andrew and asked for a sheet to cover the body. Lizzie told Bridget to get it. Whether she said anything else is in dispute; no one present testified to it, but the legend persists that our monument of straightforwardness added, "Better get two."

Bridget and Mrs. Churchill decided to search the house for Abby. They were not gone long. When they returned, a white-faced but contained Mrs. Churchill nodded at Alice Russell.

"There is another?" asked Miss Russell.

"Yes, she is upstairs," said Mrs. Churchill.

The only excited person present was Bridget.

By the Way . . .

B Y NOON, when Uncle John returned for lunch, the cops had come, and a crowd had formed in the street. Knowing of the hatred between Lizzie and Abby, Uncle John must have guessed the truth, but he chose to exhibit so much nonchalance that he became the first suspect. Instead of rushing into the house yelling, "What's the matter?" he ambled into the back yard, picked up some pears, and stood eating them in the shade of the tree.

Meanwhile, the police were questioning Lizzie, who claimed that she had gone to the barn and returned to find her father dead. What had she gone to the barn for? "To get a piece of lead for a fishing sinker."

It was the first thing that popped into her head, less a conscious deception than an ink-blot association triggered by her seaside vacation. She was playing it by ear. It never occurred to her that she could have stalled for time by pretending to faint. Women often fainted in those tightly corseted days, but she even rejected the detective's gallant offer to come back and question her later when she felt better.

"No," she said. "I can tell you all I know now as well as at any other time."

A moment later, when the detective referred to Abby as her mother, she drew herself up and said stiffly, "She is not my mother, sir, she is my stepmother. My mother died when I was a child." Before you start diagnosing "self-destructive tendencies," remember that the English novelists' favorite character is the plucky orphan, and she had just become one.

Miss Russell and Dr. Bowen took her upstairs to lie down. Lizzie asked the doctor to send a telegram to Emma in Fairhaven, adding, "Be sure to put it gently, as there is an old person there who might be disturbed." It's all right to disturb your sister as long as you don't disturb strangers; Wasps haven't kithed our kin since the Anglo-Saxon invaders wiped out the Celtic clan system.

Dr. Bowen must have sent the gentlest wire on record, because Emma did not catch the next train, nor the one after that, nor the one after *that*. She didn't return until after seven that night.

When Dr. Bowen returned, Lizzie confided to him that she had torn up a certain note and put the pieces in the kitchen trash can. He hurried downstairs and found them; he was putting them together when a detective walked in. Seeing the name "Emma," he asked Dr. Bowen what it was. "Oh, it is nothing," Dr. Bowen said nonchalantly. "It is something, I think, about my daughter going through somewhere."

Before the detective could react to this bizarre answer, Dr. Bowen, nonchalant as ever, tossed the pieces into the kitchen fire. As he lifted the stove lid, the detective saw a foot-long cylindrical stick lying in the flames. Later, in the cellar, he found a hatchet head that had been washed and rolled while wet in furnace ash to simulate the dust of long disuse.

Lizzie had been in the barn, but not to look for sinkers. The barn contained a vise, blacksmithing tools, and a water pump. Blood can be washed from metal but not from porous wood. She knew she had to separate the hatchet head from the handle and burn the latter. She did all of this in a very brief time, and without giving way to panic. Victoria Lincoln believes that because she really had been in the barn, her compulsive honesty forced her to admit it to the police. Then she had to think of an innocent reason for going there, and came up with the story about looking for sinkers. "She lied about *why* and *when* she had done things, but she never denied having done them," writes Miss Lincoln.

Alice Russell displayed the same tic: "Alice's conscience forced her to *mention* things at the trial, but not to *stress* them." The Wasp gift for making everything sound trivial, as when we introduce momentous subjects with "Oh, by the way," enabled Alice to testify about a highly incriminating fact in such a way that the prosecution missed its significance entirely.

On one of Alice's trips upstairs on the murder day, she saw Lizzie coming out of *Emma's* room, and a bundled-up blanket on the floor of *Emma's* closet. What was Lizzie doing in Emma's room? What was in the blanket? Victoria Lincoln thinks it contained blood-stained stockings, but the prosecution never tried to find out because Alice made it all sound so matter-of-fact. The same technique worked for Dr. Bowen in the matter of the note; we happy few don't destroy evidence, we just tut-tut it into oblivion.

Everyone who saw Lizzie after the murders testified that there wasn't a drop of blood on her. How did she wash the blood off her skin and hair in a house that had no running water? What trait is cherished by the people who distrust intellectuals? *Common sense* told her to sponge herself off with the diaper-like cloths Victorian women used for sanitary napkins and then put them in her slop pail, which was already full of bloody cloths because she was menstruating that week.

Now we come to the dress she wore when she murdered Abby. Where did she hide it after she changed? Some students of the crime think she committed both murders in the nude, but Victoria Lincoln disagrees and so do I. Murder is one thing, but . . .

Where would any honest Wasp hide a dress? In the dress closet, of course. Like most women, Lizzie had more clothes than hangers, so she knew how easy it is to "lose" a garment by hanging another one on top of it. Victoria Lincoln thinks she hung the blood-stained summer cotton underneath a heavy winter woolen, and then banked on the either–or male mind: the police were looking for a *summer* dress, and men never run out of hangers.

She got no blood at all on the second dress. Her tall father's Prince Albert coat reached to her ankles, and common sense decrees that blood on a *victim's* clothing is only to be expected.

Mistress of Herself

AFTER her arrest Lizzie became America's Wasp Princess. People couldn't say enough nice things about her icy calm, even the Fall River police chief: "She is a remarkable woman and possessed of a wonderful power of fortitude."

A Providence reporter and Civil War veteran: "Most women would faint at seeing her father dead, for I never saw a more horrible sight and I have walked over battlefields where thousands were dead and mangled. She is a woman of remarkable nerve and self-control."

Julian Ralph, *New York Sun*: "It was plain to see that she had complete mastery of herself, and could make her sensations and emotions invisible to an impertinent public."

To ward off a backlash, Lizzie gave an interview to the *New York Recorder* in which she managed to have her bona fides and eat them too: "They say I don't show any grief. Certainly I don't in public. I never did reveal my feelings and I cannot change my nature now."

I find this very refreshing in an age that equates self-control with elitism. If Lizzie were around today she would be reviled as the Phantom of the Oprah.

Wasp emotional repression also gave us the marvelous fight between Lizzie and Emma in Lizzie's jail cell while she was awaiting trial. Described by Mrs. Hannah Reagan, the police matron, it went like this:

"Emma, you have given me away, haven't you?"

"No, Lizzie, I have not."

"You have, and I will let you see I won't give in one inch."

Finis. Lizzie turned over on her cot and lay with her back to Emma, who remained in her chair. They stayed like that for two hours and twenty minutes, until visiting time was up and Emma left.

When Mrs. Reagan spilled this sensational colloquy to the press, Lizzie's lawyers said it was a lie and demanded she sign a retraction. Doubts arose, but Victoria Lincoln believes Mrs. Reagan: "That terse exchange followed by a two-hour-and-twenty-minute sulking silence sounds more like a typical Borden family fight than the sort of quarrel an Irish police matron would dream up from her own experience."

The Last Word

AFTER her acquittal, Lizzie bought a mansion for herself and Emma in Fall River's best neighborhood. Social acceptance was another matter. When she returned to Central Congregational, everyone was very polite, so she took the hint and stopped going.

She lived quietly until 1904, when she got pinched for shoplifting in Providence. This is what really made her an outcast. Murder is one thing, but . . .

In 1913, Emma suddenly moved out and never spoke to Lizzie again. Nobody knows what happened. Maybe Lizzie finally admitted to the murders, but I doubt it; the Protestant conscience is not programmed for pointless confession. It sounds more as if Emma found out that her sister had a sex life.

An enthusiastic theatergoer, Lizzie was a great fan of an actress named Nance O'Neill. They met in a hotel and developed an intense friendship; Lizzie threw lavish parties for Nance and her troupe and paid Nance's legal expenses in contractual disputes with theater owners. Nance was probably the intended recipient of the unmailed letter Lizzie wrote beginning "Dear Friend," and going on to juicier sentiments: "I dreamed of you the other night but I do not dare to put my dreams on paper." If Emma discovered the two were lesbian lovers, it's no wonder she moved out so precipitately. Murder is one thing, but . . .

Lizzie stayed in Fall River, living alone in her mansion, until she died of pneumonia in 1927.

Emma, living in New Hampshire, read of Lizzie's death in the paper but did not attend the funeral or send flowers. Ten days later, Emma died from a bad fall. Both sisters left the bulk of their fortunes to the Animal Rescue League. Nothing could be Waspier, except the explanation little Victoria Lincoln got when she asked her elders why no one ever spoke to their neighbor, Miss Borden. "Well, dear, she was very unkind to her mother and father."

National Review, January 18, 1993
Book Review

"The Noble White Man"

Mark Twain: Collected Tales, Sketches, Speeches & Essays,
2 vols. (Library of America, 2,126 pp., $70)

T HE INCREDULOUS, accusatory question, "You don't like
Mark Twain?" is one I heard throughout my young womanhood. The shocked inquisitor was always male. This particular gender gap has its roots in the way our schools teach Twain. In my
day, junior-high English classes read *Huckleberry Finn, Tom Sawyer*,
and the story about the frog. Little girls despise little boys and
frogs—the distinction is minimal at that age—so the damage is done.
Whatever Twain we are forced to read in college invariably runs up
against the pubertal mental block, so we spend the best years of our
lives going around saying, "I can't stand Mark Twain."

I changed my mind in my thirties when l began to prefer non-fic-
tion to novels and discovered Twain's essays. All of my old favorites,
as well as some new ones, are contained in this superbly presented
collection.

These books are secular bibles for our times—and not merely
because they are printed on elegantly thin paper. Bill Clinton's living
obituary is contained in the 1901 essay "Corn-Pone Opinions," a dis-
section of the man who "can't bear to be outside the pale; can't bear

to be in disfavor; can't endure the averted face and the cold shoulder; wants to stand well with friends, wants to be smiled upon, wants to be welcome, wants to hear the precious words 'he's on the right track!'"

The trendy masses out buying the movie edition of *The Last of the Mohicans* should first read Twain's critique of Fenimore Cooper, who "saw nearly all things as through a glass eye, darkly," and hid his lack of inventiveness under tired plot tricks.

"A favorite one was to make a moccasined person tread in the tracks of the moccasined enemy, and thus hide his own trail. Cooper wore out barrels and barrels of moccasins in working that trick." Another was the broken twig. "It is a restful chapter in any book of his when somebody doesn't step on a dry twig and alarm all the reds and whites for two hundred yards around. Every time a Cooper person is in peril, and absolute silence is worth four dollars a minute, he is sure to step on a dry twig."

Examining *The Deerslayer*, which he calls "a literary *delirium tremens*," Twains reckons that on a single page, Cooper scored 114 literary offenses out of a possible 115—a record. Of the 19 rules governing the writing of romantic fiction, Cooper violated 18—another record. Among the latter: "The talk . . . shall have a discoverable meaning, also a discoverable purpose, and a show of relevancy, and remain in the neighborhood of the subject in hand, and be interesting to the reader, and help out the tale, and stop when the people cannot think of anything more to say."

Cooper strained credulity, both out of ignorance and to suit his plot needs. In the shooting match in *The Pathfinder*, the hero hits the head of a nail driven into a tree from a hundred yards away, making him, says Twain, "a man who could hunt flies with a rifle." On another occasion, six Indians who have managed somehow to hide in a "sapling" overhanging a river try to drop silently onto a passing boat, and all six miss; "the difference between a Cooper Indian and the Indian that stands in front of the cigar shop is not spacious."

In sum: "There have been daring people in the world who claimed that Cooper could write English, but they are all dead now."

Twain believed in women's equality as long as it sprang from the kind of specialness he detected in Joan of Arc, "easily and by far the most extraordinary person the human race has ever produced." What he could not abide were mediocrities, the Eleanor Smeals and Gloria Steinems of his day, whose bollixed logic he satirized in a mock letter to the editor from a typical suffragette:

> For long years I have collected buttons, and door-plates and dictionaries, and all such things as I thought would make the poor savages of the South Seas contented with their lot and lift them out of their ignorance and degradation—and no longer than a month ago I sent them Horace Greeley's speeches and some other cheerful literature, and the pure delight I felt was only marred by the reflection that the poor creatures could not read them—and yet I may not vote!

He was devastatingly prescient about the feminization of politics that we call "negative campaigning." If women entered public life, he predicted, they "would go straight for each other's private moral character . . . it would be an established proposition that every women in the state was 'no better than she ought to be.'" The future slogans he imagines ("Vote for Judy McGinniss, the incorruptible! Nine children—one at the breast!") are close to present truth, and his anticipation of the blow-dried candidate has been realized: "And also in that day the man who hath beautiful whiskers shall beat the homely man of wisdom for Governor, and the youth who waltzes with exquisite grace shall be Chief of Police, in preference to the man of practiced sagacity and determined energy."

For peerless political incorrectness try "The Noble Red Man" (1870), which describes the Indian:

> His "wisdom" conferred upon an idiot would leave that idiot helpless indeed. . . . All history and honest observation will show that the Red Man is a skulking coward and a windy braggart . . . a creature devoid of brave or generous qualities, but cruel, treacherous, and brutal. During the Pi-Ute war the Indians often dug the sinews out of the backs of white men before they were dead. (The sinews are used for bowstrings.) But their favorite mutilations cannot be put into print. Yet it is this same Noble Red Man who is always

greeted with a wail of humanitarian sympathy from the Atlantic seaboard whenever he gets into trouble; the maids and matrons throw up their hands in horror at the bloody vengeance wreaked upon him, and the newspapers clamor for a court of inquiry to examine into the conduct of the inhuman officer who inflicted the little pleasantry upon the "poor abused Indian." (They always look at the matter from the abused-Indian point of view, never from that of the bereaved white widow and orphan.)

A last word is in order. Since few of us are in top form on our deathbeds, Twain writes in "The Last Words of Famous Men," we should prepare a memorable clincher ahead of time. His suggestion for Secretary of State Seward: "Alas!—ka."

National Review, March 1, 1993
Book Review

"The Conservative Mind"

Flaubert, by Henri Troyat, translated by Joan Pinkham
(Viking, 374 pp., $25)

I N an age that equates perfectionist standards with an undemocratic turn of mind, Gustave Flaubert would be called a "control freak." A contemporary, Théophile Gautier, did call him one, though he put it wittily:

> There is one thing for which he feels a remorse that poisons his life. It's that in *Madame Bovary* he put two genitives one on top of the other: *une couronne de fleurs d'oranger* [a crown of orange blossoms]. He is very upset over it; but there was nothing he could do, it was impossible to say it any other way.

When feminist Ellen Willis penned her now-notorious dictum, "Good writing is counterrevolutionary," she was stating a simple truth. Political liberalism and literary romanticism travel in a tandem harness of intellectual confusion and emotional excess. Conservatism and classicism are also a matched set, both governed by realism, skepticism, objectivity, order, simplicity, and restraint.

The conservative artistic temperament flowered in Gustave Flaubert, whose opinions on literature and politics were virtually interchangeable. The back-to-back flavor of "One must write coldly" and "Democracy is the exaltation of mercy at the expense of justice" lets both apply equally to voter alienation or the difference between Flaubert's *Madame Bovary* and Oprah Winfrey's "Women with Boring Husbands."

Flaubert expressed a hatred of mediocrity so early in life that he must have been born with it. "How stupid mankind is, what fools the people are!" he fulminated in a letter to a schoolboy friend. Though only 11, he was furious that Louis-Philippe, the ostentatiously middle-class "Citizen King," had the temerity to visit Rouen, birthplace of Pierre Corneille.

Though contemptuous of the King, Flaubert was even more contemptuous of the mediocrity of the speeches against him in the Revolution of 1848. His anti-republicanism was largely aesthetic, rooted in his nervous inability to hear a cliché without twitching. "I remained cold and nauseated with disgust in the midst of all the patriotic enthusiasm aroused by the 'helm of State,' the 'abyss toward which we are racing,' the 'honor of our flag,' the 'shadow of our banners,' the 'brotherhood of peoples,' and other stuff in the same vein."

He started writing *Madame Bovary* in 1851 in the middle of Louis Napoléon's coup d'état, the political upheaval strengthening his resolve to bring order out of chaos on paper. Insisting that "a good prose sentence should be like a line of poetry—*unchangeable*, just as rhythmic, just as sonorous," he frequently spent all day searching for a word that suited his stringent requirements of melody and rhythm. When he found it, "he would shout it at the top of his voice to test its music and make sure it contained no awkward combination of sounds. If he encountered the least snag, he would go back to work, scratch out, write between the lines, polish until the words flowed naturally and harmoniously."

Working seven hours a day, he produced twenty pages a month—all that remained after he had cut and tightened a much larger pile of manuscript. Ruthlessly deleting unnecessary adjectives, flowery metaphors, dialogue and descriptions that did not illuminate character or advance the plot, and, above all, taking pains to keep his own authorial voice out of the story and let his characters speak for themselves, he achieved a literary version of the maxim, "The government governs best that governs least."

He had a ready answer for friends who accused him of nitpicking. 'When I discover a disagreeable assonance or a repetition in one of my sentences, I can be sure that I'm floundering around in something false." Like George Orwell, he understood that opaque language is a tool of oppressive governments. 'When one writes well," he warned Guy de Maupassant, "one has two enemies to face: first, the public, because style forces it to think, obliges it to do some work; and second, the government, because it senses a force in us and power loves not another power."

A sensual man who saw sex as a threat to his artistic need for tranquillity, Flaubert experimented with celibacy in his twenties and practiced it periodically while living the life of a confirmed bachelor in his mother's country house outside Rouen. Occasional copulation was pleasant, but he would brook no interruptions from love-struck women. "The mere thought of being disturbed disturbs me," he said sourly.

Then he met an arty Parisian narcissist named Louise Colet, who liked to say that the arms of the Venus de Milo had been found in the sleeves of her dress. From the moment they became lovers Louise felt she owned him and demanded to see him every day. When he told her she would have to be content with a correspondence, she demanded that he write her every day, but he replied, "The very idea that you want a letter every morning will prevent me from writing it."

She clung harder, grilling him jealously about other women, complaining that he forgot her birthday, forgot to kiss her goodbye, and refused to say he would love her *forever*. To this he replied, "If despite the love that binds you to my poor self, my personality causes you too much pain, leave me."

Naturally that made her redouble her efforts. When he forgot the anniversary of their meeting, she reproached him with tears and recriminations. Next she tried to bind him to her by suggesting they collaborate on a book. Finally, when she said she wanted a child by him, he went ballistic. If she dared carry out such a mad plan, he vowed, "the Seine is here, and I would throw myself into it at this very moment with a 36-pound cannonball attached to my feet."

He concluded: "It is impossible for me to continue any longer a correspondence that is becoming epileptic. . . . I am weary of grand passions, exalted feelings, frenzied loves, and howling despairs."

He forbade her to come to his mother's house, but the desperate Louise showed up anyway—while he was writing *Bovary*. That did it. "Madame," he wrote her, "I am told that you took the trouble to call on me three times last evening. I was not in. And, fearing that if you persist in this way I shall be obliged to offer you repeated affronts, I am bound by the rules of courtesy to warn you that *I shall never be in*. Sincerely yours, G.F."

The Louise Colet episode illustrated something Flaubert knew instinctively but that today's conservatives, muzzled by America's romantic ethos, are loath to consider: there is something plebeian about sex. The agitated emotions, morbid suspicions, furious invective, wild jealousy, maudlin sentiment, and presumptuous familiarity it engenders all point to the inescapable conclusion that the behavior of the lover is the behavior of the mob.

Ironically, Flaubert's only intentional use of bad French was in the service of feminism. In letters to George Sand he addressed her as "Dear Master," using *maître*, a masculine noun, out of respect for her literary stature, but the feminine adjective *chère*, in deference to her sex. (When a conservative man respects you, you really know you've been respected.)

I discovered Henri Troyat ten years ago when I read his devastatingly perceptive and frequently hilarious life of Czar Alexander I, *Alexander of Russia: Napoleon's Conqueror*. This dazzling account of Gustave Flaubert's life reinforces my opinion that Troyat is the finest biographer now writing.

Other students of Flaubert have presented him as a literary hermit who withdrew completely from the world, but Troyat the historian reminds us that he lived through not only the Revolution of 1848 and the Bonapartist power grab, but the Second Empire, the Franco-Prussian War, and the Paris Commune—enough to make a political animal of the most rarified artist.

Both Troyat and Flaubert have been well served by a translator of uncommon common sense whose gift for grappling with the idioms and buzzwords of another time and place is—dare I say it?—awesome. Flaubert had a scatological streak and something of a dirty mind, but Mrs. Pinkham renders it all with no bumps and grinds, syntactical or otherwise. This book comes with a summa cum laude recommendation.

National Review, June 21, 1993
Book Review

"Fifty-Fifty"

The Fifties, by David Halberstam (Villard, 800 pp., $27.50)

A S AMERICA entered the 1950s, the air was full of debates about the New World Order, except that it was called "the American Century." The phrase was coined by Henry Luce, who believed it was America's duty and destiny to spread democracy around the globe.

Opposing him was Senator Robert A. Taft, the presidential choice of conservative Republicans and isolationists. Taft warned: "We would be in the same position of suppressing rebellions by force in which the British found themselves during the nineteenth century."

That is precisely what we started doing in the Fifties, thanks to a contradiction in the isolationist mindset that David Halberstam points out in the opening chapters of this richly enjoyable survey of the decade.

The Republican Right, he says, was isolationist when it came to the Atlantic, regarding it as the British ocean, the international ocean. But the Pacific was "the Republican ocean," obliquely associated with missionaries and docile, smiling Asians; a gin-and-tonic, white-linen-suit sort of world full of dreamy subcontinents, like the one that Senator Wherry of Nebraska called "Indigo China."

If I had total recall, my memory would consist of the contents of this book. I started the decade as a girl of 14 listening to the radio bulletin about the invasion of South Korea by North Korean troops, and ended it as a woman of 24 reading about the poisoned silver dollar carried, but not used, by U-2 pilot Francis Gary Powers when he was shot down and captured by the Soviets in 1960.

Halberstam uses the same landmarks, filling in the middle with a host of engaging memory promptors. His sources are secondary and derivative, but his instinct for the revealing anecdote, his ear for the memorable quote, and his awesome powers of organization add up to a variegated overview that moves seamlessly between the serious shenanigans of Chief Justice Earl Warren and the frivolous ones of *Peyton Place* author Grace Metalious.

He makes Adlai Stevenson look much better—like a New Democrat, in fact, or an earlier version of Sam Nunn. "The most conservative Democrat to run for President since John W. Davis," according to Arthur Schlesinger Jr. The media loved him nonetheless. Adlai, said Eric Sevareid in one of his trademark rolling parallelisms, "has excited the passions of the mind; he has not excited the emotions of the great bulk of half-informed voters, as had Eisenhower, who, like them, was empty of ideas or certitude."

Mordant radio wit Fred Allen called television "a device that permits people who haven't anything to do to watch people who can't do anything." The first campaign ad was aired by Ike, who said: "Yes, my Mamie gets after me about the high cost of living. It's another reason why I say it's time for a change. Time to get back to an honest dollar and an honest dollar's work."

When some purists objected to this "15-second spot," ad man Rosser Reeves countered that "Never have so many owed so much to so few" was also a 15-second spot. So was Marya Mannes's parody: "Eisenhower hits the spot; / One full General, that's a lot. / Feeling sluggish, feeling sick? / Take a dose of Ike and Dick."

Halberstam traces the decline of the Detroit auto industry from 1948, when GM president Charles Wilson signed the first union agreement guaranteeing cost-of-living raises. "In effect it made the union a junior partner of the corporation, [and] reflected the absolute confidence of a bedrock conservative who saw the economic pie so large that he wanted to forgo his ideological instincts in order to start carving it up as quickly as possible."

Forced to pass along huge labor costs to consumers, Detroit depended on "planned obsolescence," annual model changes calculated to make people ashamed of "old" cars and eager to prove their status by buying a new one every year.

The 1956 VW bug ($1,280) got a rave review in *Popular Mechanics* and "inspired" GM's disastrous rear-engine Corvair, which *Car and Driver* called "one of the nastiest-handling cars ever built." (Its tires required different pressures front and back, something few Americans outside of racing buffs understood.)

The "Model T" of housing was Levittown. The first Levitt houses sold for $7,990, with no down payment, no closing costs, no secret extras, just a $100 deposit, which was returned. "It was an unusual concept: The price was the price," Halberstam notes admiringly. Levitt built 36 houses a day. So what if they didn't have basements? The ancient Romans didn't build basements, said Bill Levitt, and who was he to challenge the ancient Romans?

Levitt houses proved unusually sturdy, but the builder was savaged by culture snobs like John Keats (*The Crack in the Picture Window*) and Lewis Mumford, who theorized that since the houses looked alike, the people inside them must be "made from a cookie cutter." Mumford's coinage quickly spread through the redoubts of bohemianism. I remember sitting on the floor deploring conformity with a bevy of tormented intellectuals, all of us wearing black turtleneck sweaters and talking about cookie cutters.

Conformity was so popular that it was defended even by rugged individualists and eccentric risk takers who honestly believed that they were just like everybody else. Halberstam rounds up a number of these for his most effective demonstration of the Zeitgeist.

Ray Kroc, organizer of the McDonald's franchise empire, combed the land for entrepreneurs without sharp edges. "We cannot trust nonconformists," he declared. "We will make conformists out of them in a hurry. . . . You cannot give them an inch. The organization cannot trust the individual; the individual must trust the organization or he shouldn't go into this kind of business."

Holiday Inns founder Kemmons Wilson modeled his hostels on his own tastes, explaining, "I like to think that I'm so damn normal that anything I like, everybody else is going to like too. The idea that my instincts are out of line just doesn't occur to me."

Hugh Hefner, driven by a belief in his own ordinariness, did not doubt that what stirred his sexual fantasies stirred every other man's. It was not pretentiousness but pride in conformity that dictated his innocent use of the royal pronoun in his first statement of the Playboy philosophy: "We like our apartment. We enjoy mixing up cocktails and an hors d'oeuvre or two, putting a little mood music on the phonograph, and inviting in a female for a quiet discussion on Picasso, Nietzsche, jazz, sex."

As the decade wore on, "alienation books" became a genre in themselves. *The Man in the Gray Flannel Suit*, a novel by Sloan Wilson, entered the language from the moment it was published in 1955. Plaid flannel shirts, on the other hand, were the trademark of Columbia sociology professor C. Wright Mills, the intellectual as lumberjack, whose books, *White Collar* and *The Power Elite*, condemned the new middle class for being affluent without purpose.

David Riesman and Nathan Glazer's *The Lonely Crowd* recast individualists and conformists as "inner-directed" and "other-directed," inspiring numerous parlor games, as well as seduction lines. (Gaze deeply into a girl's eyes and say, "You're inner-directed, I can tell.")

A feud soon erupted in the alienation industry when Riesman criticized Mills for "transferring his own need for intellectual stimulation into the minds and aspirations of people whose needs might be considerably different." Halberstam agrees; Mills, he writes, "did not understand the pride of people who had always been blue collar but who had finally moved up to the white-collar world."

The Fifties had more than one kind of alienation to deal with. Pondering the impending school-desegregation decision, *Brown* v. *Topeka Board of Education*, Chief Justice Fred Vinson said in 1952, "We face the complete abolition of the public school system." The following year he died of a heart attack and Ike replaced him with Earl Warren, "a big, dumb Swede" in the opinion of Judge Learned Hand.

Profiling Warren in 1947, John Gunther produced an assessment that is terrifying in its casual celebration of mediocrity: "honest, likable, and clean; he will never set the world on fire or even make it smoke; he has the limitations of all Americans of his type with little intellectual background, little genuine depth, or coherent political philosophy; a man who has probably never bothered with abstract thought twice in his life; a kindly man with the best of social instincts, stable, and well balanced."

Warren wanted the decision to be unanimous. "He shrewdly framed the Court's internal dialogue so that anyone who did not go along with him seemed a racist." Kentuckian Stanley Reed was an outright segregationist; Robert Jackson thought the NAACP briefs were sociology, not law, but gradually accepted the need, as he put it, to "make a judicial decision out of a political conclusion." Then he too had a heart attack, though he lived to write the concurring opinion that Warren squeezed out of him.

That left only Reed to be persuaded. He finally caved under pressure from Warren at daily lunches, insisting only that integration be allowed to take place gradually.

Halberstam organizes his section on the civil-rights movement around the story of John Daniel Rust's invention of the mechanical cotton picker, which made Southern blacks expendable. His detailed description of the machine and its many problems (how to keep the cotton from tangling in the machine's teeth and getting stuck) is one of many examples of this author's ability to make interesting what ought to be boring.

Especially enjoyable are his thumbnail biographies, including Elvis, James Dean, Tennessee Williams; Charles Van Doren, the boy-next-door star of the quiz-show scandals, who was chosen, said a CBS psychologist, to convince Americans that "We're all pretty much alike and we're all smart"; and my favorite, Grace Metalious, whom Halberstam recasts as Urfeminist, wryly pointing out that the women of *Peyton Place* were as discontented as it was possible to be.

The book has only a few faults. Halberstam identifies Whittaker Chambers as "an admitted homosexual," ignoring the very loving marriage he made after his youthful confusion.

He also overlooks the begged question in his account of the

Kinsey report's statistics on male homosexuality. Since Kinsey did the bulk of his research during World War II when the cream of American manhood was fighting overseas, could this be where the erroneous "10 per cent" came from?

One of his thumbnail biographies falls flat, but it's not his fault. When you see the word "vulnerable" all over the page, you know you're reading about Marilyn Monroe. There is simply nothing left to be said about her, so he shouldn't have bothered.

The only example of outright intellectual carelessness I found concerns my hero, Robert Taft. "Economic conservative he might have been, but he had always been a good man on civil liberties," says Halberstam, falling into the either–or of property rights versus human rights. They are the same, as our unsung Founding Father, Fisher Ames, demonstrated when he wrote: "By securing property, life and liberty can scarcely fail of being secured: where property is safe by rules and principles, there is liberty, for the objects and motives of tyranny are removed." In other words, if you can't seize property, why bother?

Other than that, Halberstam has written what is certain to be the most educational fun read of the year. My favorite of his many riveting images is that of Senator Joseph McCarthy eating a stick of butter to help him hold his liquor.

As for his best sentence, try this description of Margaret Sanger: "She was an American samurai, and she had spent her life on a wartime footing."

The American Spectator, January 1994
Book Review

"Heroine Addict"

A Woman's View: How Hollywood Spoke to Women, 1930-1960
by Janine Basinger (Alfred A. Knopf, 528 pages, $30)

E very woman of a certain age has a bone to pick with the movies. Feminists, bone-pickers par excellence, naturally do the lioness's share of it, but no woman is immune. Movies have made fools of us all at some point in our lives, usually—but not always—in adolescence. They threw us off track, made us guilty enough about something or other to try to become what we were not and never could be, and we harbor a compulsion to explain how it happened.

There is absolutely no need for another book about women 'n' movies, but they're fun to read. *A Woman's View* is especially so, and unusually well-written to boot. True, it contains a few dippy sentiments and theories, but that's the whole point, you see. No woman who grew up in the heyday of American movies is quite right in the head.

Jeanine Basinger, a film studies professor at Wesleyan University, is about the same vintage as your reviewer, and therefore just as warped. Well, almost. I identified with the Gene Tierney character in *Leave Her to Heaven* and she didn't, but she asked her mother why Mildred Pierce went back to her dopey husband instead of getting a new boyfriend, so in our separate ways we prove the theme of her book: Female moviegoers in Hollywood's golden age were not the passive, obedient zombies that feminists like to claim. We may have been distracted by inchoate romantic yearning, but we also came away from the Bijou with ideas we were not supposed to have. In other words, you didn't have to fall for it.

Of course Hollywood preached an anti-feminist message, Basinger says patiently, but look how they did it. "When morality has to dramatize its own opposite to make its point, the opposite takes on a life of its own." Maybe the heroine does give up her career in the last five minutes of the film, but for the first eighty-five the audience saw her running the world. They might have absorbed a traditionalist message when the leading man chided, "You're not a woman, Dr. Frisby, you're a machine," but they also absorbed a liberating view of female success and independence that stayed in their minds like orgy scenes in religious epics.

Taking issue with feminist film critics who pin the blanket label of "self-sacrifice" on anti-career movies, Basinger offers a testy reminder:

> As I have repeated often enough, a woman's film, in order to tell its story, has to present a central character of great importance who is out in the world doing something. Since movies encouraged audiences to identify with characters or dream about having the same experiences as were shown on the screen, women were inevitably going to project themselves into situations in which they got out and did something. To sacrifice herself. . . . she must have enough to make the sacrifice interesting—i.e., something to lose. This showed female audiences a woman of importance.

In *Old Acquaintance*, Bette Davis is a spinster careerist who accepts society's view that a woman cannot serve two masters, and resigns herself to the single life for the sake of her work. Her old friend, portrayed by Miriam Hopkins, is a married woman with a child who tries to Have It All, only to learn the hard way that a career always interferes with family life.

Both women become best-selling authors and both end up alone, but the audience knows that Davis is used to being alone, and they see Hopkins getting used to it with remarkable resiliency. In the final scene,

The two women toast each other with champagne as the camera moves back to reveal what will happen to women who don't accept love or their natural female roles in life. They will be alone—but, of course, they will also be extremely wealthy, well dressed, sought after, successful, and they will be drinking champagne.

Movie heroines not only ran the world, they occasionally destroyed it, or at least that part of it that threatened them. In *Dragon Seed*, Katharine Hepburn as Jade is the ultimate nonconformist, a Chinese feminist, a figure more at odds with her society than an American feminist could possibly be. Feminist film critics ought to love her, but because she flirts her way into the Japanese army kitchen, they get so exercised over her use of "woman's wiles" to get into a "woman's place" that they fail to give female viewers credit for understanding that she succeeded in poisoning the entire regiment.

"Were we a nation of goons forty years ago, who never noticed any subtexts?" Basinger asks. "Film scholarship has a way of making current analysts out to be geniuses, with the audiences of former times cast as idiots."

In general, Basinger believes, feminist movie criticism is skewed by too much attention to the *film noir*. She also takes our vaunted Age of Information to task; when too many over-educated and over-analytical people start combing through old movies, they over-complicate what was actually very simple when Basinger was going to the picture show back in South Dakota:

Women could ruin their lives—get free of everything—down at the movie house for twenty-five cents with butter on their popcorn. What was even more wonderful, no one cared. There were no articles written on the subject of "What Is Gold Lamé Doing to Our Mothers?" or "Will George Brent Destroy Civilization?" Society didn't feel threatened.

One reason for society's blasé attitude was that women, lacking the Walter Mitty syndrome, tailor their fantasies to fit their real-life situations, as they did when they saw the Depression-era hit, *It Happened One Night*. "They might not be able to find a Clark Gable of their own," writes Basinger, "but they certainly could get a guy with no undershirt."

Basinger is at her wittiest when she analyzes the wildly popular twin-sister movies in which the same actress played both parts. Here was "choice" beyond feminism's wildest dreams. Olivia de Havilland in *Dark Mirror* or *A Stolen Life* with Bette Davis gave women a chance to be Good Sister, Bad Sister, Bad Sister impersonating Good Sister, and Good Sister mistaken for Bad Sister. "There's two of her!" screamed the poster, heralding a frenzy of having-it-all in which Bad Sister sleeps around and wears great clothes until she drowns, whereupon Good Sister inherits her husband and her dog, only one of whom is smart enough to tell the difference.

The trio plot boiled choices down to real basics. *How To Marry a Millionaire* is about a good girl, a smart girl, and a bad girl; representing love and marriage, career, and the primrose path, or as Basinger puts it: "doing it the right way for a living, doing it the wrong way for a living, and just doing it for a living."

Naturally the movies did a lot of paternalistic preaching about good girls vs. bad girls, but shrewd viewers saw through the hackneyed props—e.g., "gum chewing becomes an effective shorthand for: she does something physical with great enthusiasm." Even funnier was the title card producers used for warning women away from really execrable behavior: "This is a story of evil. An evil woman who destroys all she touches. . . ." Bette Davis, of course, was the queen of the title card.

Basinger nails the closet elitism of feminists who are forever touting Katharine Hepburn's strength. "Hepburn could afford her strength. She was rich. She had a family to back her up." Women like Crawford, Davis, Stanwyck, and Rogers, on the other hand, had no one to rely on but themselves. Especially Crawford, who flopped in heiress roles because supposedly unsophisticated audiences "sniffed out the common clay in her":

Much has been written about how Hollywood exploited women, but most of these women would have had miserable lives without their stardom. . . . In Hollywood, they had their own money and their own clout, and not all of them went down the drain. . . . The stars who play the American woman made her strong and capable both on and off the screen.

If movies have been good for women and women have been good for movies, what is there to complain about? Basinger gives us a hint:

In movies about women, all important historical and natural events are translated into the terms of a woman's daily life. World War I is not about the Allies versus the Kaiser. It's about how unmarried women become pregnant when they have sex. The Depression is not about an economic collapse. It's about runs in stockings, no money for carfare, and being forced out onto the streets. Natural disasters like earthquakes and cholera epidemics are defined by miscarriages and dying children. Everything is couched in terms of what are presumed to be the major events of a woman's life.

This passage supports her thesis that movies have made women feel their lives are important and exciting, but to this reviewer it also describes the current feminization of American life. The news increasingly consists of "soft" features and "people stories," economics is about the two-career family, and foreign policy is driven by pictures of dying children. What started at the Bijou is now public policy.

The American Spectator, June 1994
Book Review

"3M-press"

A Woman's Place: The Freshmen Women Who Changed the Face of Congress by Majorie Margolies-Mevinsky, with Barbara Feinman (Crown, 220 pages, $22.50)

W hen a white male member of Congress jokingly referred to Rep. Marjorie Margolies-Mezvinsky as "the three-M girl," the freshman legislatrix tasted gall and wormwood. His sobriquet was "inaccurate, demeaning, and pathetically behind the times," she fumes, ignoring his accurate M count. "I took pity on my out-of-touch colleague and pulled him aside to let him know it's time to thaw out, that the ice age is over. He still didn't get it."

MMM, a 51-year-old mother of eleven—his, hers, theirs, plus three legal wards—is the former NBC-TV journalist from suburban Philadelphia who went to Congress in the Year of the Woman and fell on Bill Clinton's sword on the Night of the Long Knives, when she cast the deciding affirmative vote on his budget.

A Woman's Place, written with the aid of a former researcher for Woodward and Bernstein, is about breaking the barriers, overcoming the hurdles, finding her way, paying her dues, and what Pat Schroeder said to Leslie Byrne. Imagine *Junior Miss* recast for feminist policy wonks and you've got it.

The book begins with an introduction by Barbara Jordan in full Churchillian roll. This is followed by a foreword, which is followed by a prologue, and then we come at last to the first chapter and MMM's breathless description of how it all began:

The morning after the election, I woke up and squinted at the morning sunlight streaming through the window, yawning at the new day. Then it all came back to me. Sitting up in bed, I blurted out, "Wow! I did it. I really did it. Now I'm going to have to serve." My husband, Ed, looked at me and smiled. Ed, a former congressman himself, had been there. (Ed was serving in Congress when we met; I interviewed him for a story and came home and called my mother. I knew he was the one, from the first time we met. "Mom," I said, "if he calls me, he's a goner." We were married within the year.)

In the Year of the Woman (1992), twenty-four new congresspersons were elected, making a total of forty-eight females in the House. MMM was wiped out by the swearing in. "Imagine, twenty-four women walking down the aisle, not to get married but to be sworn in to the United States Congress." The ceremony also drew raves from Karan English (D-Ariz.), who knows a legislative snuggery when she sees one. "When we were sworn in," she recalls, "there were a lot of kids on the floor. I thought it was a delight. It did sound like an elementary schoolyard. . . . There were kids coughing and crying and young voices and everybody was excited." Some of the (white male) old timers complained of the lack of decorum, but English brushed them off. "I thought, I couldn't be more proud of all this noise, because it represents all walks of life. Sure it was disruptive, but it was real life."

But working at Laws 'R' Us was not all bliss. The first thing MMM did was count the serpents in the garden. Of 190 statues and busts in the Capitol, only seven are of women. "Everywhere I turn, I see sculptures and paintings depicting white men," she complains. "When I eat in the members' dining room, I look up and what do I see? George Washington, the father of our country, surrounded by men, staring down at me."

And then there's the cloakroom, where congressmen stretch out and take naps with their ties over their eyes. This, says Karan English, proves that males and females have different "comfort levels." Women could never feel comfortable curling up on a couch and sleeping in public. "We don't have enough power to do it. If we're asleep, we seem, look, and are vulnerable."

MMM invokes Karan English so often that the book frequently takes on the flavor of the "my best girlfriend said" testimonials in *Cosmopolitan* magazine. They seem to have forged a mutual commiseration pact and turn to each other whenever a (white male) congressman is mean to them. "I was so flabbergasted about what he was saying to me," Karan told MMM. "I was just so amazed that he was attacking me personally, because no one does that. I could hardly believe it. I lost track. . . . My voice was weak and raspy and I was totally humiliated and embarrassed."

We also meet the recovering suicide, Nydia Velazquez (D-N.Y.), who "tried to end her own life, to stifle the pain, disappointment, and frustration that had somehow enveloped her and was squeezing the hope and strength out of her." Another member of the Class of '92, Lynn Woolsey (D-Calif.), had been left destitute by the no-fault divorce that feminists demanded, with "a job that paid a pathetically inadequate salary. . . . forced to rely on welfare and food stamps to feed her children. She had to sell her house and trade in her new station wagon for a very used Volkswagen Bug."

That is really good true-confessions writing, but most of the time MMM burbles with good cheer. Freshmen congresswomen are not only bright but "incredibly bright." Their husbands are not merely supportive but "wonderfully supportive." All problems are "real problems," seeing is "perceiving," and virtually every page contains an assertion that women of the nineties are "focused"—the word is her Rosebud.

She is not above lifting a cliché from Golda Meir. "When I was at work, I felt I should be at home; when I was at home, I felt I should be at work." Elizabeth Furse (D-Ore.) lifts hers from the first issue of *Ms.* magazine. "Oh my God, laundry! Are we supposed to do that? You mean that pile in the corner of the bedroom? It certainly would be nice to have a wife."

Leslie Byrne (D-Va.) shares with MMM her thoughts on the connection between team sports and the uses of power: "Men, as little boys, get it woven into their very fabric; it seeps into their inchoate bones."

Lynn Woolsey analyzes the feminine penchant for detail: "Men are more broad-brushed, so they can go into these committee meetings and maybe they just soak it up, and they get it or it doesn't matter that they're just swishing through."

Jennifer Dunn (R-Wash.) laments: "Women often aren't taken very seriously. Maybe it's because of their speaking style." Yep, maybe it is.

MMM's chapter on The Vote is disappointingly—and suspiciously—skimpy. She caved so quickly that something else must have been said that she's not telling. All she says is that when the ayes reached 217 of the 218 needed for passage, Clinton, his voice sounding "drained and tired," phoned her and asked simply, "What would it take, Marjorie?"

When she demurred, he revved up his tone of exhausted self-pity and floored the guilt pedal. "Without your vote, I can't win. I think my administration will grind to a halt without the passage of this budget. The entire rest of our agenda depends on getting this behind us. What would it take?"

"It would really take an entitlements conference," she chirruped. That is just what she got, along with a lot of flak from her constituents. But that's okay. She says she couldn't live with herself if she "let him go down in flames, let him be cut off at the knees." And besides, the future of her children and all of America's children was at stake—the epilogue is entitled "Our Legacy to Our Children."

There also was supposed to be a postscript, but evidently it wasn't ready in time for inclusion in the reviewer's reading copy—and is missing from the hard-bound copy as well. Also missing from the final copy is the "Interview with Hillary Rodham Clinton" advertised on the book jacket. It may be that for once in her life, HRC is mad at a woman who played hard to get with Bill.

The American Spectator, August 1994
Book Review

"Sophie's Choice"

Great Catherine: The Life of Catherine the Great,
Empress of Russia by Carolly Erickson (Crown, 392 pages, $25)

Would you want your sister to marry Grand Duke Peter of Russia? Someone actually asked Frederick the Great this question. His answer was no, but his fastidious chivalry did not extend to other men's sisters. Prussia needed stronger ties with Russia, and nubile princesses were the chief export of the many tiny German states that Frederick controlled. Fifteen-year-old Sophie of Anhalt-Zerbst seemed like the best bet, and so he tossed her to the Romanovs.

Peter, the 16-year-old future czar, accepted the passably pretty Sophie, but she was definitely not his type. He liked his women lame, scarred, or one-eyed, but what really turned him on were hunchbacks. He also seems to have had Tourette's syndrome. Prone to sudden grimaces and twitches, he bellowed obscenities at court levees and laughed maniacally in church. Though puny and girlish, he imagined himself a great military commander and practiced heroic maneuvers with his vast collection of toy soldiers; when a rat gnawed on one, he court-martialed the rodent and executed it on a makeshift gallows in the royal apartments.

His aunt, Empress Elizabeth, was the daughter of Peter the Great by his second wife. The throne had originally passed to her infant cousin, Ivan VI, but Elizabeth overthrew him, imprisoned him in a remote fortress, and then spent the rest of her life worrying that someone would overthrow her. Insomnia joined paranoia when she found a barrel of gunpowder under her bed. Thereafter she thought to foil assassins by sleeping in a different room each night, but, too afraid to sleep, she made her ladies tickle her feet to keep her awake. Her superstitiousness was the despair of her ministers; she refused to read state documents if they happened to brush against one of the many holy relics on her desk; and once, when a fly landed on a treaty, she refused to sign it.

She developed a sudden, obsessive interest in lunatics after seeing a servant go mad and foam at the mouth. She turned part of her palace into a small private asylum and stocked it with inmates from her court, which, not surprisingly, yielded quite a few: a monk who castrated himself, an equerry who thought the Shah of Persia was God, and two guards officers who lost it.

Sophie did not know what to make of this wildly eccentric empress, who terrified her one moment and overwhelmed her with smarmy affection the next. Her orderly Germanic nature shrank from the chaos on which Elizabeth thrived and her businesslike Lutheran soul was repelled by the spectacle of government by omen and portent. A little voice in her head told her that this was no way to rule an empire, and gradually, almost without realizing it, she began to dream and plan.

In 1745, Sophie converted to Orthodox Christianity, changed her name to Catherine and married Peter, but whether their union was ever consummated is still debated. All we know for sure is that he made her dress in a hussar's uniform and stand sentry all night at their bedroom door. Still, she got pregnant, perhaps by Sergei Saltykov, but she miscarried when fire destroyed the imperial palace. Pregnant a second time, she gave birth to a son, Paul, but the empress took the baby away from her and raised him herself. Meanwhile, Peter found a pockmarked mistress and Catherine was left to her own devices.

"Where another woman might have gone mad or succumbed to illness or depression," writes Carolly Erickson, "Catherine retired to a small, ill-lit chamber and began to read." Like today's conservatives who turn to Albert Jay Nock and Irving Babbitt as an antidote to Billary 'R' Us, she fought down the unnerving influences of Elizabeth and Peter with the philosophers of the French

Enlightenment. It was a meeting of minds. Catherine, who was nothing if not well-adjusted, recognized in the works of Voltaire, Montesquieu, and Diderot the same instinct for the rational that she herself possessed in such abundance.

Erickson disputes the claims of some historians that Catherine went native and became more Russian than a Cossack. On the contrary, she was repelled by eastern Slav mysticism. It was

> not an honest piety, of the kind Catherine favored, but the darker sort of religion that led to intolerance, irrationality and mental aberrations. . . . Endless processions, day-long rituals, the mad ringing of the thousands of bells created an atmosphere, not so much of otherworldliness as of murky illogic, inhospitable to the concrete and the commonsensical; in Moscow, reason withered under the icy blast of the supernatural.

Catherine intended to change all this, but her plans to reign as a liberal philosopher-empress soon foundered on the shoals of Russian reality. No sooner had she murdered her husband and assumed his throne than impostors claiming to be the dead Peter III sprouted like weeds, leaving millions of hysterical peasants writhing. Then came an attempt to overthrow Catherine and crown the imprisoned and by now ga-ga Ivan VI. Next a Cossack revolt led by Emelian Pugachev, who surged around the country wearing a lace-trimmed red caftan and brandishing a silver axe.

It's bracing to watch Catherine's liberalism fade. She gave orders to Ivan VI's guards to kill him if anyone tried to liberate him. Someone did, and the guards killed him:

> She had discovered first hand how government must assert its primacy over chaos by force alone; all considerations of public good and individual liberty had to be secondary. Absolute power demanded ironclad obduracy toward traitors. Unwavering sternness alone could protect her. . . . [The peasants] were not a docile and devoted collection of willing learners, waiting to be led into the light, but an ugly combustible mass of haters, seething with murderous rage, ready to avenge themselves on their betters.

Carolly Erickson has written a highly readable biography, sometimes too readable. It occasionally reads like a novel, as when she turns passages from Catherine's memoirs into bodice-ripper dialogue. There are no notes, and she avoids discussion of the operation that may have been performed on Peter to enable him to father Paul. She states flatly that Paul was the son of Sergei Saltykov, ignoring that both Paul and his son, Alexander I, displayed several of Peter's most arresting characteristics.

Most commendably, however, she rescues Catherine from the charge of wantonness, arguing persuasively that she had only five lovers, and that the young men of her later life assuaged not her lust but her frustrated maternalism:

> With Catherine, work always came first. . . . she arranged her life so that she greeted each morning with a clear head and, if possible, a serene mind. She liked to go to bed early, to read for a while, or do a bit of needlework, then settle down for the night. She needed and craved love, but she was unwilling to let love tyrannize her or upset the balance and order of her life—at least, not for long.

National Review, September 26, 1994
Essay

"Parodic Verses"

Editor's Note: Miss King has been spendng time lately rereading the work of certain lady novelists. Inspired, she submitted the following.

HILLARIQUE SHRUGGED

After Ayn Rand

BILL CLINTON laughed. He stood naked on a soft muddy hill. It swelled out around him, the body of the hill and the body of the man blending and merging into a triumph of man over nature. He was softer than the hill.

He strode purposefully through the woods, his eyes fixed straight ahead, seeing nothing but the next election. He tried to clamp his lips shut with inflexible contempt but it was hard when you smiled all the time.

He was always striding purposefully. It was why his pasty white body was covered with scars, its soft quivering folds full of scrapes and bruises and half-healed cuts. He was always bumping into things and tripping. That's how he got his distinguishing characteristic. One day while he was striding purposefully, looking neither right nor left, he fell down and landed right on his—

That reminded him. It was time to rape Hillarique. He approached her house and stepped through the French windows into her boudoir.

She was sitting on the bed wearing a long black cape. It made her look more than ever like a witch but it came in handy for purposeful striding, and besides, it covered her legs. Glancing up, she gave him a steely smile.

"Hello, Willie." The two words fell like soft, silken waves of coiffed perfection around the tangled knot of her contempt.

"You ready for some exalted degradation, Hillarique?"

"Put your first principle away, Willie, we've got a problem. You remember that marble statue I threw out the window because I couldn't bear the thought of unworthy people looking at it?"

"You mean your highest rational value? The one you swiped from the Greek battleship last time we were in Europe?"

She gave him a look of blistering contempt. "Yes, that one. Well, it hit Joycelyn Elders on the head, and it did something to her . . . brain. She started talking and couldn't stop. Nobody can shut her up. She's been examining her premises on C-SPAN for the last sixty-three hours."

"Sixty-three hours!" exclaimed Bill with envious contempt. "Why didn't you hit me with it?"

Hillarique strode purposefully across the room, her black cape swirling with Objectivist contempt, and turned on the television. In a moment, they saw General Elders in her admiral's uniform, her jaw set in a rational clamp that made her tin-ear pronunciations sound more peculiar than ever.

"I have come here today to explain the philosophy of Ayn Ryan. My mind is on strike. I am an African-American who does not exist for others. Who is Russ Limbo? The altruist is a second-hander but the egoist won't build Greek columns because he knows you don't have to hold up the roof any more. Ayn Ryan says if you build a building and somebody builds something on top of it—blow it up! I want to hand out contempt kits in the schools. Every chyuld a purposefully striding chy-uld. Who is Russ Limbo?"

As the Surgeon General's voice clattered on, Bill Clinton sank weakly onto the bed and stared down bemusedly at his distinguishing characteristic.

"You know, Hillarique, I'm about all strided out."

Hillarique shrugged. "Who is Rush Limbaugh?"

BLUE EYES, BLACK HAIR
After Marguerite Duras

I SIT here with my face in shadow beside the window opening onto the sea. The sea, the sea, inaccessible, turbulent, crashing. The sea, the sea, murmuring always murmuring, the insomniac sea that licks the sand in the stricken, artless calamity of night.

I have blue eyes and black hair and I am running a temperature in a teapot from trying to cure a homosexual. It all started in a café by the sea, the sea, after the beauty of the day had vanished as abruptly as whisky in a book reviewer's glass.

I was sitting with a Jewish Prince from Vancouver who also has blue eyes and black hair. While we were swapping migraine stories at our table by the sea, the sea, the homosexual came in with kohl on his eyes. The prince left and the homosexual started weeping. He was alone and attractive and worn out from watching yachts on the sea, the sea, glide past his body like an infinite caress, so I asked him if he wished he were dead and he said yes.

He sat down and we wept a while, then he made me a proposition. Because I looked so much like the Jewish Prince with blue eyes and black hair, he asked me if I would move into his room and lie naked on the floor with a black veil over my face and talk about what it's like to be tired and cold and despairing by the sea, the sea. I had nothing better to do, so off we went to our zipless *Weltschmerz*.

The room was empty except for wall-to-wall sheets. Our relationship was your average existential crisis by the sea, the sea; I slept, he wept, then we switched.

"I must tell you," he said, "it's as if you were responsible for the thing inside you, that you know nothing of and that terrifies me because it seizes other things and changes them within itself without seeming to."

"It's true I'm responsible for the astral nature of my sex," I replied, "its lunar, bloody rhythm. In relation to you as to the sea."

Most of the time he walked around and around my supine body and then shrank back against the wall and wept. I got to like the idea of being repulsive when I realized how much it was adding to my sense of hopeless torment. Still, I have to admit that I got a little restless lying on the floor all day long, talking about being stricken and knowledge-less beside the sea, the sea, so one day I went out and picked up a man.

When I got back, the homosexual wanted to hear all about it, personal things like "his name, his pleasure, his skin, his member, his mouth, his cries."

That's when I started to worry. Let me tell you, when you're locked in a room with someone who calls a penis a "member," you've sunk about as low as you can get.

MORNING IN BOOK CAMP
Provoked by Joan Didion

WELCOME TO Camp Jejune. The Sublimes are lookin' for a few good novels and I got one right here. *Play It As It Lays*, by Joan Didion.

I bet you denouement-diddlers never read it, did you? Yeah, that's what I thought. You look like the kind of blurb-heads that wouldn't know an elegiac spiritual wasteland if it jumped up and bit you. Well, that's gonna change 'cause you're in Book Camp now.

Play It As It Lays is about a girl named Maria Wyeth whose hometown in Nevada has been turned into a missile range. What's that a symbol of? Lemme hear it loud and clear!

SIR! THE ARID LANDSCAPE OF THE SOUL, SIR!

Correct! Now, if there's one thing the Sublime Corps won't tolerate, it's the kind of reader who likes a novel to start out good and puts it down if it don't. If I catch you plot-suckers doin' it, I'll turn you into a slice of life quicker'n you can say "exposition." Here's how *Play It As It Lays* starts out:

"I never ask about snakes. Why should Shalimar attract kraits. Why should a coral snake need two glands of neurotoxic poison to survive while a king snake, *so similarly marked*, needs none. Where is the Darwinian logic there. You might ask that. I never would, not any more."

All right, story-ballers, whadda we got here?

SIR! NIHILISM, SIR!

Correct! Nihilism. Nada. Nothin'. That's what this whole book is about. That's how you separate Sublimes from civilians—nothin' matters to a Sublime but we'll tell you all about it anyway. It's like the Sublime Corps Manual says: You gotta read Proust when you have a fever and Joan Didion while you're havin' a miscarriage.

Now back to Maria Wyeth. Her husband's a movie maker. When he stars her in a movie about a girl who gets gang-raped by 12 motor-cycle guys, she keeps goin' back to see it over and over again. You know why she likes it so much? Because "the girl on the screen seemed to have a definite knack for controlling her own destiny." Whadda we got? Lemme hear it loud and clear!

SIR! EXISTENTIAL CHAOS, SIR!

She starred in another movie where her husband just followed her around New York and shot film: "The picture showed Maria doing a fashion sitting, Maria asleep on a couch at a party. Maria on the tele-phone arguing with the billing department at Bloomingdale's, Maria cleaning some marijuana with a kitchen strainer, Maria crying on the subway. At the end she was thrown into negative so she would look dead."

All right, Aristotle freaks, whadda you call that?

SIR! ANOMIE, SIR!

You bet your *ibids* it's anomie! It's like her husband says: "Maria has difficulty talking to people with whom she is not sleeping." She's not what civilians call an outgoin' gal. Her and her husband go to this party where she curls up in a ball until he happens to say that he likes to eat breakfast out. Then she comes to and says, real low and to nobody in particular: "In fact he doesn't always get breakfast out. In fact the last time he got breakfast out was on April 17."

All right, McMuffdivers, tell me what her problem is!

SIR! ALIENATION, SIR!

When you study the Sublime Corps Manual I want you to pay special attention to what the Lit Crits say about Joan Didion's tech-nique. Here's what General Guy "Blood and Guts" Davenport wrote: "She has given the novel a pace so violent and so powerful that its speed becomes the dominant symbol of her story."

Let's see about that. Listen to this:

Maria drove the freeway . . . it was essential (to pause was to throw herself into unspeakable peril) that she be on the freeway by ten o'clock. Not somewhere on Hollywood Boulevard, not on her way to the freeway, but actually on the freeway. If she was not she lost the day's rhythm. . . . an intricate stretch just south of the interchange . . . required a diagonal move across four lanes of traffic. On this afternoon she finally did it without once braking or once losing the beat on the radio . . . she was exhilarated, and that night she slept dreamlessly. . . . So that she would not have to stop for food she kept a hard-boiled egg on the passenger seat of the Corvette. She could shell and eat a hard-boiled egg at seventy miles an hour (crack it on the steering wheel, never mind salt, salt bloats, no matter what happened she remembered her body). . . .

All right, lube jobs, whadda the Crits call that?

SIR! VOYAGE OF SELF-DISCOVERY, SIR!

Now, lemme tell you about Joan Didion's vision. If anybody drives that much on the L.A. freeways they're gonna run into a lot of smog. That's why Maria's out there, so she can see things without a lot of sharp edges. If Sublimes find a clean window, we blow our breath on it so we can show off our exquisite sensibility. Opaque is where it's at! Heat must shimmer! You gotta have haze! You gotta have refraction! You gotta glimpse everything intermittently through squinted eyes! Squint, you lousy potboilers! *Squint!* Now tell me what you see!

SIR! AMBIGUITIES, SIR!

The Sublime Corps has racked up a lot of tributes to Joan Didion, but this one is engraved on the statue of us plantin' the flag on Pointless View that stands at the main gate of Camp Jejune. It's from Lore Segal's *New York Times* review of *Play It As It Lays*: "Her prose tends to posture like a figure from a decadent period of art, whose fingers curl toward an exposed heart or a draped bosom swelling with suspect emotion."

Whadda you print lice call that?

SIR! NEGATIVE CAPABILITY, SIR!

Correct! Now, *Semper Vortex*, as Sublimes say. Maria Wyeth turns up again in another Joan Didion novel called *A Book of Common Prayer*, only this time her name is Charlotte Douglas. After her daughter gets mixed up with terrorists and disappears, Charlotte goes to a Caribbean island named Boca Grande and waits there for the kid to turn up because Boca Grande is "the very cervix of the world, the place through which a child lost to history must eventually pass."

All right, wit-holes, whadda the Sublimes call that?

SIR! METAPHOR, SIR!

There's another woman on Boca Grande who spends her nights waitin' for her generator to break down so she can recite Matthew Arnold in the dark, so naturally she's impressed by Charlotte's energy. You wanna know about Charlotte's energy? Listen to this:

> I once saw her make the necessary incision in the trachea of an OAS field worker who was choking on a piece of steak at the Jockey Club. A doctor had been called but the OAS man was turning blue. Charlotte did it with a boning knife plunged first in a vat of boiling rice. A few nights later the OAS man caused a scene because Charlotte refused to fellate him on the Caribe terrace, but that, although suggestive of the ambiguous signals Charlotte tended to transmit, is neither here nor there.

Civilians would call that a shaggy-dog story but Sublimes have a different name for it. Lemme hear it!

SIR! ILLUMINATING THE HUMAN CONDITION, SIR!

After that Charlotte spends every day sittin' at the airport havin' hot flashbacks until a revolution closes the airport down and she has to find another place to be a symbol of futility in. Life on Boca Grande gets worse: "The bite of one fly deposits an egg which in its pupal stage causes human flesh to suppurate. The bite of another deposits a larval worm which three years later surfaces on and roams the human eyeball." That's just like Camp Jejune in August—good Sublimes like Joan Didion never forget their Book Camp days.

Finally Charlotte is shot dead in the Boca Grande birth-control clinic while she's handin' out rubbers, and her body is shipped back to the States with a red, white, and blue T-shirt draped on the coffin because nobody could find a flag—

Just a minute! I saw that smirk! All right, you cheek-tonguer, you asked for it. You're gonna do fifty *op cits* up Hostile Universe Hill before breakfast! That'll learn you to stop lookin' for a laugh in a

Sublime book! And just in case any of the rest of you get any ideas, let's go through the drill:

What did Joan Didion say when they asked who's on first?

SIR! I KNOW ABOUT FIRST, SIR!

Who's on first?

SIR! I NEVER ASK ABOUT FIRST, SIR!

Who's on first?

SIR! OTHER PEOPLE ASK THAT BUT I DON'T, SIR!

That's better! Now back to *A Book of Common Prayer*. Joan Didion never gets around to explainin' why Charlotte thought Boca Grande was the cervix of the world, so we gotta turn to the *Sublime Corps Manual* to get a straight answer from the Crits. Here's what Mark Royden "Wild Man" Winchell said: "If it is not altogether clear why Charlotte has come to Boca Grande, it is even less clear why she stays. At one level her insistence on remaining may simply be another indication of her solipsistic innocence."

Well, bookfans, what do you say to that?

SIR! ON AN OPAQUE DAY YOU CAN SEE FOREVER, SIR!

Now listen to me, because I'm only gonna say this once. There's a certain Crit that Sublimes are sworn to hate, and if I catch you readin' him, I'll cut off your classical unities and eat 'em for breakfast. His name is John Simon and this is what he said about Joan Didion: "After reading such outpourings of hypersensitivity in quotidian conflict, one feels positively relieved to be an insensitive clod."

That's a civilian for you. Now, while you're marchin' to the mess hall for breakfast, I wanna hear the Sublime Corps Hymn loud and clear. Column right, har! Forward, har!

> *From the halls of ambiguity*
> *To the shores of psychic void,*
> *We secured the arid landscape—*
> *Every sentence was destroyed!*
> *Just to fragment every story line,*
> *And to drop anomic bombs,*
> *We'll obsess through suppurating climes*
> *Until every Crit succumbs!*

The American Spectator, May 1995
Book Review

"Bulbous Brain"

Edison: Inventing the Century by Neil Baldwin
(Hyperion, 531 pages, $27.95)

After meeting Thomas Alva Edison on a transatlantic liner, Henry James described him in a letter as "the great bland simple deaf street-boy-faced Edison." True, but nineteenth-century America liked him that way. Descended from Dutch immigrants [the original name was Edeson], he had a sturdy, blue-eyed yeoman look that made him, writes Neil Baldwin, the "incarnation of Ragged Dick," hero of the Horatio Alger stories.

Young Tom was not ragged but he had other drawbacks. Expelled from school after only three months for what our age calls attention-deficit disorder and his called "addled," he was taught at home by his mother until he went off to seek his fortune at age twelve, working as a "news butch" [newsboy] on the railroad, selling snacks and the Detroit papers to passengers on the Port Huron train.

A compulsive reader who devoured Victor Hugo and technical manuals with equal pleasure, he set up a chemistry lab in a corner of the baggage car. One day his experiment started a fire, providing him with a more Algeresque explanation for his partial deafness. Loath to admit that it was a congenital defect, he blamed the conductor who boxed his ears.

His deafness drew him to the telegraph, a "clattering embrace of dots and dashes he could understand." He rose quickly to be chief telegrapher for Western Union, quitting when he found backers to finance his invention of faster techniques. Already going gray at 24, he opened his own lab at Menlo Park, New Jersey, and married 16-year-old Mary Stilwell, whom he rarely saw except when he fathered their three children. Unable to pry him away from his lab, where he regularly stayed all night, Mary took to drink and nervous break-downs while her husband benefited humanity.

This absorbing biography is a perfect blend of art and science thanks to Neil Baldwin's gift for making the technical sections as interesting as the human story. Although nominally a specialist in modern American poetry whose earlier books include a biography of William Carlos Williams, he nonetheless makes an effortless transition to Edison's laboratory, covering the major inventions of the Menlo Park heyday in clear, accessible language, illustrated with reproductions of Edison's own drawings.

One of the earliest inventions was the 1876 Electric Pen. As one wrote in the normal way, the needle tip punctured holes in the surface of a sheet of paper to create a stencil that was then placed over clean sheets of papers and inked with a roller to reproduce as many as fifty copies. Edison's P.T. Barnum streak is evident in the ad: "Like Kissing—Every Succeeding Impression is as Good as the First—Endorsed By Every One Who Has Tried It!—Only a Gentle Pressure Used." He later sold the patent to A.B. Dick of Chicago, who used it to invent the mimeograph.

The phonograph, pioneered in 1837 by a Frenchman, initially used a pig's bristle and a sheet of paper coated with lampblack rotating on a cylinder. Edison's improvement, which he called the Speaking Telegraph, consisted of a brass cylinder covered with tinfoil. One cranked it by hand while shouting into a funnel; the message was engraved as series of bumps in the foil surface, with playback achieved by a spring-held stylus. Edison demonstrated it with "Mary Had a Little Lamb," and Sarah Bernhardt traveled to Menlo Park to recite lines from *Phèdre* into it.

In developing the electric light Edison first used platinum for the filament, but it stayed lit only briefly. He switched to carbon, claiming that he got the idea by absentmindedly rolling lampblack in his fingers. This, says the author, was a lie designed to make the world see him as Archimedes in a "Eureka!" moment. Baldwin marshals a wealth of evidence to prove that Edison had been experimenting with carbon for several years, and that he abandoned platinum because of its scarcity and cost. His first carbon bulb burned for thirteen hours with the power of thirty candles; a few days later he got it up to one hundred hours by shaping the filament like a horseshoe.

Edison spoke in gnostic terms about "good" electric light and "evil" gaslight, casting himself, says Baldwin, as a knight in shining armor come to rid the world of shadows. But his chivalry did not extend to the shadows in his own home. In 1884, soon after Edison lit up New York, Mary died at 29 of "congestion of the brain," a Victorianism that Baldwin thinks may have concealed a suicide. Her death also coincided with the publication of *American Nervousness* by Dr. George Beard, who blamed "the anxiety habit" on "the trials and tribulations of modern urban civilization. . . . too many ideas being developed and introduced too rapidly."

Baldwin's analysis of Edison's workaholism runs the gamut from William Dean Howell's *The Rise of Silas Lapham* to the landmark sociological study *Homo Faber* by Andriano Tilgher. Like the prurient man who can turn any conversation around to sex, Edison could turn any conversation around to work. In Paris he complained that meager continental breakfasts of rolls and coffee were "very poor for a man to do any work upon," and pondered French *joie de vivre*: "What has struck me so far is the absolute laziness of everybody over here. When do these people work? What do they work at? People here seem to have established an elaborate system of loafing. I don't understand it at all."

He proudly punched in and out of his lab every day: a typical time card for a week in 1912 shows 111 hours. To people requesting secrets of his success he wrote: "I work 18 hours daily—have been doing this for 45 years."

He wasted no time acquiring another young wife, 20-year-old Mina Miller, daughter of an Akron industrialist. More secure than Mary, she did not try to change him, but responded to his workaholism by becoming a workaholic herself, perpetually redecorating the house and hurling herself into civic good works. She stated proudly that she never nagged him, but accepted that "his work was his life. . . . accomplishing great things for the world. . . . and if Fate had placed it within my power to be of some service to him, I feel that I have not striven in vain."

Mina guarded "his" chair lest anyone else sit in it, and always cheerfully played his favorite song, "I'll Take You Home Again, Kathleen," keeping the record at the ready so she could grab it fast the instant she sensed the savage beast needed soothing. As his deafness increased, she even learned Morse code and tapped out conversations on his knee.

Self-effacement paid off for Mina, who spent her married life "creating and burnishing the later, mellowed image of Thomas Edison; as eminence grise, he would be *her* invention."

Mina's own children by Edison turned out well—Charles was assistant secretary of the Navy, governor of New Jersey, and one of the founders of Young Americans for Freedom—but her stepchildren were a mess. Marion became an expatriate; Tom Junior changed his name twice, failed at mushroom farming, and was found dead in a hotel room; William Leslie, another failed farmer whose letters his father returned marked with spelling errors, died of cancer two years after his brother.

To hear Thomas Alva Edison tell it, he was just a regular fella who happened to become an electrical engineer. He cultivated this just-plain-folks pose assiduously, endearing himself to the American public with aw-shucks pronouncements that downplayed the importance of formal education and superior brainpower:

> Any other bright-minded fellow can accomplish just as much if he will stick like hell and remember that nothing that's any good works by itself, just to please you; you got to make the damn thing work. Genius is one per cent inspiration, ninety-nine percent perspiration. Yes, sir, it's mostly *hard work*.

Charles Steinmetz, the German-born chief engineer of General Electric, reacted to this anybody-can American modesty with European horror:

This is the attitude Edison has always taken, declaring himself a mere practical man, and the newspaper men have expanded on this and so created the popular belief that Edison does not know anything about theory and science, but merely experiments and tries anything he or anybody else can think of. There is nothing more untrue than this.

The author traces Edison's anti-intellectual intellectualism back to a national trait that was already well underway before he was born. It was articulated by Tocqueville, who discerned an ever-present tension in the American psyche between aggressiveness and withdrawn individualism. Edison personified this tension, says Baldwin, and relieved it by rationalizing his deafness and using it as a defense mechanism, claiming that it "set him apart from the masses of men, gave him an excuse to turn away from tiresome social involvements, making him a far more productive thinker."

Here then is the reason for his cold dismissal of the hundreds of deaf people who begged him to invent a hearing aid. Subconsciously aware of the split between his cerebral and practical selves, he did not want to alleviate deafness, because "he refused to surrender what was essentially his passport to the inner world."

The American Spectator, June 1995
Book Review

"Phalanx for the Memories"

John Steinbeck: A Biography by Jay Parini
(Henry Holt, 536 pages, $30)

‘ If you loved a book," Raymond Chandler always advised, "don't meet the author." The rule holds for this exhaustive biography of John Steinbeck. To Jay Parini, a poet and novelist who teaches at Middlebury College, Steinbeck can do no wrong, but his overexplained rationalizations only serve to expose his subject as a muddy thinker, derivative author, closet snob, and sycophantic toady of Democratic politicians.

John Steinbeck was born in Salinas, California, in 1902, the son of a failed businessman who had settled into a comfortable bureaucratic sinecure as county treasurer. Pushed by his parents to make something of himself, he compiled a chaotic record at Stanford before quitting to become a writer. He tried to support himself with factory jobs and write after work, but the hard physical labor left him too exhausted to think. In other respects, however, his life became easier. Socially gauche with his peers and self-conscious about his ugliness, he could relax with working-class people because his own middle-class origins made him feel a cut above them.

Steinbeck accepted an allowance from his father and went to live rent-free in his family's vacation cottage on the Monterey coast.

There he made friends with a quirky marine biologist named Ed Ricketts, who believed that people, like fish, are group-driven, and that novelists, like scientists, should forego subjective moral judgments and concentrate on random patterns of human behavior. Hardly a new idea, as the well-read Steinbeck certainly knew, but he fell completely under Ricketts's spell. He latched onto the concept of the *phalanx*, derived from the Greek word for "spider" and rejuvenated by the utopian socialist Charles Fourier, who used it to describe group behavior of any kind.

Steinbeck applied the theory in his novels of social protest. The movement of Okies to California in *The Grapes of Wrath* is a phalanx. As undifferentiated as an army of ants, they "swarm," "crawl," "creep," and "scuttle" in their instinctive march toward the place of sustenance, turning the landscape black with their old Fords and dodging inhospitable Californians who call them "a plague of locusts."

But Steinbeck was a novelist, not an entomologist. An undifferentiated swarm has a destination but no plot line; to tell a story he needed individuals. Worse, the phalanx theory clashed with his liberal-humanist belief in the dignity of man and his New Deal Democrat belief in progress. To make it fit his preconceived notions, he tinkered with it until he came up with an on-again, off-again phalanx. People, he decided, behave as individuals until circumstances drive them to "connect to a larger spirit or will that exists somewhere beyond individual response." This connection is achieved by "a keying device," signaling them that they must now respond to something bigger than themselves and do things they would not do as individuals.

The keying device goes off loud and clear in the famous last scene of *Grapes* when Rose of Sharon, whose baby has died, gives her breast to a starving man. Steinbeck's editor protested that the scene was too abrupt and asked that the role of the man be built up. Steinbeck refused, insisting that it had to be a complete stranger to make the point that the Joads, previously a separate family with selfish concerns, are now part of the phalanx, reflecting man's humanity to man in a vast connected chain.

An obsessive idea can be the grain of sand that creates the pearl, but Steinbeck's romanticized biological determinism became a stone in his shoe. Motivation, the novelist's stock in trade, was the worst casualty in his later novels. We never really find out why the businessman in *The Wayward Bus* rapes his own wife in a cave, or why the mother in *East of Eden* becomes a madam. Husbands do not hear the call of the keying device simply because they are in a cross-section-of-humanity book, and plenty of women married to cold men manage somehow without joining the world's oldest phalanx.

Steinbeck got his first fatal taste of attention from the powerful when Eleanor Roosevelt publicly praised *The Grapes of Wrath*. In 1952 Adlai Stevenson hired him as a speechwriter, an association that brought out his sycophancy, as we see in the letter he wrote Stevenson after his loss to Ike:

> I hope you will have rest without sadness. The sadness is for us who have lost our chance for greatness when greatness is needed. The Republic will not crumble. But for a little while, please don't reread Thucydides. Republics have—and in just this way.
>
> It has been an honor to work for you—and a privilege. In some future, if you have the time and or the inclination, I hope you can come to my house and settle back with a drink and—tell sad stories of the death of Kings.
>
> Thank God for the impeachment provisions.
>
> Yours in disappointment and in hope.

When he won the Nobel Prize in 1962 he received some perfunctory White House invitations from John F. Kennedy, who liked to be surrounded by intellectuals, but he hit paydirt with Lyndon Johnson, who could lap up flattery as fast as Steinbeck could pour it on. His letter praising LBJ for his 1965 civil rights speech would have embarrassed any other recipient:

> In our history there have been not more than five or six moments when the word and the determination mapped the course of the future. Such a moment was your speech, Sir, to the Congress two nights ago. Our people will be living by phrases from that speech when all the concrete and steel have long been displaced or

destroyed. It was a time of no turning back, and in my mind as well as in many others, you have placed your name among the great ones of history.

When Vietnam heated up, he wrote LBJ another fawning letter condemning war protesters ("I assure you that only mediocrity escapes criticism") and LBJ responded by inviting him and his son to the White House when young John joined the Army. Later, he went to Vietnam himself and wrote Johnson that "we have here the finest, the best trained, the most intelligent and the most dedicated soldiers I have ever seen."

Parini gingerly describes Steinbeck's letters to LBJ as "somewhat inflated," but the academic left condemned him for his hawkishness and his critical reputation plunged. What drove him to this self-defeating stance? "He believed that giving emotional support to one's president in a time of trouble was honorable," claims Parini, "and he fell hook, line, and sinker for an old-style patriotism that argued one must support one's country in a time of war, even if the war in question happened to be immoral and foolish."

His old-style patriotism was noticeably absent from his smarmy letter to Adlai about impeaching Ike merely for winning the election; evidently, GOP administrations did not stir his blood. Moreover, as Parini himself reluctantly admits, each man wanted something from the other. Johnson clung to Steinbeck to prove that all intellectuals did not hate him, and Steinbeck already had a history of clinging to powerful Democrats. Reading his sycophantic letters, one suspects that at heart he was less a patriot than a courtier.

To the intelligentsia, Steinbeck's political sins were matched by his literary disappointments. "He never wrote anything worthwhile after *The Grapes of Wrath*" became a mantra among critics, who were alternately infuriated and dismayed by his later output. *East of Eden*, which even the doting Parini calls "an exercise in secular scripture," was panned for its labyrinthine plot and baroque language. *Sweet Thursday*, about flophouses and whores with hearts of gold, was, in the memorable words of one reviewer, "at the same time highflown and flyblown."

He also tried a satire about the restoration of the Bourbon monarchy, *The Short Reign of Pippin IV*, which no one got. Even more perplexing is why he wrote it; like all earnest people he had an aversion to satirists, especially George Bernard Shaw, of whom he said: "[His] wit is so dazzling that we never stop to consider that he has never said anything very important."

In his later years he was all over the literary map. Travel books, plays, translating the Arthurian legends into modern American speech, roving sociology (*Travels With Charley*), a newspaper column. His novella, *The Pearl*, was written as a cautionary tale for a materialistic society but received as a children's story—and still is. His last novel, *The Winter of Our Discontent*, is a sustained wail against American "affluence," possibly inspired by his friendship with yet another important Democrat, John Kenneth Galbraith.

His wildly varied oeuvre earned him the contempt of the critics, and with some justification. Having a finger in so many literary pies kept him from developing a style, like Hemingway, or an artistic landscape, like Faulkner. As a result, says Parini, he rarely turns up in critical studies and is steadily disappearing from anthologies.

National Review, October 9, 1995
Book Review

"Scud Missives"

Letters of Ayn Rand, edited by Michael S. Berliner, with an
introduction by Leonard Peikoff (Dutton, 681 pp., $34.95)

I F ANYONE needs a makeover it's Ayn Rand. After her death in
1982, her one-time protégés, Nathaniel and Barbara Branden,
both published biographies portraying her as an abusive monster
who held facts instead of opinions, drove her husband to drink, and
held purge trials in her living room whenever one of her acolytes got
philosophically out of line.

The centerpiece of both books is Miss Rand's affair with
Nathaniel, begun when she was 50 and he 24, and continuing until
they were 63 and 37. The story goes that she gathered the Brandens
together with her husband, Frank O'Connor, announced that she and
Nathaniel wanted to have an affair, and then opened the floor to discussion, which she dominated, analyzing the proposed adultery to
prove that it was rational according to the principles of Objectivism,
her home-cooked contribution to Western thought.

When the inevitable explosion came, Miss Rand publicly repudiated and denounced the Brandens, who soon divorced. Her think
tank, largely their work, fell apart, as did many of her emotionally
dependent acolytes, some of whom discussed whether it was rational
to assassinate Nathaniel.

No hint of any of this appears in *Letters of Ayn Rand*, a labor of
love by Leonard Peikoff, her leading loyalist (and sole heir under her
will, according to Barbara Branden), and Michael S. Berliner, execu-

tive director of the Ayn Rand Institute, newly restored to promote
Objectivism. They give us a new, improved Ayn Rand.

A 1936 letter to her husband opens "Cubby Sweet!" with a drawing of a lion cub, and closes with "Good night, Tweet! XXXXXXX
Your Fluff."

She is risquée when she sends Mickey Spillane her address, 36 East
36th Street: "A good way to remember it is to think of a perfect 36."

A dinner guest received a note that sounds like Mrs. Clinton in
campaign mode: "Here are the recipes for the Beef Stroganoff and the
salad dressing."

To Barbara Branden's mother, who praised her work, a gracious
AR replied: "I must tell you in return that I am very much impressed
with your work—namely, Barbara."

She was admirably conscientious about answering her fan mail,
and one reply is touching: "I was glad to hear that you consider me a
desirable relative, but I am sorry to disappoint you, because Rand is
only my pen name; so we are not related. We can still be friends,
however, and I am glad that you liked *Love Letters* [AR's 1945
screenplay]."

She hit it off with Barbara Stanwyck, who wanted to play
Dominique in *The Fountainhead* and left Warner Brothers when they
refused to give her the part. AR's letters prove it was Miss Stanwyck
who first brought the book to the studio's attention—not Gary
Cooper's wife, as some sources have claimed. Cooper, who played
Roark in the 1949 movie, was AR's ideal man, but by 1962 she preferred Robert Stack. She wrote Stack that he was "the only one" she
wanted for Roark in a TV miniseries of the novel then being discussed.

When her mask slips, we see the old Ayn Rand in full throttle. To
a fan who argued for humanitarianism, she wrote pithily, "Please
notice that the humanitarians are among the loudest advocates of dictatorship." But pith isn't enough. The letter begins to pulsate. As her
fury mounts she capitalizes CONTEMPT, italicizes trigger words, and
clinches the argument with her favorite scene from *The
Fountainhead*: "Didn't you understand that it was a *housing project*
which he blew up to hell, where it belonged?"

Professor John Hospers demanded a disclaimer before he would hand over her letters. It says in part: "I am afraid the reader who reads what Ayn wrote to me, and not what I wrote to her, would gather I was a bloody fool."

He has a point. In one letter she wrote: "Please reread your note and see whether it can be intelligible without the implicit definition which you now repudiate." Then: "I will refer you to Roark's speech, specifically to: page 737, paragraph 2—page 738, paragraphs 2, 3, 4, 5, 6, 7, 9—page 740, paragraphs 2, 3, 6—page 741, paragraphs 1, 2, 3."

Writing to Barry Goldwater about his book, *The Conscience of a Conservative*, she upbraids him for saying that conservatism rests on faith instead of on reason. Magnanimously, she absolves Goldwater and blames his ghostwriter for stressing the importance of religion; then, some italics later, she launches a salvo at the magazine she loved to hate.

> This leads me to the subject of the NATIONAL REVIEW. I am profoundly opposed to it—not because it is a religious magazine, but because it *pretends that it is not.* . . . But the fact that the NATIONAL REVIEW poses as a secular political magazine, while following a strictly religious "party line," can have but one purpose: to slip religious goals by stealth on those who would not accept them openly, to "bore from within," to tie Conservatism to religion, and thus to take over the American Conservatives.

She castigates *NR* for running a review of *Atlas Shrugged* by Whittaker Chambers, "this former Communist spy," and two defamatory articles about her, one of which "*denounced me for advocating capitalism.*" Along the same line, she refused a fan permission to name a chapter of YAF after her: "I am opposed to the organization known as Young Americans for Freedom. That organization is controlled by, or shares the policies of, the NATIONAL REVIEW magazine and is my avowed enemy."

The 1980 election infuriated her. To a television producer who wanted her to appear in a series called *Cultural Conservatism* she wrote: "This year in particular, I would be ashamed to be connected with the so-called Conservatives in any way. Their anti-abortion stand is outrageous—and so is their mixture of politics with religion."

In view of all this, one quakes for the fan who asked her to decorate an Easter egg for his collection, but she's gentle with him—and uncharacteristically arch: "Unfortunately, my schedule is such that this is the first chance I had to answer you, let alone to permit myself the luxury of attempting to paint. Since you needed the egg by March 15, shall I send it back to you undecorated?"

Her most notorious trait emerges in a letter to Archibald Ogden, editor of *The Fountainhead*, who was to supply an introduction to the 25th-anniversary edition. In his draft he made the mistake of relating the funny things that happened during the editing of the book, and was promptly hit by a Scud missive: "You are entitled to your own views about humor. But you know mine, and you chose to ignore them—and there is no meeting ground." She cast him out and wrote the introduction herself.

This book reeks of the sycophancy that Miss Rand always inspired, from its terse little editor's notes to Leonard Peikoff's grim promise that "an authorized biography of Ayn Rand will appear in due course." Considering that her birthday is given incorrectly here, it would appear that Peikoff and Berliner aren't even very good sycophants.

The American Spectator, November 1995
Book Review

"Catotonic State"

Cato's Letters: Or Essays on Liberty, Civil and
Religious and Other Important Subjects
by John Trenchard and Thomas Gordon
Edited and annonated by Ronald Hamowy
(Liberty Classics, 2 volumes, $30 cloth; $15 paper)

Nowadays the only Cato most Americans have heard of is Kato Kaelin, yet this statement poses a fascinating question: How did Kato hear of Cato? He must have, else he could not have chosen it for his stage name. He probably got it from a boxer, human or canine, but where did they get it? These are bizarre links in an unbroken chain stretching back to the Colonial era. The name has lived on in all sorts of unlikely ways, because once every American knew who Cato was.

He was Marcus Porcius Cato Uticensis [95–46 B.C.], known as Cato the Younger. A staunch defender of republican principles, he was so opposed to Julius Caesar that, when the latter triumphed, Cato committed suicide. His story inspired the Continental army. Joseph Addison's play Cato [1713] was read aloud around the campfires of Valley Forge, and one of its lines—"What pity is it that we can die but once to save our country"—was recycled by Nathan Hale.

Colonial America also knew another Cato, the pen name of two polemicists, John Trenchard and Thomas Gordon, who met in a London coffeehouse in 1720 and collaborated on a weekly letter to the London Journal that ran for three years. At first they concentrated their fire on the South Sea Bubble scandal, but quickly turned to treatises on radical Whig politics. Their letters, later published in book form, were wildly popular in the American colonies and became a major inspiration in the struggle for independence.

The Roman Republic was their touchstone, the ideal against which they judged all governance. Their knowledge of its history and language is staggering; the text is liberally sprinkled with Latin quotations, translated in footnotes here but not in the originals. That this was considered standard journalistic fare in the 18th century speaks volumes in defense of Western classical education. The letters are bracingly masculine, free of the equivocations of today's tepid op-eds. Cato "feels" not, he thinks; neither does he "tend." The febrile primness of American "values" is alien to him. He speaks of "virtues," whose root [*vir* means "male"] imposes stark certainty on the maxim of Juvenal: *Nobilitas sola est atque unica virtus*—virtue is the one and only nobility.

More succinct than Jefferson, Cato sums up Locke's theory of natural rights with Roman brevity: *Salus populi suprema lex esto*—"The benefit and safety to the people constitute the supreme law." The government that ceases to believe this "is not government but usurpation."

It is tempting to speculate what would happen if these volumes fell into the hands of our current crop of tribunes. Cato's Cromwellian puritanism and his hatred of the licentious Stuarts, the liberal elite of that day, need only a little editing to make the perfect anti-Hollywood speech for Phil Gramm:

> They will promote luxury, idleness, and expence, and a general depravation of manners [my Momma told me]. In order to do this, they will bring into fashion gaming, drunkenness, gluttony, and profuse and costly dress. They will debauch their country with foreign vices, and foreign instruments of vicious pleasures; and will contrive and encourage publick revels, nightly disguises, and debauched mummeries [just like my Momma always said].

There are plenty of zingers for Pat Buchanan: "The state of tyranny is a state of war"; "Tyranny is not government but a dissolution of it"; "It is wickedness not to destroy a destroyer."

These will do for the stump. For a convention keynote speech guaranteed to spark fears of an *auto da fe*, widen the gender gap, and offend animal-rights groups—all at the same time—Buchanan can use Cato's explanation of why a good cause need not fear a bad press: "A church is not the less sacred because curs frequently lift up their leg against it, and affront the wall: It is the nature of dogs."

When the new, improved Bob Dole is ready to satisfy the legions of people who are waiting for him to crack, he can turn to "Letter from John Ketch," in which Cato imagines England's legendary executioner harboring thoughts of dispatching the perpetrators of the South Sea Bubble.

> I did likewise bespeak, at least, a dozen curious axes, spick and span new, with rare steel edges; the fittest that could be made, for dividing nobly betwixt the head and the shoulders of any dignified and illustrious customer of mine. . . . Being bred a butcher, I can comfort my said customers with an assurance, that I have a delicate and ready hand at cutting and tying; so let them take heart, the pain is nothing, and will be soon over. . . . And so, for the ease of my mind, I beg that I may have those sent me, whom I may truss up with a safe conscience. My teeth particularly water, and my bowels yearn, at the name of the brokers; for God's sake, let me have the brokers.

Jesse Jackson's fatal attraction to seesawing parallelisms will get a big boost from Valerius: *Quid ergo libertas sine Catone? Non magis quam Cato sine libertate*—"What liberty without Cato? No more than Cato without liberty."

Rescue is at hand for Lamar Alexander. All he has to do is announce that absolutism destroys eloquence, and then say, "La Bruyère complains that the French are cramped in satire." This is guaranteed to deflect attention from that plaid shirt.

Ross Perot will pounce on Cato's praise of Cincinnatus, early Rome's ultimate outside-the-Beltway politician, who looked under the hood not once but twice, fixed the trouble, and skedaddled back to his farm to beat his swords into plowshares. "Government was not in those days [519 B.C.] a trade. The office he executed honestly and successfully, without the grimace and gains of a statesman. Nor did he afterwards continue obstinately at the head of affairs. *As he came to it with universal consent, he resigned it with universal applause.*" [Perot's italics]

A resolute Protestant, Cato was obsessed with the danger posed by the Jacobites, the Catholic supporters of James II, who wanted to put the Stuarts back on the throne. In "The Necessary Decay of Popish States Shewn from the Nature of the Popish Religion," he lists every charge ever leveled against the Catholic Church: ostentatious wealth, licentious priests, riotous feast days, etc.—plus a new one. The candidate willing to use it would be credited with the freshest, most original gaffe in American political history: The Catholic practice of giving sanctuary, says Cato, makes bandits part of the establishment.

He also has a message for the freshman class of the 1994 Congress. "Personal virtue is fatal in a corrupt state," as the Emperor Galba discovered when he succeeded Nero. As a first step toward reforming Rome, Galba made a public vow not to bribe anyone, but the moment he said, "I will choose my soldiers, not buy them," the army assassinated him. Wrote Tacitus: *Nocuit antiquus rigor, et nimia severitas, cui jam pares non sumus*—"He was resented for his old-fashioned harshness and excessive severity, qualities to which we are no longer equal."

Students of our big lovable lug of a president will empathize with Cato's aversion to the feckless Stuarts, especially his take on James I, who was "such a wild mixture of timidity and pride, and familiarity, that many hated him, more despised him, and yet none feared him . . . His tongue was never still. He delighted in sifting metaphysical questions and in discussing dark points in divinity. Foreign princes derided him. In their treaties with one another they either took no notice of this keeper of the balance of Europe, or always outwitted him."

National Review, November 6, 1995
Book Review

"Their Town"

*Seasons of War: The Ordeal of a Confederate Community,
1861-1865*, by Daniel E. Sutherland (Free Press, 400 pp., $25)

C ULPEPER, Virginia, is thirty miles west of Fredericksburg where I live. To get there you drive out toward Spotsylvania Mall and continue on past other burgeoning retail centers at Chancellorsville and Wilderness. As these once-hallowed names attest, you are on what some developer sooner or later will call the "Civil War Strip": shop till you drop in the midst of dead where they fell.

Unlike the other places along our route, Culpeper does not have "battle of" in front of its name. No battle was ever fought in Culpeper, and unlike Atlanta it was never burned. A single, unequivocal event would have been easier to bear, but Culpeper remained the eye of the storm for over three years.

Situated on the southern bank of the Rappahannock river midway between Chesapeake Bay and the Blue Ridge, Culpeper with its fords was a natural invasion point, and the launch pad for some of the most important campaigns, starting with First Manassas. It was the place both armies went through to get somewhere else, where they retreated after battles, where they set up their headquarters and winter encampments. Cemetery, morgue, hospital; experimental station for Nurse Clara Barton, inspirational station for Nurse Walt Whitman, railroad station for Libbie Custer at conjugal-visit time. If CNN and *Hard Copy* had existed, they would have been in Culpeper, too.

This orgy of to-ing and fro-ing is skillfully shaped and artfully dramatized by Daniel E. Sutherland, chairman of the history department at the University of Arkansas. Writing in the present tense from the viewpoint of a few representative Culpeper families, he infuses his vast scholarly research with gossipy immediacy and displays a gift for envisaged narration that most screenwriters would envy, not to mention most Civil War historians.

He wastes no time deploring slavery, but does show that its tensions had produced some interesting eccentricities. By 1860 some people refused to own slaves but did rent them; Culpeper had three auction houses that went unused as buyers quietly resorted to private transactions. Efforts at emancipation usually produced tragi-comic situations. A nice old lady freed her slaves in her will, but stipulated that they could be sold if the law at the time of her death prohibited manumission. A well-meaning planter spared no expense to colonize his freed slaves in Pennsylvania, but they came back.

After First Manassas, Culpeper received the Confederate casualties and some Union ones as well, sparking the first of many debates about how to behave toward the enemy. Anyone displaying too much kindness came under suspicion, but the town established a medical ward in its poorhouse for wounded Yankees.

Meanwhile, healthy Yankees camped across the river slipped over at night and raided crops and barns. The townspeople responded with guerrilla warfare, which led to Union General John Pope's notorious Order No. 11 providing for the execution of Rebel civilians. When Pope's forces invaded Culpeper in 1862, his men interpreted the order as carte blanche for wanton destruction of civilian homes and crops.

Captain Charles Francis Adams Jr. did what he could to control his Massachusetts company, but most officers were like the New York chaplain who wrote his wife, "We are so far into the heart of secessia now that we don't try to restrain the men much but let them forage to their hearts' content." He regretted only that they had demolished a church.

At the height of these depredations a Yankee trooper wrote home, "Secession is more rabid and bitter here than in any place we have been in Virginia." He was especially offended by female bitterness, expressed by a "contemptuous and disdainful sneer."

The disdainful sneer, a by-product of the region's aristocratic self-image, is the Southern woman's specialty. But she has another, even more celebrated specialty that cannot be long frustrated, else she will suffer withdrawal pains: she must flirt or die.

Two years later, as Confederate troops massed near Culpeper, an incensed patriot hauled some young ladies before Robert E. Lee and told him they had been overly friendly to Yankee officers and even attended parties at General John Sedgwick's headquarters.

Lee's unruffled reply shows to what extent the Civil War was one big West Point class reunion: "I know General Sedgwick very well. It is just like him to be so kindly and considerate, and to have his band there to entertain them. So, young ladies, if the music is good, go and hear it as often as you can, and enjoy yourselves. You will find that General Sedgwick will have none but agreeable gentlemen about him."

When Culpeper was occupied for the third time by General George Meade, it seemed that the Yankees would take permanent root. Officers' wives visited at Christmas of 1863, to the vicarious pleasure of the enlisted men. "It does seem so good to catch a view of the ladies occasionally," one confided to his diary. "It is a variety that softens the harsh, coarse, everyday life in the army, so full of everything hostile to society, and evils that blunt the finer sensibilities and feelings." That an ordinary soldier could express such mature ideas so well stuns a later age, but these troops were Victorians who revered the diarist's art.

The soldiers stationed in Culpeper that Christmas also learned something that Pat Schroeder and her women-in-combat allies have yet to grasp. They decided to have a dance, correcting the dearth of females by arraying some of their comrades in dresses confiscated from Rebel women. At first it was pleasantly silly, but when a fight broke out something primitive happened—suddenly, just for a moment, the "males" found themselves instinctively protecting their "female" partners.

Mr. Sutherland fleshes out his characters so deftly that they seem to be at our elbow. We are tense around the perpetually irritable Jubal Early, shocked by macho Jeb Stuart's intense interest in a handsome

Alabama captain, repelled by Nurse Cornelia Hancock of New Jersey, who seemed to enjoy looking at corpses.

He never gets bogged down in military strategy. In describing the battle of Cedar Mountain he concentrates not on the battle itself but on its aftermath, when "bullet-riddled trees look as though they have been devoured by termites." The details are ghoulish, but the controlled prose strips horror of its shock value and evokes the stark pity of the classical epic: "One officer, having lost his hat, spots a likely replacement lying beside a dead man. He picks it up and is about to crown himself when he sees the inside smeared with the brains of its previous owner."

National Review, December 31, 1995
Book Review

"Crashing Gore"

Palimpsest: A Memoir, by Gore Vidal
(Random House, 435 pp., $27.50)

G IVING one's memoirs a title that has to be explained must
be a status symbol among the leftist literati. First there was
Lillian Hellman's *Pentimento*; now comes Gore Vidal's
Palimpsest. Miss Hellman's title at least sounded pretty, but Maitre
Vidal's sounds like an arcane sexual practice involving an inflated
condom that explodes like the *Hindenburg* in the tradesmen's
entrance of some hired Apollo, sending ecstasy and other things
washing over Maître Vidal.

But no. A palimpsest is a special kind of paper that can be written on and wiped clean again, like a slate; or paper that has been written on twice, the original writing having been rubbed out. Maître
Vidal adapts the word to the task of remembering and recording one's
life in the face of memory's familiar tricks.

He likens the process to the writer's task of revision in which one
deletes something here, adds something there, or scratches out and
starts all over again. But revision also includes pulling discrete material together into a logically ordered narrative, and this he doesn't
always do.

A case in point is his account of Hillary Clinton's visit to his
Italian villa last year. The local papers treated it as a pilgrimage
("*Lady Clinton nel paradiso di Vidal*"), so he takes pains to resurrect
the moment with all due pomp. After describing himself waiting

seigneurially at the gates, he fashions a solemn interior monologue suitable for the occasion.

> The Clintons are now under attack because they would improve a society that is a heaven for, perhaps, one-tenth of the people and a hell, of varying degrees, for the rest. I doubt if he will survive his first term. He will experience either the bullet or a sudden resignation, and then cousin Albert, the Cromwell of Washington's Fairfax Hotel, will be Lord Protector.

That is Mrs. Clinton's cue, but instead of bringing her on and finishing the story, he suddenly flashes back to his childhood and does a palimpsest. The next sentence reads: "The only reason I was born was that rats had chewed on Mother's douche bag, or so she told me."

The floodgates of Maitre Vidal's memory open wide, as they must to accommodate the multitudes that pass through. Returning from World War II, he patronized New York's Everard bathhouse, which offered "sex at its rawest and most exciting. . . . Newly invented penicillin had removed fears of venereal disease, and we were enjoying perhaps the freest sexuality that Americans would ever know. Most of the boys knew that they would soon be home for good, and married, and that this was a last chance to do what they were designed to do with each other."

At 23 he wrote *The City and the Pillar*, America's first openly homosexual novel. It was published in 1948, the same year that Dr. Alfred C. Kinsey published *Sexual Behavior in the Human Male*. Vidal was interviewed by Kinsey, who used the lobby of the Astor Hotel as an office so that he could catch the patrons of the gay Astor Bar. "I like to think," writes Vidal, "that it was by observing the easy trafficking at the Astor that he figured out what was obvious to most of us, though as yet undreamed of by American society at large: perfectly 'normal' young men, placed outside the usual round of family and work, will run riot with each other."

Kinsey was intrigued by Vidal's lack of sexual guilt. "I told him that it was probably a matter of class . . . guilt [was] a middle-class disorder from which power people seem exempt."

Vidal is the grandson of Sen. Thomas P. Gore of Oklahoma and the stepson of Hugh D. Auchincloss. These credentials combined with his early literary success gave him an entrée into the highest social and intellectual circles on two continents, enabling him to become the contradiction that he remains today: a misanthrope who knows everybody.

Let the name-dropping begin. In Europe he met Eddie Bismarck, the chancellor's grandson, who said of him, "He's brilliant, but in a way more like us"—that is, at home in aristocratic salons, instead of plagued by self-doubt like the middle-class Tennessee Williams. Through the Bismarcks he met the Windsors. "I got the duchess in a reminiscent mood," he boasts, claiming she told him: "I never wanted to get married. This was all *his* idea."

Princess Margaret has stayed at his villa and he has stayed at Windsor, where the two of them saved a swarm of bees from drowning in the pool and Margaret shouted, "Go forth and make honey!" She also confided, "Queen Mary hated us. We were royal and she was not." Alas, Maître Vidal doesn't pay enough attention to poor Margaret, who told a mutual friend, "He never rings up! Kick him in the shins for me, and then give him a big kiss."

On the literary side he met Gide, realizing "my lifelong dream of shaking the hand that had shaken the hand of Oscar Wilde." (All right, you little devils, stop thinking what I'm thinking.) Describing his audience with the frail, ethereal Santayana in his cell at a convent, he quotes from another memoirist, Frederick Prokosch, to prove that Prokosch was lying when *he* claimed to have met Santayana: only the unerring Vidal ear can render the subtle intonations of the great philosopher's speech and bring him to life on the page. (He quotes from numerous other memoirists to prove things of this sort.)

He hated Truman Capote ("the round pale fetus face") for his addiction to vicious gossip, but he dishes up plenty of vicious gossip himself, especially about his Auchincloss stepsister, Jacqueline Kennedy Onassis. Like a loutish frat rat he says she lost her virginity to a friend of his in a stalled elevator. He tells a particularly ghoulish story about her last days: "From the family, I hear that the cancer had gone to her brain and that she had had a hole drilled in her skull so that radium—or whatever—could be put in."

He is drawn to the dark. Visiting a male brothel in Paris that was founded by Proust to satisfy his voyeurism (the holes are still in the walls), he relishes a morbid anecdote: "Proust had once become ecstatic when he watched a rat bite a youth's hand—or was it the other way around?"

Naturally he knew Greta Garbo, who provides him with the most outlandish story in the book.

> But she was very funny about her visit to the White House. Early on, Jackie had told me, "One of the few nice things about being here is we can get to meet everyone we've ever wanted to meet." So, inevitably, Garbo came to dinner. "The President took me into his bedroom. So romantic. Then he gave me a whale's tooth and we went back to Mrs. Jah-kee, who said, 'He never gave me a whale's tooth.'"

Can this be? Why is there no mention of it in all those Kennedy books? Could Garbo possibly have visited the White House without its being discovered? No matter how many threats and bribes were made, it would have come out, wouldn't it? Or did I miss the whole thing during my years in the Gobi Desert?

But I digress, as Maître Palimpsest would say. He digresses often, never missing a chance to take a swipe at those out of his favor: "*lumpen*-imperialists of the far right like Buckley Jr."; "Jesus-Christers" (Christians); and Charlton Heston: "all the charm of a wooden Indian." That's a middle-class cliché but not his only one. Seated next to Jack Kerouac, with whom he had a one-night stand, he confesses, "I feel the heat from his body."

He practices his own form of political correctness. In the past he rejected "homosexual" as a noun and termed himself a "homosexualist." Now he prefers "same-sexualist" and shows his disdain for "straight" and "gay" by putting them in quotation marks. His preferred adjective is "homoerotic."

His only interests were and are "reading, writing, and anonymous sex," though turning seventy has broadened his horizons to include his blood pressure and his blood-sugar count. He records them in the book along with a list of his medicines, leaving the reader with a picture of a worn-out Regency buck taking the waters at a German spa.

The American Spectator, January 1996
Book Review

"Diaper Dandy"

Big Babies by Michael Kinsley
(William Morow, 336 pages, $23)

I f our leading liberal pundits could travel back in time to comment on the *Titanic* . . .

Richard Cohen would apologize for damage to the iceberg.

Ellen Goodman: Have you noticed how white males keep saying, "*She* hit an iceberg"?

Anthony Lewis: Thoughtful people everywhere are sensitive to the nuances of five thousand tons of steel crashing into five thousand tons of ice.

Clarence Page: A white iceberg destroyed a black ship the other night. We still have a long way to go.

Michael Kinsley: Oh, spare me the shock and surprise! First-class was weighted down with enough fat-cat Republicans to sink the *Titanic* and that's exactly what happened.

If Michael Kinsley were a Dickens character his name would be Barnaby Sneerly. He seems to be aware of his identifying trait, at least subconsciously, judging from his frequent use of "sneer" and its derivatives to describe other people. His new book contains at least four instances of this classic projection mechanism. There may be more, but I stopped counting once I got the picture.

Big Babies is a collection of Kinsley's columns from 1986 to early 1995. The title refers to American voters, whom he blames for democracy's current discontents. They want their taxes cut, their benefits preserved, and the budget balanced, all at the same time, and if it doesn't happen they stamp their feet and bawl. He professes "annoyance at the fatuous populism that dominates American politics," defining populism as "the politicians are terrible but the people are wonderful." He has a point, but only an unabashed elitist can infuse such sentiments with Hamiltonian élan. Kinsley, a closet elitist, merely sounds like a snob, and a confused one at that.

On the defeat of his man Dukakis: "I have enough respect for the political intelligence of the public [?] that I hope a majority may come to agree with me the next time around."

On himself as the Ayn Rand of the left: "My own political views are more or less liberal. . . . I hold them under no form of compulsion except reason. It seems to me they're the sort of views a reasonable, intelligent person would hold . . . the mystery to me is not why journalists tend to be liberals but why so many other reasonable, intelligent people are not."

Elsewhere, however, he admits to several other political compulsions. Liberals, he says, are motivated by "an instinct to oppose," "a fear of seeming boosterish," and a "knee-jerk iconoclasm," which can be set in motion by a mere word or phrase that "starts the facial nerves twitching into the formation of a cynical sneer."

When all these compulsions come together in Kinsley, he goes into a tailspin. He twitches on cue in columns about the 1988 Bush-Dukakis race, contemptuously dismissing the debates over flag burning and the pledge of allegiance as "the flag flap" and "the pledge nonsense." These, he insists, are mere "symbolic issues" calculated to stir up an emotional populace—and an emotional Kinsley, who suddenly gives vent to a Learish howl: "Is there no one eloquent enough to make people weep with gratitude that we live in a country where people are free enough to burn the flag?"

The case he makes to prove that Dan Quayle was wrong about Murphy Brown recalls those "Crossfire" moments when we long to reach into the TV and grab him by the throat.

1. If people waited for perfect conditions before bringing kids into the world, no one would ever have kids. Therefore, "Murphy Brown has nothing to feel guilty about."

2. What Quayle called "indulgence and self-gratification," the Founding Fathers called the pursuit of happiness. "They were for it," Kinsley reminds us. Therefore, we should rejoice that the pill, gay rights, no-fault divorce, and toleration of single motherhood "have offered paths to happiness for millions who would otherwise be trapped by the conventions that provide the plots of so many gloomy nineteenth-century novels."

3. "The very decision to give Murphy Brown a fatherless baby was more a product of capitalist forces—the quest for ratings—than any leftover 1960's ideology."

4. The family values issue is "a convenient excuse for the failure of two Republican presidents to do much of anything about the cities and the underclass."

5. Now comes the tongue-in-cheek clincher, a perfect *argumentum ad sneer*: "No wonder we're running a $400 billion deficit when unmarried middle-aged women think they can just go off and have babies by themselves."

One of his best-known columns, "Who Killed Vincent Foster?" is a classic paralepsis—the rhetorical device whereby one says something by announcing that he is not going to say it:

> I have no real evidence that deputy White House counsel Vincent Foster was driven to suicide by a series of viciously unfair and hypocritical editorials in the *Wall Street Journal*. In fact, I don't even really believe it. But it would be easy enough to make the case, if one were willing to use against the *Journal* the same techniques of innuendo and demagogy that the *Journal* editors used against Foster and his colleagues in recent weeks.

That said, he flies into a search-and-seizure and trots out everything the "howling" *WSJ* editors ever wrote about the Rose Law Firm, breathlessly revealing what the *WSJ* "breathlessly revealed" about these fine Arkansans, reiterating every "heinous" and "unctuous" slur and innuendo, right up to that final, "tastelessly sneery" headline, "A Washington Death."

Then, his *J'accuse* spent, he abruptly reverts to speak-no-evil prudence in his last paragraph:

Did the *Journal* editorials have anything to do with Foster's suicide? It's always possible that, being inexperienced in the ways of
the Beltway Big Leagues, he took them more to heart than he
should have. Even if so, the *Wall Street Journal* deserves no blame
for his death. Public debate cannot be conducted on the assumption
that public officials are overly sensitive. But the *Journal* and its
editors can be blamed for trashy journalism. They tarred themselves without leaving a single real mark on Vincent Foster.

(In a footnote to this column Kinsley simultaneously acknowl-
edges its flaws and crows that his paralepsis was right on the money:
"This column is the ultimate flowering of my neurotic obsession with
the *Wall Street Journal* editorial page. It was written before the
reports of Foster's 'suicide note,' in which he did indeed blame '*WSJ*
editors' for his troubles.")

Kinsley is astute on the "fatalistic insouciance" of Britons faced
with national decline; mordant on the opportunism of spinmeisters
James Carville and Mary Matalin ("They are strip-mining their
lives"); and hilarious on the ironclad *New York Times* rule that a cor-
rection must avoid repeating the original error ("It was Mr. Bennett
who called Mr. Rangel a 'gasbag,' not the other way around"). This
Kinsley displays a Johnsonian wit, but not even Dr. Johnson was
"on" every time.

Like all collections, *Big Babies* is uneven, mingling the author's
best efforts with second-rate, dashed-off material that reviewers normally ignore unless there is too much of it. There are two such
columns here, smart-alecky riffs that seemed to have no apparent significance until the *Washington Post* reported that Kinsley is quitting
"Crossfire" and joining Microsoft to edit a magazine that will exist
only in cyberspace.

Suddenly I realized that the two flippant columns I had overlooked were pregnant with planted cues. The first, written in 1991 but
for some unexplained reason never published, is called "Term Limits
for Columnists." Masquerading as a jab at George Will for changing
his mind and favoring term limits for politicians, it is clearly what the
compassion gang calls a cry for help, though Kinsley couches it in
one of his projections: "If an obscure congressman is likely to suffer

from swollen self-importance after twelve years, a member of 'The McLaughlin Group' is unlikely to avoid the curse."

In the second, "Mamas, Don't Let Your Babies Grow Up to Be Pundits," which appeared in the *New Yorker* in 1992, a kvetching Kinsley asks us to feel his pain:

> It's opine, opine, day in and day out; until you never want to have another opinion again. What used to be one of the day's great pleasures—perusing the newspapers over morning coffee—becomes a nightmare. . . . TV punditry adds a whole extra layer of terror, mainly of being exposed as an ignoramus. It's ten seconds to showtime and you suddenly realize you have no idea where Somalia is.

He's going to live in Redmond, Washington, Bill Gates's neck of the woods—and formerly this reviewer's. What populism calls "the real people" are thick on the ground out there, but Kinsley won't be troubled by them. One click of the mouse and he will soar, trailing a little puff of smoke, into cyberspace, to edit a magazine that is, yet isn't. There he will lodge, writing on unpaper, and astronomers gazing at the heavens will point to his constellation and say, "Look, it's the Little Sneer."

National Review, January 29, 1996
Book Review

"The Mud Turtle's Progress"

The Education of a Woman: The Life of Gloria Steinem,
by Carolyn G. Heilbrun (Dial, 451 pp., $24.95)

T he parable of the mud turtle comes at the end of this hagio-
graphic book, but it so perfectly illustrates the feminist blind
spot of both biographer and subject that I shall start with it.

Here is how Gloria Steinem claims she learned to respect the
right to self-determination:

During a science field trip in college, she found a turtle beside a
road. Afraid that it would get run over, she picked it up and carried it
back into the woods where it would be safe—only to be told by her
professor that it had probably taken the turtle weeks to reach the
muddy shoulder where she wanted to lay her eggs, but now, thanks to
Miss Steinem's help, she would have to start all over again.

"It was a lesson Steinem never forgot," writes Carolyn G.
Heilbrun.

Really? Coulda fooled me. Miss Steinem has made a career of
meddling in women's egg-laying habits and taking them where she
thinks they ought to be. Now, in what is tactfully known as post-
feminism, they are faced with the task of starting all over again.

Writing a biography of a still-living subject whose friends, enemies,
and lovers are still alive is a delicate operation, but Carolyn G. Heilbrun

is eminently qualified to jump in with both feet. The author of *Writing a Woman's Life*, she is widely regarded as the leading expert on female biography. She is also a salted-in-the-shell feminist who used to teach at Columbia until the "boys' treehouse gang," as she calls male English professors, drove her away. "Women who speak out," she reminds us, "usually end up punished or dead." Note that "usually." Both Miss Heilbrun and Miss Steinem have flourished like the green bay tree.

Gloria Steinem was born in 1934 into a solid middle-class Toledo family, but her father's wild financial schemes and her mother's nervous breakdowns landed them in not-so-genteel poverty. After her parents divorced, she lived with her increasingly delusional mother in a ratty apartment and attended a working-class high school, earning extra money tap dancing at the Lion's Club. These gritty experiences shaped her politics. Years later, watching Chicago police beat up protestors at the 1968 Democratic Convention, she said, "Those cops are the boys I went to high school with."

Life improved in 1951 when her older sister institutionalized their mother and took Miss Steinem to live with her in Washington, where she entered the city's elite public school, Western High in Georgetown. No more tap dancing for Babbitts; secure in her improved social status, she became a swimming instructor at the segregated city's Negro pool. Lady Bountiful on the half shell.

To pay her tuition at Smith, the family sold a piece of property they had managed to hang onto. She graduated in 1956 and won a Chester Bowles fellowship to study in India, spending half of the $1,000 stipend en route on an abortion in London. Avoiding all Westerners, she sought out "the real India," her solo trek through remote regions facilitated by railroad cars reserved for women only. She went completely native; dyed her hair black, wore saris—and had a karma reading. It said she had "lived in Bengal in a previous incarnation, and that she had done something disastrous to have been born in the United States."

When she returned to New York, the guilt she had felt in India at being pulled in a tonga (rickshaw) by another human being made her resolve to ride in the front seat of cabs, but she soon gave it up for reasons not hard to imagine.

She conquered male-dominated publishing like a Marxist Scarlett O'Hara. Her best early writing had a Nellie Bly flair, especially her 1963 exposé of Playboy Clubs, "A Bunny's Tale," but even the worshipful Miss Heilbrun admits that *The Beach Book* was "clearly not a book any serious publisher in his right mind would have agreed to." But Viking's Tom Guinzberg was not in his right mind, he was in Miss Steinem's bed. We aren't sure where John Kenneth Galbraith was, but he wrote the introduction to her sandy anthology, explaining that he did so because "I like the girl who put it together." Sold with a sun screen inside the cover, *The Beach Book* contained suggested fantasies: "You have just dealt a crushing defeat in public debate to (choose one: William Buckley Jr., Hugh Hefner, David Susskind, Ayn Rand), who is being laughed off the stage."

But she was never frivolous for long. Given some stock in *New York* magazine, she used it as collateral to bail women out of prison to get abortions when the prison hospital refused to perform them. Even more earnestly, she told a new bride: "You married that man? I would have stopped you; he's another conservative central European."

When she founded *Ms.* she vowed to run "a communal, cooperative, nonhierarchical, democratic" magazine patterned on the "strict structurelessness" of early radical feminism. Nobody had a title and there was no masthead, just an alphabetical list of "workers" with the now-famous Miss Steinem buried under S. This egalitarian code was broken when a worker's mother said, "I saw your boss on television."

Private offices with doors were verboten; everyone worked in a communal room which also served as the nursery for single mothers on the staff. Editorial duties were assigned by lot; all the workers read all the copy and everyone got to express an opinion, including the receptionist. When a reviewer panned Kate Millett's book some workers didn't want to run the review because it might hurt Miss Millett's feelings; another warned, "Kate might have a nervous breakdown" unless they cut the mean parts.

By 1979 *Ms.* had lost so much money that Miss Steinem had to file for non-profit status. This enabled her to get a $300,000 grant from the Ford Foundation. Whether it helped that she had had an affair with Ford Foundation president Franklin Thomas is not known.

Her last important lover was real-estate tycoon Mortimer Zuckerman, whose limo made her feel so guilty that she asked him to replace it with a van. Normally she would not have slept with a man who believed in trade with countries whose embassies she picketed, but he knew how to break down her resistance: he told her he had had an emotionally deprived childhood. It worked. She decided to "help" him, telling herself, "Once happy, he would give all his money to the poor." He didn't—nor did he get rid of the limo.

The only enjoyable parts of this book are the quoted passages by other writers. Miss Heilbrun herself is maddening. Three examples will suffice.

Miss Steinem's gullibility in business matters: "Those who despise all group hatreds, all racial and sexual stereotypes, are more easily duped."

Miss Steinem takes up feminism: "Like Paul after his vision on the road to Damascus, but like him in no other way, she decided to go forth and speak, to spread the message."

Miss Steinem today: "She has, furthermore, shocked many people in frankly stating that her sexual drive has diminished."

What is so shocking about a woman of 61 saying that? It's the only sensible thing she's ever said.

The American Spectator, March 1996
Book Review

"Great Character, Nice Quads"

Founding Father: Rediscovering George Washington
by Richard Brookhiser
(The Free Press, 230 pages, $25)

I f George Washington is no longer first in the hearts of his countrymen, it is due in part to his major biographies. One consists of
seven volumes, another contains four; still another begins with
Columbus's discovery of America. Between the hush of veneration
and the drone of land surveying, we lose access, and then interest.

Even less successful are those biographies that dispense with veneration and look for vulnerability. Clinton has facilitators and Newt
has Tofflers, but Washington had only Seneca, the Roman stoic who
advised, "Scorn pain; either it will go away or you will." Never one
to read for pleasure, Washington read for information; and he read
Seneca to perfect that bane of tell-all biographers, control of his emotions. Late in life, when told that his pleasurable anticipation of
retirement showed in his face, Washington replied: "You are wrong,
my countenance never yet betrayed my feelings." Nor, in the long
run, did his pen: the only personal remarks he ever committed to
paper were cut up by a worshipful nineteenth-century historian for
handwriting samples.

The aloof and majestic Washington lends himself to only one type of biography: the moral essay in the tradition of Plutarch, the first-century student of exalted human nature who wrote *Parallel Lives of the Noble Greeks and Romans*. Interested less in historical narrative than in the portrayal of character for instructive purposes, Plutarch took biography into the realm of ethics, setting forth his aims thus: "The virtues of these great men serve me as a sort of looking glass in which I may see how to adjust and adorn my own life."

The last sighting of the Plutarchian form was reported by Victorian schoolboys, but it is here brilliantly revived and simulated by Richard Brookhiser, who blends classical concision with engaging modern touches in this less-is-more examination of the Washington we ought to know.

Like Plutarch, Brookhiser uses personal details only as they relate to public career. But Plutarch placed high value on the psychological benefits of manly form, so Brookhiser showed a portrait of Washington on horseback to a lady body builder, who took one look at the bulging saddle muscles in his thighs and reverently breathed, "*Nice* quads." Our age, which travels by auto and harbors political fears of the "man on horseback," is left cold by an aspect of Washington that enchanted his contemporaries: the image of the centaur. He rode so well, says Brookhiser, that his soldiers imagined that man and horse were one. A minor, indeed arcane, point to us, but a godlike asset in a century saturated in classical antiquity.

He had the ease and composure of the big man (six-foot-three-and-a-half), though his large-framed physique had a disconcerting flaw: wide hips. Was this an outward clue of his "undoubted sterility"? If so, it was the only one; "There is not a king in Europe," said Benjamin Rush, "that would not look like a *valet de chambre* by his side."

Nor could royalty top his manners. Our age worries about authenticity but the eighteenth century worried about reputation, defining character as "a role one played until one became it"—what we call hypocrisy. Washington cultivated his reputation assiduously; at 16 he copied out advice from etiquette books, playing the role of gentleman until, as president, he thought of the nation as an expanded Mount Vernon guest list whom he must treat properly. "The way men behave in polite society is related to how they order society," Brookhiser writes. "Politeness is the first form of politics."

Polite, yes—but his mere presence at the day-care center would have ruined Ted Kennedy's rendition of the spider song. According to Martha Washington's granddaughter Nelly Custis: "His own near relatives feared to speak or laugh before him, not from severity, but out of awe and respect. When he entered a room where we were all mirth and in high conversation, all were instantly mute. He would sit a short time and then retire, quite provoked and disappointed."

He had the same effect on the Constitutional Convention. When the duties of the president were opened to discussion, silence reigned; all the delegates were loath to discuss in Washington's presence what everyone knew would be his next job. He did not help matters when he found a copy of some proposed resolutions on the floor. Placing it on the table, he warned the members to be careful lest the business of the Convention get into the hands of the press and "disturb the public repose by premature speculations." Then he bowed and left, "with a dignity so severe that every Person seemed alarmed," recalled one delegate, who rushed back to his room to make sure he still had his copy. Nobody ever claimed the lost one.

The delegate from South Carolina, Pierce Butler, thought that the powers of the presidency had been made too great because they were adopted with Washington's character in mind, thereby making the savior of his country "the Innocent means of its being, when He is lay'd low, oppress'd."

Although Washington was, in Brookhiser's description, "a conspicuous example of moderation and disinterestedness," he had no patience with unhappy freedmen. Shay's Rebellion of 1786, the tax revolt by Massachusetts farmers during the Confederation period, moved Washington close to petulance: "It is but the other day that we were shedding our blood to obtain the Constitutions under which we now live; Constitutions of our own choice and making; and now we are unsheathing the sword to overturn them. The thing is so unaccountable, that I hardly know how to realize it."

Likewise, 1794's Whiskey Rebellion "struck him as an attack on the legacy of the Revolution, all the more serious because it mimicked its arguments." Both involved taxes, but the first were levied on Americans without their consent; the second were levied by them through their elected representatives. It was one thing to rebel against a foreign tax collector; but when men make their own tax laws they must abide by them. He put down both rebellions like an impatient father knocking heads.

In *Burr*, Gore Vidal paints Washington as a provincial Eisenhower, but Brookhiser offers the interesting speculation that in the matter of Jay's Treaty, Washington may have benefited from being less cosmopolitan than Jefferson, who had spent five years in Paris, and Hamilton, who was born in the West Indies. Never having left America except for a trip to Barbados with his half-brother, Washington could focus on the welfare of the United States as Jefferson the Francophile and Hamilton the Anglophile could not. The roiling hatred between these two was not lost on Washington, who signed the imperfect treaty with the pointed comment: "Men are very apt to run into extremes. Hatred to England may carry some into an excess of Confidence in France. . . . But it is a maxim founded on the universal experience of mankind, that no nation is to be trusted farther than it is bound by its interests."

Brookhiser's deft brushstroke portraits of Jefferson the radical-chic liberal and Hamilton the overwrought Burkean elitist point up Washington's biographical problem: he was surrounded by so many complex intellectuals that he comes off as boring. Neurotics make better theater, but Washington's gift to his country was a temperament rooted in undemonstrative steadiness. Richard Brookhiser's wise analysis of it is a timely lesson for a contemporary America that worships shallow image and shrinks from the sternness of maturity.

National Review, May 20, 1996
Book Review

"The Man Man"

The Sibling Society, by Robert Bly
(Addison-Wesley, 272 pp., $25)

ROBERT Bly is known as "the woods man," "the tom-tom man," or simply "the man man" thanks to the movement he founded to help men rediscover what he calls the "mythopoetic" roots of masculinity through reenactments of primitive male-group rituals. It involves campfires, animal skins, reverence for the tribal elder (Bly), and enough spears for round-the-clock performances of *Aïda* in the major opera houses of the world. Bly described it all in his first book, *Iron John*, which cried out for satirization—and got it. The funniest send-up was Iron Joe Bob, by my partner in columny, Joe Bob Briggs.

In his new book, *The Sibling Society*, Bly analyzes our fatherless era and concludes that the Oedipus complex has been downsized. Without fathers to struggle against, more and more boys are being deprived of the maturing experience that the Oedipal situation imposes. Aiding and abetting this literal fatherlessness is the figurative fatherlessness that has plagued us since the Sixties destroyed hierarchy, authority, and tradition. With nothing and no one to look up to, we have become a "horizontal" society of perpetual siblings whose level gaze is locked on passive Mother Television, where two fatherless sons, Clinton and Gingrich, vie for our attention.

Trimmed down to its essentials, Bly's thesis would make an interesting five-thousand-word magazine article, but he doesn't pack a blue pencil in his old kit bag. He approaches the writing craft like Thomas Wolfe, who, asked to cut his manuscripts, replied: "Flaubert me no Flauberts, Bovary me no Bovarys, I'm a putter-inner, not a taker-outer."

Among the things Bly puts in this book are the complete text of "Jack and the Beanstalk," poems by everyone from Emily Dickinson to Hadewijch of Antwerp, Greek myths, Sioux rituals, Nordic sagas, and Hindu legends that read like early *Ms.* magazine: "If the elephant relates Ganesha to the magnificent areas of male divinity, the cow's head relates the Sister to the Great Goddess, to the Goddess of Life and Death."

Matters go from bad to worse when he stops ponying other writers and speaks for himself. He doesn't seem to be in the habit of revising and polishing his work—or even rereading it. Real men write rough drafts, and his prose style provides comic relief on nearly every page.

> Elvis was a part of what women had longed for, not militaristic, not rigid in feeling, not exclusionary toward mothers and young women, but lighthearted, open to impulses rising from below his belt, playful, and yet grounded in sexuality, heavier than Peter Pan, more human than the stiff-faced old grandfather who wound clocks. Young women felt themselves losing some of their Doris Day rigidity. . . . Why shouldn't she give up her mother's stuff about waiting until the ring is on the hand before having fun with zippers?

Whether from an excess of testosterone or simply a tin ear, his comparisons read like a clash of titans: "Why should desire disappear, like the red wolf, the passenger pigeon, and the Irish elk, into extinction?" Like heroism, sacrifice, and chivalry? Like faith, hope, and charity? The sentence requires three emotions, or three ethics. To go from desire to elks conjures a bellowing rut.

An incorrigible romantic in the Jean-Jacques Rousseau mold, he periodically slips over the line into metaphorical hysteria: "The big mother is the breasty mother, or the woolly mammoth mother, or the flooding mother. She is moorish, spongy. She is great."

"Ronald Reagan was a sort of Grand Central Station for the trains of disaster."

This very short book takes a very long time to read because one keeps stopping and saying, "Huh?" Bly's howlers are memorable, as when he states that Oedipus "puts out his eyes with a hatpin," leaving the reader to reflect on an ancient Thebes full of Floradora girls. In the play, Oedipus uses the shoulder brooches that he tears from the dead Jocasta's robes.

In a tangled discussion of "vertical thought" and hierarchy, Bly tells us that the former has to do with longing and the latter with power, a distinction that was lost when the Catholic Church "conflated the two" and destroyed metaphorical thinking with its doctrine, "No salvation outside of the church." Bly renders this as "*Ex exclessi-am nulla sallus*," proving that a little Latin is a dangerous thing.

He really goes off the rails in his overview of the various male movements that have shaped American life. The first of these was the cult of the western with its solitary rogue-male hero who practiced silence and stoicism and shunned introspection.

> The movement produced books with titles like *Riders of the Purple Sage* instead of *A Room of One's Own*. We remember President Reagan's fondness for Louis L'Amour. We could say that Ronald Reagan was a late-coming Phyllis Schlafly for this group, although true to the western type, he spoke very little and it was mostly jokes. President Reagan was probably reading westerns when he invaded Grenada and sent illegal arms to the *contras*. President Bush could also be said to have been "west of every-thing" during the Gulf War.

What, besides an inept Homeric simile, is a "late-coming Phyllis Schlafly"? If he's using her as a symbol of political reaction, does he mean that Reagan made it okay for men to read westerns the way Mrs. Schlafly made it okay for women to be anti-feminist? Or that he stopped men from reading westerns the way Mrs. Schlafly stopped the ERA? And if speaking very little made him true to the western type, what does that "although" mean? And what does Virginia Woolf's book have to do with all of this?

Turning to the male-feminist movement, Bly writes: "They want attention drawn, and against male violence in the home and in the world at large." He doesn't like male feminists because they are "full of judgment," meaning, I suppose, that he tried to say "opinionated" and missed; and because they are "idea fighters." Like narrow-minded fire fighters.

Of his own mythopoetic movement he says, "It cares for elegant and expressive language in poetry and storytelling," explaining: "Through story, men can recognize spiritual energy or warrior energy or lover energy come up, and men then have a choice of how to live that energy."

The latest men's movement is the Promise Keepers, founded by a former University of Colorado football coach, who dedicate themselves to staying married and home at night. They meet in football stadia, Bly says, because men feel more comfortable there. Why? "Emotion is allowed for men in sports stadiums, even though the emotion tends not to be very personal or inner."

We can expect to see Bly on the passive Mother Television he claims to despise, promoting *The Sibling Society* amid kudos of "original," "groundbreaking," and "seminal." It is none of these. It's a padded cell between hard covers, but I can't leave you with that. Those, after all, are my own words, and we must be mythopoetic, so I'll quote something.

The story of Lazarus in John 11:39 contains an apt appraisal of Robert Bly's book: "Lord, by now he stinketh, for he hath been dead four days."

National Review, June 17, 1996
Book Review

"Onward and Downward"

Dumbing Down: Essays on the Strip-Mining of American Culture,
by Katharine Washburn and John Thornton
(Norton, 332 pp., $22.50)

NOVELIST James M. Cain complained of "the curse of American literature: the sympathetic character." It's worse than he thought. Our determined national optimism has long since extended beyond fiction to the upbeat final paragraph demanded by editors of mass-market articles, and, in politics, to morning-in-America sunniness in the shadow of Damoclean swords.

The smile-button spell is broken in *Dumbing Down*, a collection of savagely witty essays by a hardy band of cultural commentators who believe things are bad, really bad, out there, and are not at all reluctant to say so.

The volume's refreshing tone of cynical pessimism is established in the introduction by *NR*'s John Simon, who sees no point in worrying about people whose idea of repartee is talking back to a movie screen. Concurring with Pascal's dictum that all human unhappiness stems from the inability to stay calmly put inside a room, Simon predicts the total collapse of American education "unless the cult of excellence takes over in the land or hell freezes over—whichever comes first. To expect things to improve is like asking for the return of the five-cent beer."

Cynthia Ozick demonstrates that universal literacy was a fluke from the beginning. Borne on the confluence of the reform movement and the industrial revolution, it lasted barely a century, from about 1830 to 1930. During this period the shop girl with her pulp romance and the laborer with his penny-dreadful gave the erroneous impression that reading was here to stay, but when radio and movies came along the little people promptly abandoned their printed entertainment. Thereafter the centuries started slipping away. Now, writes Miss Ozick, television is "the simple speaking face" of pre-literary epochs and the VCR has returned us to "the world of traveling mummers."

Phillip Lopate's essay is called "The Last Taboo," a reference to the only thing left that Hollywood won't show: an intelligent person who is *not* a mad bomber.

Early Hollywood, says Lopate, had a reverence for intelligence. The moviemakers of the Thirties and Forties were German refugees who, missing Europe and depressed by American cultural blandness, compensated by creating worldly, cultivated supporting characters (the Claude Rains and Maria Ouspenskaya parts), sprinkled their films with references to the Louvre, and "wrote in countless minor comic roles for displaced European character actors, as violin repairers, Pushkin-quoting janitors, etc."

By contrast, today's moviemakers pour out of film schools with no cultural memory except a fascination for poor white trash (called "extreme white people" by politically correct screenwriters) and a belief that "people without brains are cool." The result is today's film noir in color about "a pair of greasers . . . stranded in a nowhere town who meet cute, fall in love, and go find a gun." The "idiot genre," as Lopate calls it, keeps dialogue to a minimum so as not to sound literary: "More and more, I am told, action movies go into production without a final script; the gaps are patched over with last-minute wisecracks."

Poor white trash are the only whites that today's audiences willingly identify with. Gone from the screen is our national archetype, the Common Man, the ordinary American portrayed by James

Stewart who rises to a moment of moral excellence in the course of coping with his travails. But national archetypes are historically white figures, so the Common Man has been rejected by newer immigrants and minorities. In so doing, says Lopate, they reject as well the premise of a shared humanity on which all good drama is based. Without a model of commonality, moviemakers "attempt to locate universality in a pre-adult child mind." Hence, Forrest Gump.

What ever happened to high art? It collided, says Joseph Epstein, with our secret knowledge that artistic talent is unequally distributed by a capricious Mother Nature with no interest whatever in being fair. To right this wrong, multiculturalists "have made the arts avenues to progress and encouraged the downtrodden to practice them." As a result, "the avant garde has largely turned away from technique and toward content"—i.e., the kind of people who once gave us ground-breaking movements like Impressionism and stream-of-consciousness now give us chocolate-covered feminists. Victimhood art, says Epstein, is "ultimately uncriticizable," as witness the thriving career of Maya Angelou, who "probably has more honorary degrees than James Joyce had outstanding debts."

Forget the novel, says Kent Carroll, erstwhile editor at Grove Press. Confessional talk shows have destroyed the whole concept of fictive structure. When Sally Jessy announces, "Today we're doing lesbian shoplifters who seduced their stepmothers," everything that traditionally has propelled a narrative line—suspense, conflict, motive, mistaken identity, the dog that doesn't bark—becomes academic.

NR's David Klinghoffer takes on theological dumbing down in "Kitsch Religion." He first became aware of it at his bar mitzvah when he found himself reciting Hebrew he had memorized but did not understand, imperfectly taught at a Reform temple more interested in politics and "social action" than in the Torah. Klinghoffer's essay is notable for his highly effective narrative technique, familiar to readers of his *NR* vignettes on urban life: the sudden punchy detail that brings everything into focus. His quick sketch of the environmentally sensitive Reform rabbi selling low-flow shower heads in his temple shop illuminates all that is wrong with trying to make religion "relevant."

Dumb has even invaded cooking. Nahum Waxman contrasts the tone of respect and confidence in Colonial-era recipes with the paranoid admonitions in today's: mash anchovies with the *back* of a fork, rub avocados with the *cut* side of a lemon, discard the pits, discard the bouquet garni, remove the string from the roast, and—a pinch of sagacity for the truly witless—"Lower the heat if the pan threatens to burn."

David R. Slavitt traces the dumbing of higher education to the passage of the GI Bill, when "the whole country declared itself to be middle class." As going to college replaced learning, Slavitt, who worked at *Newsweek*, had to help readers along with appositives, changing stand-alone references to "Plato" to "Plato, the Greek philosopher," and writing the "Summing Up" squibs at the end of long articles, a job he calls "reducing all experience to fifty words of pith and vinegar."

The dim views fly so fast and furious that Oswald Spengler would go mad trying to pick his favorite. Sven Birkerts's "Homo Virtualis" examines "the pinball fixity" of the Net user and notes that "getting off-line is like coming down from a high," a brand-new addiction for which counseling is already available. Heather MacDonald describes a writing class in the "peer teaching" program at CUNY where essays by the semi-literate serve as models for the cretinous. James B. Twitchell, blaming advertising for the "carnivalization of culture," suggests that the real reason why books are ad-free is that "the prime audience for advertisers, namely the young, is functionally illiterate."

And on and on, or as Jeremiah might say, "It's all here." The editors, a poet and a literary agent, who set out to find curmudgeons immune to facile nostalgia, err only once. Striving for "balance"—an evil goal—they include "I'll Take My Stand: In Defense of Popular Culture," by Anthony DeCurtis, who goes all muzzy as he attempts to explain why he likes rock 'n' roll.

DeCurtis's essay was also too much for John Simon, who slams it in his introduction—proving, like this review, that misery loves company.

The American Spectator, September 1996
Book Review

"Still Growing: The Girl Governor from Pontefract"

Growing Up Republican: Christie Whitman:
The Politics of Character by Patricia Beard
(HarperCollins, 262 pages, $25)

When Colin Powell called himself a "Rockefeller Republican" last year, pundits found nothing odd about his use of such an antiquated term to claim membership in the liberal wing of the GOP. Yet it was decidedly off-key. Given the short memory and abysmal ignorance of the American public, why did the savvy Powell latch onto a tag associated with a Republican nomination battle that took place three decades ago?

He may well have picked it up from Christine Todd Whitman. Powell and New Jersey's first woman governor have become thick lately, and Nelson Rockefeller runs through her life like a trout line. She and her mother were among the original Rockefeller Republicans; her mother was chairman of Citizens for Rockefeller in 1960, 1964, and 1968, and Christie's first paid job was in Rocky's last campaign.

None of this sat well with Christie's father, Webster Todd, who was passed over for an ambassadorship when his man, Nixon, decided to punish him for the disloyalty of the Todd womenfolk. Losing out on the diplomatic post no doubt made Web remember the first time Nelson Rockefeller caused trouble for the Todd men. It happened during the Depression, when Web and his father, John R. Todd, built Rockefeller Center for Nelson's grandfather, John D. Rockefeller.

Nelson, an art fancier, had been given the job of commissioning a mural for the main entrance. He chose the Mexican artist Diego Rivera. When the finished mural was delivered, Nelson had it installed and covered it with a curtain to await the official unveiling. But John R. Todd peeked—and recoiled. Rivera's mural showed a parade of workers representing "the Proletariat" marching joyously toward Lenin.

The horrified Todd told his son, "Bring a crew of men you can trust and meet me here at two o'clock in the morning." When they were assembled, John R. Todd personally jackhammered the mural off the wall and had it dumped in the East River.

The next day he went to Old John D., confessed what he had done, and insisted that he take back the Rockefeller Center stock that had been his fee. He obviously expected the tycoon to admire him for his honor, thank him for defending capitalism, and tell him to keep the stock, but Old John D., tight as a tick, took it back.

Did Christie and her mother become Rockefeller Republicans out of a subconscious wish to reward the gadfly Nelson for putting one over on their oppressive menfolk? It makes psychological sense, but making psychological sense cuts too close to the bone for this gang of hardy WASPs. Get too analytical and they will simply diagnose you as being what they call "off your feed," and send you out to play field hockey or ride a horse until you stop thinking so hard.

Biographer and subject were never better matched than in *Growing Up Republican* by Patricia Beard, an editor at *Town & Country*. Beard herself is a Democrat but otherwise she and Christie Todd Whitman are virtual clones; same age (fiftyish), same background ("comfortable"), same number and type of children (one boy and one girl), and same good-sport feminism: "A woman can do it all provided she doesn't try to do it all at once." Both stayed home when their children were small and launched their careers later.

They hit it off so well that Christie gave Beard unrestricted access to the Todd papers stashed in the attic at the family farm in Oldwick, New Jersey. The farm is named "Pontefract," after the English village whence the first Todd emigrated to the colonies in the seventeenth century. The village happens to be named for the neighboring castle where Richard II was murdered, but as unpleasant things are best put out of the mind, neither biographer nor subject brings this up.

It's quite possible that Christie doesn't know it. After all, the only papers she refused to let Beard see are her old report cards. This is a family that seems to have read nothing but position papers, and there is no evidence that Christie ever let down the side by opening a book. She inadvertently reveals her condition in her introduction when she describes finding a letter to one of her forebears thanking him for his help in relieving the 1892 Russian famine.

"Nobody in the family knew that letter was there or remembered the reason," she marvels, but one day while poking around in the attic she found it and saw that it was from "Count Leo Tolstoy." Only two kinds of people would use the title with that name. One is a status seeker, which Christie most definitely is not. The other is someone who doesn't know that Tolstoy was anything besides a Russian count.

Christine Todd Whitman is old blood and new money. Both grandfathers started out poor and made "respectable, but not flashy, fortunes," the Todds in building and the Schleys in banking; her maternal grandfather, Reeve Schley, was vice-president of Chase.

The Republican Party has always been central to the ideal of public service held by both families: between them, they ran the New Jersey GOP. Christie's parents, Webster Todd and Eleanor Schley, met at the 1932 national convention when Web was 33 and Eleanor 21. They married the following year and produced their first three children within the standard time frame: Kate in 1934, John in 1936, and Dan in 1938. Then came a fallow period that ended with the birth of Christine Temple Todd in 1946, when Web was 47 and Eleanor 36. It would have been natural enough had Web been absent during the war, but he wasn't. In all likelihood Christie was what was tactfully known in those days as a "surprise."

Biographer Beard tactfully avoids the dilemma of the unwanted child, opting instead for interviews with the Todd children's friends, people now in their fifties, to paint a general picture of family life at Pontefract. It was a household of "dictatorial men and complicated women, flawed by the insularity, repression, and inflexibility that were the hallmarks of their class." Christie's friends found Eleanor cold and frightening, while Web was famous among his sons' friends for the beatings he gave the boys, taking them upstairs and whipping them so hard with his belt that guests heard the lashes.

This is more like it, but just when we feel we are getting somewhere, Beard takes it all back with a tortured rationalization: "Yet the reason those who grew up with the Todds have so many of these stories to tell is that the children always brought their friends home, even when they were old enough—in college and after—to have avoided going home much themselves if they had wanted to."

Christie's childhood memory of her father is a classic. First she issues a disclaimer, saying she doesn't really remember all that much about him from her early years, then nonchalantly adds, "for some reason he always seemed to be in an ill humor on Sunday morning, and he'd vacuum. I mean, the house was immaculate."

Web never hit Christie, but he did write her letters when she was away at boarding school. Here is one about her pet animals that Beard calls "jocular":

> Drummer Boy is fine. I expect to shoot him any day. Angel, if she keeps barking every morning, will also get shot. Next on the list will be the ducks because they are getting to be a nuisance also. All of which means that when you come back you won't recognize the place. I may decide to shoot both horses (but not Greyleg now that you want him) over the week-end, Angel I will save until you arrive home, and probably the old woman the week after.

The "jocular" reference to shooting Christie's mother is intriguing in view of something that had happened a few years earlier. In 1952 Web delivered the New Jersey vote for Eisenhower, who rewarded him with a NATO job. The Todds moved to Paris and enrolled Christie, then seven, in a school for children of American diplomatic personnel:

> I did not like the school and—apparently in order to overcome, I presume, boredom—I told some relatively outrageous stories at "show and tell" about the relationship between Mother and Dad, which caused the headmistress to call Mother in one day to ask how they got along.
>
> Mother said, "Fine, as far as I know."
>
> The headmistress said, "Well, it disturbs Christie when Mr. Todd chases you around the house with a hatchet; she's been telling us about it at show-and-tell."
>
> Mother thought anyone who was dumb enough to believe a seven-year-old about stories like that was too dumb to educate me. So she pulled me out.

This story is—apparently—a tin-eared attempt to—presumably—convince us that there was absolutely nothing to it, just a relatively silly misunderstanding that we must not think too hard about lest it put us off our feed.

Christie's grandmother called her a "spoiled brat" because her parents indulged her hatred of school. After the show-and-tell contretemps they enrolled her in a French school. She quickly became fluent in the language but complained that the other children refused to play with her, so the Todds withdrew her and sent her to the Marymount nuns. But the gentle sisters locked disobedient pupils in the dog run and made Christie eat fish eyes, and the other girls made fun of her father's name being Webster. She ran away several times, until finally her mother gave up and hired a full-time nanny. The horse-struck Christie was now free to go to the races.

Another crisis erupted when they sent her to summer camp in the French Alps; "Christie's reaction was to hold on to the dashboard and scream until Eleanor and Dan pried her out of the car and delivered her to her bunk."

Returning to America, the Todds enrolled her in Far Hills Country Day School, where she received a conditional eighth-grade diploma due to an Incomplete in Latin.

On to boarding school at Foxcroft in Virginia, where her mother had been Class of '29. Once academically rigorous, it was now little more than a finishing school run by what one alumna called "a bizarre group of maiden ladies."

An inherent contradiction existed between the school's guiding principle, "Dare to be a Daniel"—i.e., an individual—and its para-military flavor. The girls wore dresses styled like uniforms and Civil War-era billed caps. They had a drill team, a color guard, a drum corps, and daily inspection wherein senior Daniels lifted the skirts of lesser Daniels to see if they were wearing slips. Students were per-mitted to keep horses, which Christie liked, but she hated the living arrangements. The girls had to sleep in sleeping bags on cots on unheated screened porches—three to a porch, which, she believed, made her the odd-girl out.

It was while she was at Foxcroft that her father wrote her "jocu-lar" letters about shooting her pets and her mother.

She finagled a leave of absence from Foxcroft and attended the Chapin School in Manhattan as a day student. When her parents tried to make her return to Foxcroft, she hid under the bed covers and cried until they agreed to let her go to Chapin. She graduated and enrolled at Wheaton College outside of Boston, majoring in political science and graduating in 1968.

"Christie knew she wanted to get married and have children," writes Patricia Beard; "her family was so close, she was looking for-ward to trying to replicate it."

When Christie met John Whitman in 1971 he was "playing the field"—i.e., dating lots of girls. He and Christie did not get along, but despite their personality clash she thought he was "a very studly guy." Two years later, needing a date for the Nixon inaugural ball, she invited John. They were married the following year.

John is Yale, Harvard Business School, and the grandson of a New York governor. During their early married years while Christie wifed and mothered, John supported the family, first as a Citibank executive and later as a venture capitalist. He did extremely well, so well that if Christie seeks national office we can expect a marathon press conference *à la* Geraldine Ferraro. Christie's will last even longer, because John Whitman has done much better than John Zacarro.

After he left Citibank he became chairman and CEO of Prudential-Bache Interfunding, which successfully invested a pool of $800 million in leveraged buyouts. In one deal, John put in $78,211 and made $981,553. Next he started a consulting company whose clients included Ford Motor Company, the U. S. Agency for International Development, and the Hungarian-American Enterprise Fund. Now he heads Sycamore Partners, which concentrates on investments in the U.S. and Asia.

He certainly has the financial expertise to be the brains behind Christie's governorship, especially her famously successful 36-percent tax cut. But Steve Forbes and Lawrence Kudlow also attended the meeting that produced it so we can't be sure who her Pygmalion is, only that she needs one.

The couple's public statements about their marriage run the usual gamut in praise of independent women and the strong, secure men who love them. But to know the real Whitmans we must see them on the tennis courts, where they seethe and fume and curse each other *sotto voce* in eternal competition. Unremarkable enough, if only Patricia Beard had let it pass, but she cannot resist an offhand explanation that arouses the very suspicions she tries to douse: "This is not unusual in the milieu in which they were both brought up, where emotions that are closely guarded are often expressed through sports."

John is known for his gruffness, especially with the media. Asked if Christie was scared when she faced an operation for an ovarian cyst, he replied, "How should I know? She's a politician." Asked why he fell in love with her, he replied, "It doesn't sound romantic, but it was the right time."

The indefatigable Beard also has an explanation for this, attributing it to "Protestant distantness." An awkward word, but less awkward than wondering if Christie, in her zest for replicating her family, set out to find another "jocular" sadist like her father—and did.

Governor Christie, in the opinion of the late Malcolm Forbes, is "on her way to becoming the American Margaret Thatcher." At the moment the way is marked by teddy bears—one behind her desk at the state house and the others in the governor's mansion—gifts from her grandmother's friend, A.A. Milne, author of *Winnie the Pooh*. The snuggliness has spread to some of New Jersey's toll takers, who have been known to rush out of their booths at the sight of a state car, crying, "Got Christie with you? I love her. Tell her I love her."

The growing assumption that this woman is a seasoned pro seems to be based more on her lifelong exposure to power politics than anything else. True, she's seen and heard a lot, but it emerges as a boiler-room, summer-intern kind of knowledge when filtered through her bland personality.

She has a feminine dread of offending people and a jittery compulsion to make nice on all fronts. Bob Grant endorsed her for governor, but after he was accused of racist remarks she issued a statement that she would not appear on his show again. When Grant subsequently attacked her, Christie decided to go on his show to explain why she wouldn't go on his show. Now, he has said, he's "through with her."

Ever since Ed Rollins boasted about bribing black ministers to "suppress" the inner-city vote in her gubernatorial election, her desperation to please Jesse Jackson & Company has been palpable. How she will manage to keep on growing up Republican with this albatross around her neck is uncertain, to say the least, for little New Jersey contains Newark, Camden, Jersey City, and Trenton, the capital, whose per capita income is $11,018.

Indistinguishable from a starry-eyed liberal, she is heading into an abyss of tough love and task forces, pushing programs like "Second-Chance Homes" and "Work First" that spend a fortune on welfare to keep from spending a fortune on welfare, and a juvenile-detention center whose director proudly explained his innovative system of "norms" thus: "These kids break rules, so we have norms instead."

Growing Up Republican is "emphatically not" a campaign biography, as Beard states emphatically on page one. Nonetheless, she does all she can to help Christie tone down her patrician image, to the extent of ramming politically correct buzzwords into the most sacred aristocratic preserves, e.g., "Foxhunting is more cooperative than competitive; it's too dangerous a sport for one rider to try to outdo the others."

Christie also plays the leveling game, and shares Beard's propensity for making things worse. Here she is laboring to prove that Pontefract is not an estate but a hardscrabble farm and she but a simple milkmaid:

> One of the reasons I loved growing up on a farm is that there's no hierarchy; people are respected for the work they can do. A farmer is a good farmer or a bad farmer; it's not what his last name is. Farming gives you a perspective that no one is inherently better than anyone else, and you can work side by side with anybody. My first model for that was the relationship my father had with our farmer, Merle Stiles; Merle worked for us but he was the professional and we took direction from him.

These people are more fun than a barrel, but the best line in the book belongs to Christie's daughter, Kate: "I don't think she should do vice president."

National Review, September 2, 1996
Book Review

"Tent City"

Powertown, by Michael Lind (HarperCollins, 272 pp., $23)

' **W**HAT is written with ease is seldom read with plea-sure," said Samuel Johnson. "Make haste slowly," said Augustus Caesar. "If something is worth doing, it's worth doing well," said your mother. Pick any old saw from the haste/waste school of thought and you will have an apt description of Michael Lind's problem. Somebody should take away his laptop and give him a quill.

Powertown is a Washington political novel about the good, the bad, the ugly, and the mentored. Lind uses the "Grand Hotel" format: take a group of disparate people who would not ordinarily meet and make their paths cross. It sounds easy, but this mode of storytelling demands the balance of a juggler and the patience of a chess player. Lacking a protagonist to hold the story together, the writer must take pains to move the right character into the right place at the right time so that the action unfolds in an orderly manner. In a carefully crafted Grand Hotel novel, the characters are synchronized as precisely as the statues that strike the hour on German cathedrals: the trumpeters come forward, the archangels turn right, King Wenceslaus turns left, and St. Boniface changes places with St. Stephen.

But painstaking writing takes time, so Michael Lind had to find a quicker technique. If I had to guess, I'd say he played "52 Pickup" with his Rolodex and put everybody who landed face up into this book.

The two most important male characters are both gay

Republicans, one white and one black. The former is Ross Drummond of Mississippi, a K Street lobbyist who never loses sight of the fiscal. "The real division in the world is not between heterosexuals and homosexuals. It's between tops and bottoms," he explains. "If you're a top, why the hell would you be in favor of gay marriage? You're probably bringing in most of the income, right? So . . . even though you're pulling in 80 per cent of the money, the male wife gets 50 per cent of the household assets. F— that s—."

Ross's lover is Avery Brackenridge, a black elitist conservative who is drawn to the Aryan imagery of Wagnerian music and has fantasies of a blond Anglo-Saxon beau ideal he calls "the man in the Burberrys coat."

Stephanie Schonfeld is the hot-shot careerist who has mastered the art of carrying a drink, a cigarette, and finger food at cocktail parties without dropping anything. Homely Stef has an affair with Bruce Brandt, an aide to the Drug Czar. Bruce's reason for sleeping with Stef, while not the only cliché in the book, is definitely the oldest; "in his experience ordinary girls had often been the best lovers. They were determined to compensate—and also desperate to keep a guy as good looking as him [sic]."

Stef works at *Perspective*, a small-circulation opinion journal owned by a Greek-Australian, Des Kazakis, whose do-gooder sister, Aglaia Kazakis, wants to train monkeys to help the handicapped. *Perspective*'s editor is Sir Robin Blair, an imported Brit who thinks the civil-rights movement took place in "Binghamton" and was led by "Malcolm Luther King."

This ménage cries out for satirical development, but Lind gives them a lick and a promise and moves on to Ouida Covington, a black activist who works for D.C. Statehood; Darryl Shelton, a white gunrunner to the ghetto; Graciela Herrera, an illegal immigrant who is seduced in a warehouse owned by financier Jay Prentice Pierce, the subject of Stef's exposé, "Piercegate," that will make her a world-famous journalist after Bruce rejects her for Allison and she opts for the brittle world represented by Claudia, etc., etc.

The underclass blacks include Velma Hawkins, who keeps saying "Lawd a'mercy," her husband Curtis, a security guard who beats up the elitist Avery, their nephew Evander, who sees himself as Salamander Man, impervious to fire; his mother Sharonda, his girl-friends Teesha and Eunique, and a pride of gang members with names like Jamal, Twon, and Lookout.

No real connection is ever forged between the white and black characters. The ghetto scenes serve the purpose of showing off Lind's knowledge of street-smart dialects and provide him with inordinate-ly lubricious black-on-black sex scenes that hint of a cherubic Southern white boy imagining forbidden dusky pleasures.

Lind introduces so many characters so fast that we feel we are being held hostage in a receiving line. Especially frustrating are the ones who are named and described as if they're going to play a large role, only to have little or no importance. In this group we find Senators Ed Shaunnessey of Massachusetts and his pal, Brad Doyle of Connecticut, obviously Ted Kennedy and Chris Dodd, who have a drunken donut fight and then disappear from the book.

But worse than the revolving door, worse than the confusing tran-sitions, is Lind's style. He strains so hard for metaphors and similes that the book needs a truss instead of a dust jacket:

"The room is suffused with an amber effulgence."

"Blood-colored light seeps through clouds textured like gauze."

"Soon she is clenched in pleasure again as his eager bucking flares coals of burning pleasure in her core."

". . . that moment when the sun has set but the blue sky has not yet forgotten the day, and the cloud-foam, piled beyond the darkening trees, appears to have the weight and texture as well as the color of clay."

". . . pants tented by a rebellious reflex [an erection]."

"The shadow of a pteranodon tents them [lovers in the Museum of Natural History]."

". . . his stomach twisted, pregnant with fear."

This is what happens when you just let it come: the rosy fingers of dawn, a certain slant of light, two *pleasures* in the same sentence, a pregnant man, and tent city.

Powertown is being hyped as another *Bonfire of the Vanities*, but in fact it's a cast of thousands looking for a novel. If they ever find it, they can call it a gas leak of the incongruities.

National Review, September 30, 1996
Book Review

"That Lovely Couple"

Hellman and Hammett,
by Joan Mellen (HarperCollins, 572 pp., $32)

L OVE on the Left tends to validate the adage, "For every old sock there's an old shoe." Lillian Hellman was no oil painting, though Louis Kronenberger always said she looked like Gilbert Stuart's portrait of George Washington; another man imagined that making love to her "would be like going to bed with Justice Frankfurter." Thwarted at being desirable by a clock-stopping face, narrow hips, and no derrière to speak of, she settled for being available.

At six-foot-two and 141 pounds, the prematurely white-haired Dashiell Hammett looked like a tubercular stork, but the former Pinkerton operative had created Sam Spade, the fictional private eye who, in the words of Dorothy Parker, was "so hard-boiled you could roll him on the White House lawn." Hammett and Miss Hellman met in a Hollywood nightclub in 1930. On their second date he punched her in the jaw and knocked her down. She arose sweetly, with the soft coquettish laugh of the Southern belles she had envied back home in New Orleans, and moved in with him.

A fledgling writer, she began at once to suck forth his soul. He wanted to do a play based on a Scottish slander case about two headmistresses accused of lesbianism by their pupils, but instead gave the plot to Miss Hellman and guided her through the writing of *The Children's Hour*, her first Broadway hit.

Biographer Joan Mellen's thoroughgoing literary detective work leaves little doubt that Hammett, not Miss Hellman, wrote this play, and *The Little Foxes* as well. With so many drafts, each heavily edited and revised by him, the final draft had to be all his work. In an attempt to sound feminine, Miss Hellman boasted that he steered her through every line, but it was her name, not his, that ended up in lights. The self-destructive Hammett, who never wrote another book after she entered his life, had collaborated in his own castration.

He got even by never letting her forget that she was an ugly duckling. He beat her, disappeared on benders, patronized black brothels in Harlem, caught gonorrhea, arranged for her to find him in bed with other women, forced her to have lesbian sex so he could watch, and promised to get a divorce and marry her when he made her pregnant, only to change his mind and force her to have an abortion.

Worse than his abuse were his cold moods. During one, her fear of rejection drove her to proposition novelist Nathanael West, but it couldn't have been much of an ego boost in view of what West said afterward: "I did it because she asked me and men are not taught how to turn a woman down."

Politically, she behaved like a teenage girl carefully tailoring her opinions to please a boy, making sure she liked what he liked whether she liked it or not. Her favorite comic strip was "Li'l Abner" but Hammett said it was "fascist" and ordered her to stop reading it. She stopped.

He was a committed Communist for a tangle of reasons: guilt over his strikebreaking days with Pinkerton, anger at the government for a red-tape delay in his World War I pension, a nihilistic worldview, and a monkish need for the dedication and obedience Communism demanded. "He was monogamous in politics as he could not be sexually," says Joan Mellen. She believes his aversion to introspection, which made him such a successful writer of detective stories, also explains his unquestioning acceptance of Party orders.

Hammett and Miss Hellman both joined the CP in 1938 during

the period of low-profile respectability known as the Popular Front, when Stalin ordered American party members to eschew violent revolution and support the New Deal. Communism without danger or grubbiness suited the Hollywood crowd to a tee: "Amid paeans to Americanism, Lillian could display her mink coat."

In 1942 the 48-year-old Hammett joined the Army and was stationed in the Aleutians with other subversives, among them Irving Howe. On her own and rich from movie money (she could write a good screenplay), Miss Hellman went on a cultural jaunt to the Soviet Union and had a wild affair with John Melby, third secretary at the American embassy.

Flying over Siberia with a Russian pilot, her plane was forced down in a blizzard. Aroused by their brush with death, she and the pilot stumbled from the wreckage and copulated in the snow while a young boy watched them curiously. Years later she met Yevgeny Yevtushenko, who confessed that he was that young boy. It's a small world.

In 1951 Hammett was jailed for contempt of court for refusing to identify subversives. Fearing for her career, Miss Hellman abandoned him; she later claimed she pawned her jewels for his bail, but in fact she left the country. Called before HUAC in 1952, she simpered that she had joined the CP at the urging of "a misguided lady" but soon quit on realizing she was not political. She refused to name names, however, and gained an undeserved reputation for courage with one catchy metaphor: "I cannot and will not cut my conscience to fit this year's fashions."

She weathered the McCarthy years, but Hammett, impoverished by IRS liens and drinking a quart of Scotch a day, was finished. She didn't want him now, but she needed him on tap to maintain the legend she was constructing, of Hellman and Hammett, the Brownings of America's literary Left.

She kept him around as her trophy deadbeat, more or less supporting him until his death in 1961 freed her to burnish their tawdry romance to a still higher gloss. She got it up to Tristan-and-Isolde speed in two volumes of memoirs, threatening Hammett's biographers with lawsuits if they departed from her lies.

Her dotage was a saga of geriatric lubricity that reads like Suetonius's account of Tiberius at Capri. Looking ninety-some instead of seventy-some, smoking four packs a day, she propositioned men in a Baby Snooks voice, showed herself in the nude to a deckhand on a cruise, asked a screenwriter to hold a mirror while she inspected her genitals, undressed under a towel on the beach, coyly warning her guests not to peek ("Who wants to peek?" groaned Leonard Bernstein), and accused Norman Mailer of trying to rape her. William Styron, a target of her advances, confessed that he "wound up hating her."

Everyone was afraid of her unparalleled viciousness, never more in evidence than when she sued Mary McCarthy for libel, vowing, "I'll bleed and impoverish her." The suit died with Miss Hellman, who died of natural causes, but one finishes this book wishing that she, like Tiberius, had been smothered.

The American Spectator, October 1996
Book Review

"The Un-Alchemist: Suffering Fools Deliciously"

Fools' Names, Fools' Faces by Andrew Ferguson
Introduction by P.J. O'Rourke
(Atlantic Monthly Press, 213 pages, $22)

Among the noteworthy qualities of Andrew Ferguson's writing is its freedom from clichés, bromides, and lazy phrasing. No state-of-the-art this or that, no devils in the details, no rocket-scientist analogies, no Yogi Berra-isms, no calls for "more education," and no interminable quotations from punditry's favorite pony, Alexis de Tocqueville.

This is because Ferguson is a writer who makes haste slowly. Unlike syndicated columnists, he does not write three times a week; most of the time he doesn't even write once a week. He writes when he writes, i.e., when he has something to say and is ready to say it, for opinion journals such as *TAS*, the *New Republic*, *National Review* (where he was my roommate, so to speak, on the back page we alternated), *Forbes MediaCritic*, and, most recently, the *Weekly Standard*, where he is a senior editor.

This collection of thirty-two previously published columns and essays is rich with those distinctive freshets of prose that I have come to think of as "Andyisms": former NOW president Molly Yard is "the Mammy Yokum of the choice people"; the bland Nineties are "a zeit with no geist"; Barbra Streisand's signature song is "People Who Read *People*." Grace notes like these usually don't come to a writer the first time around, but emerge in the fine-tuning of a second or third draft.

His attention to craftsmanship also produces zany anecdotes of such invisible construction and perfect timing that we aren't always prepared for the punchline. Be forewarned: reading Ferguson at the table can be fatal, or at least messy.

His account of his talk-show appearance with Gennifer Flowers initially makes the reader expect some sort of ultimate pronouncement on the character of Bill Clinton, but instead he suddenly makes us privy to an off-air exchange between Flowers and himself:

"I'll tell you," she hissed, "whoever said the truth will set you free was full of s---."

"I think that was Jesus," he replied.

This is where I had to mop up coffee, clear my windpipe of donut crumbs, and change my T-shirt. *Fools' Names, Fools' Faces* is that kind of book.

A refusal to suffer fools has been the defining trait of satirists since Juvenal, but pre-millennium America has added a new wrinkle: our biggest fools are the people called "national treasures." Ferguson the Un-Alchemist returns them to their original states of dross and paste, beginning with Bill Moyers, "an Elmer Gantry for the New Age." The soft-spoken PBS producer-host-ego of *Bill Moyers' America* has gone from being LBJ's henchman to being "concerned," the preferred condition of the furrowed-brow set he now commands, who nod solemnly over his runny pieties about "an ethic of cooperation," "a renewal of community," and "the conversation of democracy" around "the national campfire."

Campfires have loomed large in Moyers's life since he took up spiritualism and pop psychology in his six-part *omnium tedium*, "The Power of Myth with Bill Moyers." He followed this with "A Gathering of Men," in which he went hunting for his lost manhood with the founder of the male mythopoetic movement, Robert Bly, "a plump poet from Minnesota who serenades men's seminars with an untuned lyre."

What of the hope, long cherished by the usual suspects, that Moyers will run for president? Doubtful, said Ferguson in this 1991 profile; "To Democrats he is a Henry Wallace for the 1990's." But that was five years ago, before Bill Clinton became a Bill Clinton for all time. Now Ferguson's analysis takes on an eerie prescience: "Moyers has left behind a seamy past to take to the airwaves, where he tells tall tales to the gullible, appropriating their confusions, only to administer a salve of undemanding reassurance . . ."

He does not spare conservatives if they display what he regards as an unforgivable sin: *unseemliness*. The anachronistic word suits the Lord Chesterfield streak underlying Ferguson's easygoing, puckish nature—a duality as interesting as it is rare, and the likely source of the psychological tension that makes his style so rigorous.

Bill Bennett is unseemly because the virtue-oil salesman "has become a brand name." Bennett's literary tonics, *The Book of Virtues* and *The Devaluing of America*, have a truth-in-labeling problem that is obvious to anyone who knows how to spot a ghost job:

> One of the few pleasures of reading such books comes from the acknowledgments, in which, shoved up among the encomiums to wife, kids, typists, and high-school track coaches, the name of the book's true author is slyly revealed. The surest clue is an excess of praise. On page 15 of *Devaluing* we read: "A very special debt of gratitude is owed to Peter Wehner. Over the years, I have come to respect and rely on him in many ways, but this was never more so than when I embarked full-time on this enterprise . . ." Etc. And on page 16 of *Virtues* we read: "As to John Cribb, I cannot thank him enough for his efforts to make this book a reality . . ." And so on. Getting away with this, and thinking nothing of it, is part of what it means to be a brand name.

(It proves Ferguson's point that Beltway ethicists were offended when Hillary Rodham Clinton did not even bother to sneak the name of her own ghost into the acknowledgments of *It Takes a Village*, thereby giving dishonesty a bad name.)

The biggest fools are those who do the most talking, closely followed by those who lack the brains to realize that the talkers aren't saying anything. Ferguson's America is bent double with a massive attack of logorrhea. "I talk on the phone, therefore I am," is the *raison d'être* of "yuppies with portable phones attached to their ears, stopping traffic, tripping over hydrants, bumping into lampposts." Celebrity interviews tell us little about the celebrity because the interviewer talks about himself. With Clinton thinking aloud, Newt Gingrich explaining what the Tofflers meant, and everyone trying to define "self-esteem," merry cynics like Ferguson are tempted to conclude that the examined life is not worth living.

America is hooked on talking cures, Ferguson believes, because our Protestant heritage deprived us of the sacrament of Confession. In that case the diversity workshop is our counter-reformation. The one he attended was packed with corporate types listening to windy speeches about "Unleashing the Power of Your Workforce by Managing Diversity," and obediently chanting after their facilitators, "I accept the 'onion theory' that I will continue to peel away layers of my own racism for the rest of my life."

That the most conservative members of society, the business community, are themselves seasoned veterans of soul-searching workshops, explains why Clinton has gotten away with his emotion-wracked, hysteria-prone presidency; "the button-down squares whose hackles should have been raised, had been doing precisely the same thing for years."

The spectacle of latter-day Babbitts on expense-account guilt trips activated Ferguson's "what's wrong with this picture?" test of conservative values. His answer is bleak: "The revolution proceeds without a shot being fired, with scarcely a peep of protest . . . [T]he white-male power structure of late-twentieth-century America [is] the first to pay people to dismantle itself."

National Review, October 28, 1996
Essay

"Good Ol' Clothes"

W HEN a child first thinks of living to see the century turn, he always does some arithmetic to figure out how old he will be when it happens. I was in the second grade when I did my calculations: 2,000 take away 1936 equals 64.

I stared at the figure, trying to imagine myself at that age. My grandmother was about 64 at this time so I based my mental picture on her. The facial features were easy to sketch in because I already looked like her that way. Then I started on the clothes.

A jersey dress with a self-fabric belt, a lace fichu tucked under the collar and spread across the bosom like a giant snowflake, service-weight stockings, and black oxfords called "EnnaJetticks." Underneath were a satin slip that had to be ironed wet; something she called a "shimmy" which was a kind of camisole undershirt; and the holy of holies, a "foundation garment," a cross between a girdle and a corset.

As I write this defense of traditional fashion in the shadow of the millennium, I am wearing polyester pants with a drawstring waist, a pullover, underpants, knee-highs, and Hush Puppies. When I go out I add a bra, but that's it.

I am physically more comfortable than Granny, but I am pinched and chafed by psychosartorial conflicts she never knew. I disapprove of myself; all that is rigid in me cries out against the way I dress and the society that lets me get away with it, but Granny was in sync with her clothes and her time.

She bought her frankly fusty duds in old-lady departments called "Stylish Stout" and "Grande Dame." The euphemisms fooled no one; shoppers new to a store would ask, "Where's the old-lady department?"

They were comfortable places to shop. The salesladies were the same age as the customers and the stock reflected a sense of historical connectedness. The racks were full of purple dresses because it had been the color of "second mourning" for Victorian widows after an initial year spent in black. The custom died out well before Granny's generation grew old, but by then purple was so thoroughly associated with old ladies that people referred to it as an "old-lady color."

Historical connectedness has turned into hysterical fritz. "Classical is back!" means Caesar's legions are back, every knee bared. "Romantic is back!" means the coachman is back, three capes to the wind. "Traditional is back!" means the bellhop is back, double rows of buttons playing Russian roulette with nipples. When they trot out something that looks like Quentin Durward in drag, it means "Femininity is back!"

In my case, "Pyrrhic victory is back!" If I worked in an office instead of at home I would have to buy some dressy clothes, but nothing would change. Looking undignified in a thigh-high skirt is no different from looking undignified in drawstring pants, except that I show a lot less leg. Dignity, not youthful illusion, is what I want now, but dignity is the only fashion look considered outré.

If the personal is political, the imperious is impossible when women past a certain age eagerly adopt the same fashions worn by sweet young things. It would not matter so much were it merely a matter of clothes per se, but something more important is involved.

The Roman Matron has to be serene before she can do her stuff; if she's constantly tugging her skirt down and yanking at her neckline to cover her cleavage, it won't be long before she ceases to be a Roman Matron.

This sort of woman, whom Americans used to call a "dowager"

and a "rock," or "the duchess" and "the old battleaxe," has now been replaced by geriatric gamines like Helen Gurley Brown.

Throughout history, societies that honored their old battleaxes have tended to flourish, but America is fast running out of the breed. We could replenish our supply if we brought back the old-lady department, but of course we won't. Cut-off points and lines of demarcation are conservative by definition. The enthusiastic promotion of one-age-fits-all clothing is the sartorial equivalent of the socialistic leveling we find so chic.

When people say a woman "looks conservative" they usually mean she looks frumpy. Said of a man, it's a backhanded compliment; it means he looks dignified, authoritative, prosperous, capable, powerful, and stern—just what men aren't supposed to be nowadays. If clothes make the man, anyone wishing to destroy the man can simply destroy his clothes. Social historians always look to women's fashions for their harbingers, but some of the most significant battles of the sartorial war on tradition have been fought in men's closets. Take, for example, the number of anti-conservative metaphors based on articles of male clothing.

Basic, all-round conservatism is conveyed by "blue suit" and "wingtips."

Repression and unhappiness springing from conformity and suburban life are conveyed by "gray flannel suit."

Paper-pushing boredom and the calcified attitudes that go with it are conveyed by "white collar."

Setting arbitrary standards, telling people what to do, and being judgmental are summed up by "coat-and-tie."

A conservative political candidate is an "empty suit."

In a democracy, the only men who can get away with looking conservative are liberals. When John F. Kennedy wore cutaway-and-stripes and a silk topper at his Inauguration, the media purred and the other officials on the dais, Democrats and Republicans alike, went along without a murmur. That it was the correct attire did not matter to them, only that Kennedy chose to wear it.

Yet when Ronald Reagan announced the same intention, the media was up in arms with dark murmurings about snobbery and exclusiveness, and GOP congressmen such as Sen. Howard Baker did the "Aw, shucks, I'm just a country boy" routine. Whatever Reagan had planned originally, he ended up wearing stripes, short coat, and no hat, which made him look like a butler.

The latest victim of the sartorial levelers is Bob Dole, who probably will wear Cotton Dockers to his Inauguration if he has one.

Dole's main purpose in going casual was to narrow the gender gap by making women feel warmed and secure in his open-collar, rump-sprung presence. But it doesn't work that way. Another midwesterner, Sinclair Lewis, came nearer to the mark in *Main Street*:

> She was close in her husband's arms; she clung to him; whatever of strangeness and slowness and insularity she might find in him, none of that mattered so long as she could slip her hands beneath his coat, run her fingers over the warm smoothness of the satin back of his waistcoat, seem almost to creep into his body, find in him strength, find in the courage and kindness of her man a shelter from the perplexing world.

That traditional fashions are a boon to morality and good manners seems to me inarguable. Even Bill Clinton agrees; whether or not he meant what he said about school uniforms, he had the good sense to say it, suggesting that he knows it's true whether he believes it or not.

I would go further and recommend knickers and long socks for pre-teen boys. I'm just old enough to remember the tag end of this fashion from my elementary-school days. Nothing else says "boy" with such devastating effect. Knickers may be the best line of demarcation ever invented: it's virtually impossible to smart-mouth teachers and cops while wearing them.

The button fly, still favored by Savile Row tailors, will not reduce casual sex, but it might reduce coarseness in movies and television. I am always appalled when actors casually unzip and remove their pants, or put them on and zip up, while facing the camera. They wouldn't be able to do this with a button fly; it would take too long and waste dramatic time.

The button fly also inculcates a genteel habit, though we're probably too far gone for it to take. The pants my father bought before

World War II all had button flies, and he always turned his back on us females—even my mother—while he did them up. Once, when I asked, I was told all gentlemen did. I believe it. A zipper provides a man with a jaunty gesture, but buttons force him to keep his hands at his crotch long enough to make him feel awkward and a little foolish: most men will turn their backs.

Traditional fashions have done wonders for female chastity, and even when they didn't, the fun was hardly worth the trouble.

Whenever I read a period novel, I always wonder how a woman unable to dress and undress without a maid could manage the logistics of an assignation. How could she get out of all those clothes, and then get back into them? What about the whalebone stays? Either her lover did them up for her, or else she knotted the strings around the bedpost and made like a dray horse, either of which would shatter illusions.

I imagine she didn't have to. There were some blithe spirits, but most women behaved themselves, and at least some of that virtue had less to do with godliness than with the daunting barriers presented by clothes that layered them like geological eras.

If you're thinking that the Victorian adulteress might have removed nothing except the most necessary garment, say one word: hoopskirt.

The American Spectator, December 1996
Book Review

"Resurrecting Harding"

The Strange Deaths of President Harding
by Robert H. Ferrell
(University of Missouri Press, 208 pages, $24.95)

T he parallels are intriguing: a big, white-haired, womanizing president with a shrouded medical history, an aggressive First Lady with an interest in spiritualism, a scandal-ridden administration, a mysterious suicide, and a shelf of tell-all books.

So far, so good. But if we add rumors that the First Lady poisoned the president, that he was sterile, that he had Negro blood, and that he signed over government oil leases to his cronies while drunk, we realize this is not the politically correct, calorie-counting White House of current ill fame but that of Warren Gamaliel Harding three-quarters of a century ago.

Harding invariably has placed last in presidential ratings, trailing even Millard Fillmore. His obloquy has been total and seemingly beyond the reach of revisionist rescue, but now relief has arrived. *The Strange Deaths of President Harding* is a scrupulously researched and vividly told overview by Robert H. Ferrell, emeritus professor of history at Indiana University, who demolishes or casts doubt on most of the accusations and suspicions surrounding America's twenty-ninth president.

Ferrell, author of *Ill Advised: Presidential Health and Public Trust*, is on his surest ground with the poison rumor. Harding died on August 2, 1923, in the Palace Hotel in San Francisco after a cross-country train trip to Tacoma, where he boarded a Navy ship for Alaska. This voyage was memorable for two macabre reasons. One was the coffin that the White House doctor had ordered placed in the ship's hold—not for the president but for Mrs. Harding, who was seriously ill with the nephritis that would kill her the following year. The other was shellfish, always the chief suspect when someone gets sick. When Harding vomited, it put the words "food poisoning" on the wire, and that, as later events would prove, was enough.

The 58-year-old president was actually a prime candidate for a heart attack, says Ferrell, and showed all the signs during the western trip. Overwhelmed by the presidency, he had sought to banish fears of inadequacy with frenetic "busyness" until he was exhausted, yet refused to admit it for fear of sending down the stock market. Now the western trip wore him out, the turning point coming in a Seattle motorcade when he pumped his arm up and down for hours as he tipped his hat, straining a heart that his doctor afterwards discovered was enlarged.

He collapsed as the train neared San Francisco, but loath to let people see him being carried, he insisted on donning morning dress and walked unaided up the steps of the Palace. As soon as he entered his suite he fell headfirst across the bed, where he would die three days later of what his doctors called "apoplexy," the old name for stroke and a common mistaken diagnosis in an era when cardiology was in its infancy. But stroke victims don't die instantly, and Harding did, of a massive coronary.

His funeral train is the one we never hear about. In Cheyenne crowds stood in a dust storm, in Chicago they filled the freight yards until the train could not move; silent awestruck masses who remembered the funeral procession of the Unknown Soldier two years before, when Harding had presented the very picture of a noble Roman. After the bulbous Taft and the wizened Wilson, the man who "looked like a president" had stirred their spirits and won their hearts.

The Teapot Dome scandals changed the perception, and Mrs. Harding's death in 1924 opened the floodgates of calumny. The first book to advance the poison theory was a 1926 novel, *Revelry*, by Samuel Hopkins Adams, about a president who accidentally poisons himself when he takes the wrong medicine and then decides not to tell his doctors, choosing a martyr's death to escape his political scandals. One of the many taken in by it was Herbert Hoover, Harding's secretary of commerce, who read it in manuscript and told a friend it described "many things which are not known."

The success of the Adams novel prompted a bimbo eruption. Her name was Nan Britton. Born in 1896, she had grown up in Marion, Ohio, and had known Harding all her life. A giddy teenager when Harding was editor of the town paper, Nan had developed such an intense crush on him that her father had seen fit to warn him about it. Harding no doubt was tempted by the warning because Nan had a well-established reputation among the townsfolk for being "fast." Something very likely happened between them, but Ferrell believes it was less a case of Harding seducing her than of her pestering him until he weakened, and produces enough old hotel registers to dispute the assignations she described in *The President's Daughter* (1927).

In 1919 Nan gave birth to Elizabeth Ann Christian, ostensibly conceived in Harding's Senate office. The child was adopted by Nan's sister and brother-in-law. In her book she claimed she continued her affair with Harding, who wrote her letters promising to marry her. She never could produce any of these letters, having destroyed them, she said, out of discretion.

Plenty of letters were written, but all by Nan and none of them discreet. With the help of a little-known memoir published in 1959 (*"Dear Mr. President . . .": The Story of Fifty Years in the White House Mail Room*, by Ira R.T. Smith), Ferrell shows that she was blackmailing Harding, and after his death tried to put the screws on his sister as well. As for her famous claim that she and Harding used a White House closet for their amours, Ferrell unearths Secret Service files showing it to be impossible. He also proves, conclusively and hilariously, that Nan's book was ghostwritten by an ex-minister engaged in selling stock in a Mexican gold mine.

The most incredible book was *The Strange Death of President Harding* (1930) by Gaston B. Means, called by J. Edgar Hoover "the greatest faker of all time." A former Burns detective who had worked in Harding's Justice Department, Means conned a writer from the true-confessions magazines to ghostwrite his book. Claiming to have been a frequent White House visitor on intimate terms with the late president and his wife, Means's account presents a power-maddened Mrs. Harding intent on poisoning her husband in the cause of feminism. Speaking in a voice "like the purring of a female tiger, intent, threatening," she tells him:

> This is the age of woman. For the first time in American history, a woman shall be recorded as a real factor—a power—and not have to go by that insipid and uninteresting and moth-eaten title: First Lady of the Land! Silly!

If that reminds you of someone you know, try the suicide on Memorial Day, 1923, of Jess Smith, who was found on the bedroom floor of the apartment he shared with Attorney General Daugherty; his legs under the bed, a bullet through his temple, and his head in a wastebasket (he had evidently fallen forward into it).

Smith's suicide was the only hint Harding had of brewing administration scandals, but Ferrell's account of it, based on papers recently made available, suggests a murky personal reason might have prompted it. Smith worked for Daugherty and was involved in his bribes and banking irregularities, but he also lived with him. Their arrangement began when Daugherty's invalid wife entered a hospital and Smith's wife of one year divorced him. The older Daugherty invited the younger Smith to share his apartment, launching what sounds suspiciously like a master-slave relationship.

According to the papers of White House physician Dr. Joel T. Boone, Smith was pathetically eager to perform chores for Daugherty; "a word of praise or expression of appreciation from Daugherty would cause Jess to 'purr' happily." One day, however, the attorney general was displeased with Smith and spoke harshly to him: "If you do not discontinue your seeming assumptiveness and do nothing to change your ways down at the Department of Justice, and in and outside of Washington, you will have to cease to live with me and move out of this apartment." Smith shriveled visibly, Dr. Boone noted, and thereafter became subdued and withdrawn. More rejections followed as Daugherty and others in the administration, put off by Smith's overbearing behavior and wild partying, cooled toward him and eased him out of official functions until he was sunk in self-loathing. It was neurotic insecurity, Dr. Boone believed, not political malfeasance, that led him to shoot himself.

Ferrell is at his best when he dissects the "debunkers" of the 1920's, the media elite of an earlier time who did to Harding what their descendants did to Nixon and Reagan:

> The debunkers had what a later generation would call a hidden agenda. They did not like any American president of their generation and did not mind if they tore reputations to shreds, in gentlemanly prose if possible, in humor if that suited them, but with no real effort to search out the truth. Behind these tactics it might be said that they did not much like, not to mention admire, the American people, and considered democracy an impossible form of government.

Ferrell's rogues gallery includes:

1. H.L. Mencken, who called Harding "a third-rate political wheel-horse, with the face of a moving-picture actor, the intelligence of a respectable agricultural implement dealer, and the imagination of a lodge joiner."

Mencken admitted he voted for Harding. Ferrell suggests he did so to guarantee himself four years' worth of column material.

2. William Allen White, editor of the Emporia, Kansas *Gazette*, called Harding a "he-harlot," and repeated in print the rumor that he had signed over oil reserves while drunk.

White, says Ferrell, was jealous that another small-town newspaper editor had beaten him to the White House.

3. Allan Nevins, the historian, worshipped Woodrow Wilson and was a passionate supporter of the League of Nations, which Senator Harding helped to defeat. Moreover, Nevins had once worked for the Dayton editor, James M. Cox, who ran against Harding in the 1920 presidential election.

4. Alice Roosevelt Longworth uttered the deathless, "Harding

was not a bad man, he was just a slob," but some thought she was consumed by the belief that another Ohio politician should have been president: her husband, Speaker of the House Nicholas Longworth—who, Ferrell adds, drank up all of Harding's liquor.

The Harding debunkers quoted each other—and Nan Britton—over and over until their undocumented claims entered the national consciousness like a computer virus. Their hatred of Harding was as passionate and unrelenting as the adoration of today's cultural elite for Bill Clinton, yet the two presidents are practically clones. Why the different reactions? The simplest explanation is that Harding was a Republican whose cultural elite were all Wilsonians, whereas Clinton is a Democrat among McGoverniks and worse.

Another difference is timing. Harding's presidency coincided with the publication of *Main Street* and *Babbitt*, and it was his misfortune to fit both. He was the "Typical American," a gregarious booster from a small Midwestern town who graduated from a cow college and had neither the time nor the inclination to read books—all the things his elite despised. By contrast, Bill Clinton is the atypical small-town American who went to the right schools, lives in an era that calls gregariousness "caring" and "reaching out," and stages photo-ops in bookstores.

The biggest difference is the change that has come over the elite's opinions of politicians. Harding's elite looked down on them and harbored, says Ferrell, "a refusal to believe that ability at politics is a mark of intelligence." Today's elite, enamored of government *über alles*, regards Bill Clinton and his ilk as the architects of their fondest dreams.

Harding's reputation will never be completely restored, but Ferrell has done a superb job of debunking his debunkers and ferreting out facts from the tangle of calumny that no other historian has thought worthy of attention. I have always had a certain fondness for Mrs. Harding because her maiden name was Florence Kling, but now, thanks to Ferrell's sympathetic portrait, I like her husband as well.

National Review, December 23, 1996
Essay

"The Joys of Re-Reading"

'C HARACTER," said J. C. Watts, "is doing the right thing when nobody is watching." Recommending books is a golden opportunity to do the sublime thing while everybody is watching, which is why so many book lists kick off with the Bible or *War and Peace* and pitch "the complete works of" with such lofty certitude.

Oh, please. Breathes there a man with soul so dead that he could read the complete works of Sir Walter Scott? Nobody has read all of Scott except Scott, and that only because he had to read proof.

I've read my share of classics and reviewed countless new books in the last 15 years, but the books I enjoy most are old favorites that I re-read when I'm too tired to do anything else but not tired enough to go to bed. Most are out of print now, but they sold so many copies in their day that they continue to turn up regularly in used-book stores. They might be a little dog-eared but they still make good stocking stuffers. If your loved ones object to secondhand presents, keep the old books and get some new loved ones.

☐ "It was on an afternoon in May of 1844 that the letter came from Dragonwyck." I challenge anyone to read that opening sentence and put this novel down. Its structure is flawless. By the end of the first page we know who the heroine is, her age, her appearance, where she

lives, and what she's like—all the things that Joan Didion may or
may not get around to revealing by the last page of hers. My initial
reaction to Anya Seton's Dragonwyck (1944) corroborates the feminist group on the Internet who called me an elitist psychopath. The
villain of this gothic tale is Nicholas Van Ryn, a reactionary Hudson
River patroon who murders his wife with oleander leaves ground up
in a nutmeg mill, but the first time I read it at the age of 13 I thought
he was the hero and didn't realize my mistake for several years.

The aristocratic Nicholas is still my idea of Mr. Right, and so is
the real-life enemy of populist democracy who makes a cameo
appearance in the book: James Fenimore Cooper.

☐   Another favorite Anya Seton novel is *Katherine* (1954), about
the love affair between John of Gaunt, the ambitious younger son of
Edward III, and Lady Katherine Swynford, whose four bastard children became the progenitors of the York and Tudor lines in fulfill-
ment of the ancient prophecy, "Thou shalt get kings though thou be
none." Richly descriptive of medieval life, the story dramatizes major
events of late-fourteenth-century England—the Black Plague, the
Lollard heresy, the storming of the Savoy palace in the Peasants'
Revolt—and presents a brilliant fictional portrait of Katherine's
brother-in-law, Geoffrey Chaucer.

Like many who read *Katherine* the year it came out, I thought
Charlton Heston and Susan Hayward should star in the movie, but it
was never made, probably because Katherine lived openly as John's
mistress and produced those four bastards. They were legitimized by
Richard II when John married Katherine late in life, but even so, this
movie wasn't possible in the Fifties. Ironically, the sex scenes in the
book achieve an exquisite balance between eroticism and sweetness
that isn't possible in the Nineties.

☐   The town in *Kings Row* was modeled on Fulton, Missouri, which
erupted when native son Henry Bellamann published his 1941 novel
of sex and sadism in the heartland. Fulton got better press in 1946
when Winston Churchill made his "iron curtain" speech at its
Westminster College (Aberdeen College in the book), but by then

Ronald Reagan's performance in the movie had immortalized another line of demarcation.

Reagan's character is far from the only medical victim in the book. Omitted from the movie are Patty Graves, who becomes a fanatic housekeeper after Dr. Gordon spays her; Ludie Sims, the complaisant grass widow whose face is disfigured after Dr. Gordon treats her earache; and the excitable Lucy Carr, who dies after Dr. Gordon gives her a sedative.

In contrast to Dr. Gordon's busy HillaryCare practice, Dr. Alexander Q. Tower has no patients at all, just a worn shingle flapping outside his gloomy house. In the movie Dr. Tower shoots himself after poisoning his daughter Cassandra to save her from the insanity she has inherited from her mother, but that's a toned-down Hollywood version of what happens in the book. My lips are sealed. Suffice to say that *Kings Row* is immensely satisfying to read during political campaigns when the Trad Vals pile up too high.

☐   Betty Smith's first novel, *A Tree Grows in Brooklyn*, was such a smash hit that her later work was never fully appreciated. My favorite is her third novel, *Maggie-Now* (1957). As usual it's set in pre–World War I Brooklyn, but for once we get a Smith heroine who is not a compulsive reader.

Maggie Moore (her childhood reprimand, "Maggie, now," becomes her nickname) is a simple Irish-Catholic girl who wants only to marry a good man and have children. But along comes Claude Basset, a Protestant-agnostic college graduate with an ironic wit that goes over her head and a wanderlust she doesn't find out about until after she marries him.

The O. Henry–like twist here is the blissful marriage of this mismatched pair. Under normal conditions they would grow to hate each other, but their strange modus vivendi inadvertently keeps the dew on the rose.

Claude lives with Maggie in Brooklyn during the cold months and takes off as soon as the weather turns warm. She doesn't know where he goes but he always comes back, and when he does it's like a honeymoon again. They go on like this for years, until Claude finds

what he's looking for, and the provincial Maggie, her vistas expanded by their unconventional life, is able at last to understand him.

☐   Sisterhood eludes feminist novelists, but it fairly leaps off the
pages of Gwen Bristow's *Jubilee Trail* (1950), a good girl/bad girl
western in which the male characters are all satellites.

Garnet Cameron of Washington Square, a privileged daughter of
Old Knickerbocker society who won the politeness medal at finishing school, and Florinda Grove, a dancehall girl on the lam from a
murder rap, are members of a covered wagon train headed for
California.

Garnet soon loses confidence in her handsome but weak young
bridegroom and turns to Florinda for companionship. Together they
do men's work—shooting, dressing game, building fires, reading
Indian prints, and fighting off the savage hordes. When Garnet takes
an arrow in the shoulder, Florinda helps in the cauterization even
though she has a terror of fire and hideously burned hands from a
mysterious incident in her past. Each crisis they meet together
increases their mutual admiration. They learn to take pride in their
strength, both moral and physical, especially the ladylike Garnet,
who can't help gloating, "The men I used to dance with—I could
break them in two."

Much, much more happens—Garnet's husband is murdered, she
and Florinda open a saloon, etc.—but her ultimate liberated moment
comes when she contemplates her cauterized wound: "She was going
to be proud of that scar when she got back to New York. She was glad
she had been wounded in the arm, instead of some unmentionable
spot that she could not boast about."

☐   Henry Morton Robinson touches on partial-birth abortion in *The
Cardinal* (1950), except that it's called a "craniotomy" and involves
crushing the skull while the entire baby is still in the womb.

Father Stephen Fermoyle's brother-in-law is a Catholic doctor
who loses his hard-won residency at a Protestant hospital when he
refuses to perform the operation. Later on, when Steve's erring sister
Monica is taken in labor to the same hospital, he must decide whether

to let them kill the baby to save her life. He cannot, and gives her the last rites as the baby is born.

The Cardinal opens in 1915 and traces Steve's rise from Boston parish priest to prince of the church. My favorite parts are the behind-the scenes accounts of how the Vatican works, and the descriptions of the Roman contessa's salon: a hierarchy of ecclesiastical guests, their rank denoted by the colors of their flowing capes and birettas (the book answers all the Protestant questions about vestments), soignée women kissing rings, learned Jesuits swapping bons mots, and Cardinal Merry del Val capping quotations from Horace while juggling oranges. That's what I call a party. It's enough to make me religious.

☐   Today we have constipated little novels that tell the story of a three-hour car trip. In 1942 we had *The Valley of Decision* by Marcia Davenport. It begins with 15-year-old Mary Rafferty's first day as a maid in the Scott family's Pittsburgh mansion in 1873, and ends with her listening to the news of Pearl Harbor with a Scott great-granddaughter.

In between, Mary becomes the mainstay of the Scotts. As strong as the steel they produce, she devotes her life to bringing out the best in them, saving them from themselves, and loving Paul Scott even though she must withhold herself from him in penance for the terrible event that keeps them from marrying.

This novel has everything: sex amid the Johnstown Flood, labor-union strife, an expatriate adventuress, a playboy turned monk, a society wife who goes mad, a Czech violinist fleeing the Nazis. And if all this weren't enough, the author even keeps us glued to the page when she describes the operation of the open-hearth furnace, a tour de force of "writing like a man" that won her high praise from male reviewers in that benighted pre-feminist age.

I could go on, but I've reached my word limit and it's 3:00 A.M. so I'm going to have a drink and unwind with *Forever Amber*. Its descriptions of seventeenth-century London goldsmiths allow economists to skip the sex and read the good parts.

National Review, April 21, 1997
Essay

"South Mouth: Why Liberals Hate Dixie"

I N 1906, Varina Howell Davis, widow of Confederate President Jefferson Davis, died in New York. She had moved there for financial reasons after her husband's death in 1889. Needing to earn her living but reluctant to embarrass her fellow Mississippians by doing it in their midst, she accepted an offer from her cousin's husband, Joseph Pulitzer, to review books for his paper.

Now that New York Gov. George Pataki has ripped the Georgia state flag from the Albany capitol, it is instructive to learn how an earlier New York responded to the passing of the First Lady of the Confederacy.

Her funeral, described in Gerry Van der Heuvel's excellent biography, stopped traffic:

> New York honored Varina without any prompting. . . . The mayor sent an escort of mounted police to accompany her body to the station, where it was placed aboard a special train [to Richmond]. The casket was draped in the Confederate flag. A military band marched before the hearse playing "Dixie," "Maryland, My Maryland," and "The Bonnie Blue Flag." . . . General Frederick Grant, son of the Union general-in-chief, ordered a company of artillery from Governors Island to escort the cortège. This was the first time in history federal troops had accorded this honor to a woman.

It is a commentary on our times that this passage could serve as a checklist of all the things that are now in the process of being banned.

Attitudes were different in 1906. Back then, the North held the Old Confederacy in high esteem. The halcyon days of Southern good repute had begun almost immediately after the Civil War. The image-makers were Union veterans, whose stories of Confederate valor spread respect for the former enemy at a time when Americans invested the good loser with nobility and the martial grand gesture stirred every schoolboy's heart.

By the end of the nineteenth century memories were fading and veterans were dying off, but the South won the country's admiration again in 1898 when war with Spain broke out. Southerners enlisted in droves, earning ardent tributes to their patriotism. The spirit of 1898, when Northern and Southern men fought side by side under the American flag for the first time since the Mexican War, lingered into the twentieth century and explains the send-off New York gave Varina Davis.

The era of good feeling ended when America contracted South Mouth, a recurring infection that causes its sufferers to spout criticism, drip invective, ooze sanctimony, and chew rugs.

It began in 1925 with the Scopes "Monkey Trial" in Dayton, Tennessee, when fundamentalist Christians succeeded in banning the teaching of evolution. Liberal intellectuals, who had caught Midwest Mouth when Sinclair Lewis published *Main Street* and *Babbitt* a few years earlier, now had a whole Southful of Bible-quoting hicks to make fun of.

Once the Depression and the New Deal got underway, South Mouth turned into a pandemic with something for every taste. Communists had lynching, socialists had sharecropping, unions had textile barons, social-workers had Appalachia ("the South's South"), political scientists had Huey Long, geneticists had the novels of Erskine Caldwell, liberals had segregation, and Eleanor Roosevelt had everything.

During World War II, race riots in Detroit and Chicago were blamed on Southerners who had moved North. In the Fifties the South was constantly reminded that "the eyes of the world" were trained on the school integration struggle, and in the Sixties that its response to the civil-rights movement was being tried in "the court of world opinion"—lofty threats that South Mouth was going global.

The Seventies seemed to hold out hope, but Southerners who thought the election of Jimmy Carter had any meaning beyond Watergate were soon disabused. In deference to the new President, the media exchanged malignant South Mouth for benign South Mouth.

It showed in their mantralike repetition of the false claim that Carter was "the first Southern President since the Civil War." Woodrow Wilson was born in Staunton, Virginia, in 1856 and grew up in Georgia, making him the first and only President to lose his American citizenship, but that pales beside his other credentials. Wilson, after all, was president of Princeton and governor of New Jersey, which proves that he was polished and urbane and hence not a "real" Southerner like Jimmy Carter.

South Mouth eased up when the Left discovered multiculturalism. Beginning in the Eighties, the South was absorbed into broader categories of villainy such as "Eurocentrism," "Dead White Males," and "angry white men." At last Southerners and ethnic Catholics got a chance to bond; now we were all Europeans together.

Evidently the multiculturalists just realized their error, because South Mouth is back.

A suspicious suddenness surrounds the current outbreak. It started less than a year ago when the Citadel lost its court battle over admitting women and the decision spilled over onto the Virginia Military Institute. The defeat of these two bastions of everything Southern seemed to send the Left into a foaming frenzy.

On a single day in February, the front page of the *Washington Times* contained South Carolina's Confederate flag fight, the Georgia–Pataki flag fight, the Maryland Sons of the Confederacy flag fight—and something new. As if the forces of sensitivity had suddenly realized that flags don't weigh much, a group of blacks in Walterboro, South Carolina, demanded that the town move the Confederate statue.

While the flag fights raged, the state song crisis struck. For more than twenty years now, "Carry Me Back to Ol' Virginny" has been played but not sung because it contains the words "darky" and "old massa." The legislature had always hoped to substitute new lyrics, but that idea collapsed recently when some blacks complained that the tune now upsets them: they can still hear the words in their heads even if nobody sings them. That did it. After years of procrastination, the legislature suddenly—i.e., while the flag fights raged—voted to banish the song entirely.

The very next day, Maryland's song came under attack. The PC patrol considers this one a twofer. Its tune is that of a Christmas carol, "O Tannenbaum," and its lyrics are an incitement to secession: *"From shore to shore, from creek to creek, Potomac calls to Chesapeake, 'tis time to give the rebel shriek, Maryland, my Maryland."*

Before the week was out, Florida was debating whether to shelve Stephen Foster's "Old Folks at Home."

I have a hunch that this latest outbreak of South Mouth was triggered in part by the implications of the Citadel–VMI decision. Feminists were coming awfully close to turning the Land of Racism into the Land of Sexism, so blacks went on an ethnic-cleansing spree to keep the South's rap sheet unchanged.

T HE larger causes of South Mouth have held steady over the years. If the South ever secedes again, she could get a good national motto out of the three qualities she embodies that have made her the target of twentieth-century America's envious rage: Identity, Eccentricity, Complexity.

Identity: "Analysts are scared to death of Southerners," wrote Mississippi novelist Willie Morris. It's hard to have a fruitful session with someone who feels no need to explain himself. Why do you feel that way? "I just do." Why is it so important to you? "It just is." Why are you so angry? "I just am."

Often mistaken for stupidity, these responses reflect a granite sense of self powered by a value-control center of pre-set codes guaranteed to threaten the kind of people who attend alienation conferences.

Eccentricity: Get a Southerner talking and sooner or later he will claim to know somebody who rode a horse through a hotel lobby. This has been the *ne plus ultra* of what the South calls "colorful" behavior ever since mad, bad Sally Ward did it in Louisville in the 1840s. Other favorites include drinking in a cemetery—a staple of John Berendt's Savannah book, *Midnight in the Garden of Good and Evil*—and the kind of family incidents that non-Southerners keep quiet about. (I wrote a whole book about my family but didn't think I had said anything particularly unusual until "eccentric" turned up in all the reviews.)

The South cherishes her eccentrics as Italy cherishes her singers and France her lovers. I remember one called the "Left-Turn Lady" for her habit of making left turns from the right lane. She didn't do it by mistake; it was just the way she liked to make left turns. She caused several collisions but nobody ever did anything about her. Our streets would have been safer if her license had been lifted, but then we wouldn't have had a Left-Turn Lady. She was ours, by God.

"Eccentricity," wrote John Stuart Mill, "has always abounded when and where strength of character has abounded; and the amount of eccentricity in a society has generally been proportional to the amount of genius, mental vigor, and moral courage which it contained."

Big Brother and the Nanny State hate eccentrics. They're too hard to control and they identify with aristocrats.

Complexity: "The Gothic Mall: Conflict and Duality in the New South" is the kind of topic Southern writers are invited to tackle in panel discussions. A whiff of attraction-repulsion always hangs over these gatherings, emerging full-force in the question period when a Yankee graduate student asks, "Are you presently tormented by anything, and if so, what?"

America likes simple open personalities who inspire instant childlike trust. We used to call them "straight shooters"; now we use the computer-graphics term WYSIWYG—"what you see is what you get." WYSIWYGs never shop at the Gothic mall. Southerners, on the other hand, must constantly be explained. Our warring traits—manners and mayhem, for instance—and our tolerance for self-contradiction drive observers to distraction.

"What are we to make of Thomas Jefferson?" asks Kenneth Auchincloss in *Newsweek*. The question saturated the media in February in conjunction with Ken Burns's PBS documentary and the publication of a new biography, *American Sphinx*, by Joseph J. Ellis, whose reviews have featured "contradiction," "puzzle," "conundrum," "enigma," and "labyrinth."

Jefferson died for the second time in February, a victim of "shaken Southerner syndrome." Like a distraught au pair tending a baby who has destroyed her nerves, America picked him up by his lace jabot and demanded, "How could you believe in liberty and equality and still own slaves?"

If he answered us he might say, "I just could."

If you are wondering where Bill Clinton fits into all of this, wonder no more. He doesn't. Oakland has no *there* and Clinton has no *from*. This is the "what it is about Clinton" that people can't put their finger on: he doesn't seem Southern. His desperate need for the approval of others has robbed him of identity; his compulsion to succeed has turned eccentricity into a third rail (what Carolina-born David Brinkley meant when he called him "boring"); and his substitute for complexity is calculated confusion. On a scale of mottos he assays out at Fluidity, Conformity, and Flux.

As we look to the future of America's ethnic-cleansing movement we see environmentalists doing their best to spread West Mouth, but at the moment it's South Mouth that ought to worry people. Anyone who is now neutral on the subject may find himself uttering a new version of a famous apologia:

"They came for the Confederate flags but I had none, so I did nothing. Then they came for the Confederate statues, but I had never even seen one, so I did nothing. Next they came for the state songs, but I didn't even know what my state song was, so I did nothing. Now they've come for me, and there are no Southerners left to be Europeans with."

The American Spectator, August 1997
Book Review

"Queen Victoria's German Prince Charming"

The Uncrowned King: The Life of Prince Albert
by Stanley Weintraub (The Free Press, 478 pages, $27.50)

' T he stud farm of Europe" was Bismarck's name for the Duchy of Saxe-Coburg. One of many independent states in the patchwork quilt of the German Confederation, it was *the* place for royalty with marriageable daughters to shop for willing and able princelings to carry on the line.

The greatest coup in the history of this one-export Ruritania was the marriage in 1840 of Prince Albert, younger son of the reigning duke, and England's Queen Victoria. They were first cousins; his father and her mother were brother and sister. DNA aside, they had little in common; at their first meeting in 1836 the only discernible chemistry between them was metabolic. Victoria, who loved to dance the night away and sleep until noon, "never saw the dawn but through a ballroom window," but Albert the early bird could not stay awake after ten and frequently nodded off at late suppers.

She had a hearty appetite; he picked at his food and had a weak stomach. She liked brisk English room temperatures and thought it a sign of weakness to light a fire; Albert was always cold. He was also a bookworm. Despite his good looks he displayed a "marked indifference to women" and abstained from the time-honored Teutonic tradition of student princing while at the University of Bonn. To the amazement of classmates and professors alike, Albert preferred studying to wenching.

The marriage of these two chaste 20-year-olds (both were born in 1819 but Victoria was three months older) inspired many a ribald joke, mostly at Albert's expense. "His virtue," said one wag, "was indeed appalling; not a single vice redeemed it." But virtue had the last laugh. That the young couple's lack of sexual experience did them no harm is evident from the Blue Lagoon sweetness of Victoria's diary entry for their wedding night: "When day dawned (for we did not sleep much) and I beheld that beautiful angelic face by my side, it was more than I can express! He does look so beautiful in his shirt only, with his beautiful throat seen. . . . Never did I think I could be so loved."

During their honeymoon at Windsor Castle, the couple were seen taking an early-morning walk, prompting Lord Greville to tell Lady Palmerston, "This is not the way to provide us with a Prince of Wales." He didn't reckon with the Saxe-Coburg sperm count. Nine months later Victoria gave birth to the first of nine children (four boys and five girls), but the real augury of the marital dominance Albert would achieve is that walk: He got her up.

Stanley Weintraub's earlier biography, *Victoria*, follows the queen to the end of her long life when she had become a grand old lady who "wrapped the nation in her warm Scotch shawl," so beloved that even London's prostitutes wore black when she died. In his new biography of her husband, he is limited to the younger Victoria, who was often less than lovable and occasionally a hysterical shrew. To keep her from dominating the book, Weintraub had to do what Albert himself had to do and put her firmly in her place. Both of them succeeded. *The Uncrowned King* is a concentrated look at a man of astonishing intellect and ability that gives Albert his long-overdue place on center stage and offers proof on every page that England, at least, got two for the price of one.

Albert got off to a bad start. The English people were sick of foreigners, having endured German sovereigns since 1714 when Queen Anne, the last of the Stuarts, died childless and the Crown went to her distant cousin, the Elector of Hanover, who became George I. The first George never learned English; Albert did, but he never lost his heavy German accent, and the news that he and Victoria always spoke German together did not please.

Nor was he popular with the powerful, except for the wrong reasons. Victoria's ministers, jealous of their influence over her, welcomed the unthreatening youth but refused to do anything to enhance his status, including giving him a title. As for useful work, his job was to sire the Succession, nothing more.

They did not bargain on Albert's extraordinary conscientiousness. Like all members of the royal family, he was given honorary chairmanships and invited to lend his name to committees, but unlike them, he actually went to the meetings. The Association for the Abolition of the Slave Trade, the Association for Relief of the Poor, the Committee to Redecorate the Houses of Parliament, Sponsors of the Boys' Mechanical Institute, every Royal Society for this-or-that—wherever improvers gathered Albert was there; taking notes, asking questions, listening and learning.

It was while he was at one of these meetings that he received a message saying, "The Queen desires HRH to return to Buckingham Palace." Albert ignored it. A little while later came another that said, "The Queen awaits HRH . . ." Still he ignored it. Finally, there came a third message: "The Queen commands HRH . . ." Knowing that Victoria simply wanted him home, Albert ignored this one as well and spent the night—alone—at another royal residence. His refusal to be "managed" won the respect of male members of Victoria's court, who knew her imperious ways.

Albert followed up on what he learned, researching topics with a Germanic thoroughness that flattered and impressed his audiences, leading an awed glass manufacturer to exclaim, "Why, he knows more about glass than I do." The aristocracy, less impressed, saw in Albert what a later age would call a geek. "Almost the only time the Prince came alive at dinner," writes Weintraub, "was when he could discuss problems of drainage and heating."

Albert's consuming interest in science and industry dragged England into the nineteenth century. Made an honorary chancellor of Cambridge, where Latin and Greek were sacrosanct and a professor of Oriental languages lectured in Sanskrit, he moved higher education into the "ungentlemanly" areas of applied science and engineering. Whenever he encountered an antiquated practice that offended his methodical mind—a frequent occurrence—he urged change. Learning that all of Britain's screws were made by hand in a quaint Yorkshire workshop, he imported an American screw-making machine. This and many other mechanical innovations were displayed in 1851 at the Great Exhibition, a living museum of modern industry conceived and designed by Albert, which became the inspiration for the World's Fair.

Having by now earned the trust of Victoria's ministers, he read state papers, drafted her replies, and sat in on audiences, taking notes which he labeled and filed in his meticulous fashion. He even read and clipped the newspapers for her. All this on top of his continuing round of committees, societies, and associations, and cornerstone layings without end (his collection of ceremonial trowels has never been equaled).

This was Albert the Good of Victoria's italic-strewn diary ("Dear, *dear* Albert, so *faultless*, so *perfect*, such an *angel*!"), but though serious and responsible, he was never a bluenose. The prudishness for which he has been blamed was actually the work of the Wesleyan Methodist movement, which, Weintraub points out, saw his "foreign" influence in every pleasure. When he approved free Sunday concerts by military bands, "Leaders of the movement for strict Sabbath observance were outraged that the working classes might be drawn away from prayer, and promoters of penitential Sundays also objected to the bands as a German sacrilege introduced by Prince Albert."

Albert himself was an organist whose playing, said Felix Mendelssohn, "would have done credit to any professional." (During this private recital some sheets of music fell to the floor and were picked up by Victoria.)

He could be quite witty, especially at the expense of the English who criticized him. In a letter to his brother he wrote: "Sentimentality is a plant which cannot grow in England, and an Englishman, when he finds he is being sentimental, becomes frightened at the idea, as of having a dangerous illness, and he shoots himself."

His married life was subject to the extremes of Victoria's nervous system. Disliking everything about motherhood except conception (the couple filled their boudoir with nude paintings and statuary and had a device that permitted them to lock the doors without getting out of bed), she suffered frightening episodes of post-partum depression which she took out on Albert, who, like all husbands, sought peace and quiet by burying himself in his work—in his case, the settlement of the Sepoy Mutiny.

By 1860, when he addressed the fourth International Statistical Congress, his life resembled an eternal C-Span gig. Though only 41, he looked like an old man, and his stomach trouble worsened. Nonetheless, he found time to tutor his oldest and favorite child, the Princess Royal Victoria ("Vicky"), who alone of all his progeny had inherited his brilliant mind and answered his deep need for intellectual companionship at a time when Victoria, worn out from childbearing, expected him to read *Jane Eyre* to her. On top of this, it also fell to Albert to explain the facts of life to another daughter before her betrothal when Victoria sidestepped the duty herself ("Papa told her all," she noted in a letter).

The following year he collapsed as England faced a *casus belli*: the seizure of HMS *Trent* by the USS *San Jacinto* and the forcible removal of two Confederate envoys from the British vessel. Dragging himself literally from his deathbed, Albert defied the jingoistic politicians and found the perfect diplomatic loophole to prevent England from entering the American Civil War on the side of the Confederacy.

The American captain had taken the Confederate envoys back to blockaded Norfolk and jailed them. Although this was technically impressment, enemy communications were proper contraband of war, and since the envoys were traveling with oral instructions only, they could be considered "the embodiment of dispatches." Moreover, the Americans did not take HMS *Trent* into port but allowed her to sail on, making the offense against the British flag illegal in form but not in substance.

Albert latched onto these mitigating circumstances and combined them with common sense: Surely, he pointed out, no country that had just split in half would deliberately add to its troubles by provoking a war with England. In his letter to Secretary of State Seward he said that HM's Government was unwilling to believe that this could be the case, and felt that the American naval commander had acted on his own rather than on official orders, in which case HM's Government would accept "the restoration of the unfortunate passengers and a suitable apology."

The letter, dated December 1, 1861, was a masterpiece of diplomacy that let the Lincoln government off the hook and saved face all around. "This draft was the last the beloved Prince ever wrote," Victoria noted in the margin. On December 14 he died.

Weintraub argues convincingly that Albert died of the kind of stomach cancer that starts with ulcers—he was a classic ulcer type—not from the long-assumed typhoid, and certainly not from a chill caught while lecturing the erring Prince of Wales on prostitutes (Victoria's theory).

Victoria survived him by thirty-nine years. At first she slept clutching his nightshirt; later she mourned him by insisting that all future male successors to the Throne bear "Albert" as one of their names. All did, but none, Weintraub reminds us, dared rule under it. "They recognized the risks. The Prince's vision for the modern monarchy died with him. It could not have been sustained without his intellectual qualities and his intensity of purpose, and he left no such potential in his spouse or progeny."

The Uncrowned King is one of those rare books that thoroughly justifies its title. As Disraeli said in his eulogy: "With Prince Albert we have buried our Sovereign. This German Prince has governed England for twenty-one years with a wisdom and energy such as none of our Kings have ever shown."

National Review, August 11, 1997
Book Review

"A Girl for
All Seasons"

An Army of Angels: A Novel of Joan of Arc,
by Pamela Marcantel (St. Martin's, 578 pp., $24.95)

I T IS only fair to warn you that this review will violate the standards of objectivity, detachment, and ironic distance demanded by literary criticism. I've reviewed many books that I've liked and some that I've loved, but this time I have a masterpiece on my hands and I'm still reeling from it.

An Army of Angels is a first novel by Pamela Marcantel, a Louisiana native who was raised in the French Catholic tradition. Although she wrote a great deal of fiction and poetry while in college, none of it was published, and eventually she gave it up and joined the English Department at the University of Virginia. It was here that thoughts and images of Joan of Arc began to come to her, intensifying over time until she was compelled to embark on the research that led to this book.

Not the least of her many gifts is an instinct for literary structure that gets her right into the story. It opens with Jehanne (the medieval version of her name) being kicked awake in her prison cell by a brutal English guard who tells her, "We're going to burn you, witch," then flashes back to the day six years earlier when Jehanne first hears her Voices while tending her family's cows.

The manner in which the author handles the Voices of Sts. Michel, Catherine, and Marguerite will reaffirm the devout while convincing the most recalcitrant freethinker. To avoid the cheapening ghost-story effect of letting them appear as characters who speak within quotation marks, she renders them as light, the heat of a summer day, the wind against the face of a running child, a swarm of bees humming with an otherworldly intensity; and puts their words into type faces—dominant bold, feathery italic, bleak sans serif—that match the content of their messages.

To relieve the ethereality of medieval mysticism she also gives Jehanne vivid dreams full of modern allusions that make us thrill with recognition:

> Jehanne saw a spacious city rising to meet her. The inhabitants were strangely dressed and rode in bizarre carriages that moved without being pulled by horses. A tremendous statue of a knight on horseback stood in the center of the city's square, and when she asked who he was, she heard, "That is no man; that is Jehanne the Maid, who saved France from the English."

The future saint who is brought so superbly to life on these pages is a tomboy with a healthy ego who enjoys being one of the guys. "So this was what it was like to have one's legs encased in cloth!" she thinks the first time she puts on male attire. "She had never imagined what a liberating feeling it could be. No wonder men felt so vigorous and masterful, wearing such wonderfully freeing things." To the troops she leads she is "as down-to-earth and approachable as a sister," but women are another matter, especially after she becomes famous. Pestered by a wannabe mystic who claims that she, too, hears voices, Jehanne impatiently tells her, "Your place is with your husband and children." Womanly duties are not for Jehanne; "There are plenty of other women to do them," she blurts out to a hostile cleric. "Only I can do the work I was charged to do by the King of Heaven."

Incapable of suffering fools, she was allied by destiny with the biggest fool in Christendom: the Dauphin Charles, declared a bastard by his own mother and robbed of his inheritance by his father, the mad Charles VI, who signed over the throne of France to England's Henry V after the latter's triumph at Agincourt.

The combination of parental rejection and physical unattractiveness has given the Dauphin a paralyzing inferiority complex that worsens when he is exposed to Jehanne's utter certainty of purpose. She is all for attacking Paris *now*; he dithers in endless brainstorming sessions, forever polling his advisors. She wants to hold his coronation in Reims *now;* "Charles kept stalling, moving in baby steps . . . she felt as if she was trying to roll a large stone uphill." Exhausted by his need for constant reassurance, sick of his imploring glances, Jehanne comes across as Margaret Thatcher trying to keep George Bush from going wobbly.

When she finally gets him to the church, he has one of those spurts of strength to which the weak are prone and insists that Jehanne stand beside him at his coronation, an honor never before granted even to the peers of France. During the ceremony her Voices come to her in a passage of breathtaking beauty:

> Through the delicately spinning vortex she saw the domain where she most desired to be, ageless, loving; and a serenity overcame her, all at once expelling fear and reducing everything human to the level of a child's game. In the center of that eternal Moment nothing else mattered; the only thing real was that blinding, singing warmth that pulsed in her ears and whistled through her like a wind from Forever.

That the spineless Charles would betray her was in the cards. The mediocre always hold the superior back even when they are on the same side. Eisenhower did it to Patton, and Charles did it to Jehanne, relieving her as commander of the army and appointing the doddering Archbishop de Chartres in her place. In a final, incredible display of self-hatred the newly crowned Charles gave the Duc de Bourgogne, England's ally, permission to take Compiègne, one of the towns Jehanne had won, to use as a supply base for the English forces holding Paris. Said Jehanne's gallant comrade, the Bastard of Orleans: "Charles has managed to betray himself."

The account of Jehanne's capture and imprisonment contains

some of the most evocative prose I have ever read. "An Englishman in a hatlike helmet threw a rotting head of cabbage at her, and it smacked wetly against her cheek, then plopped into the dust. With her arms bound, she could not wipe away the mess, which would later dry into a greenish-brown crust that cracked when she spoke."

The author uses the physical filth of the Middle Ages as metaphors for the spiritual rankness of Jehanne's enemies. Her English jailer's body "emitted the nauseating odors of urine that had dried to a dark patch across his codpiece"; when Jehanne removes the boots she has not had off for a year, "they took a layer of damp, wrinkled skin, leaving pink patches on the bottoms of her feet." Everything the medieval world took for granted—foul breath, rotten teeth, grease-laden hair, ubiquitous rats—becomes a symbol of the darkness and corruption closing in on her.

Chained to the wall in a cell in Rouen castle, deprived of food by her guards, defecated upon by one of them, she still found the wisdom and strength to give her magnificent answer to the inquisitor's trick question, "Are you in a state of grace?" A straight answer either way would have been fatal, but for once she didn't mouth off. Facing down her tormentor, she replied: "If I am not, may God put me there. If I am, may He so keep me." Was it the legendary shrewdness of the French peasant? Finesse picked up from exposure to the Dauphin's courtiers? Or her Voices guiding her answers as they had promised? It makes you wonder.

On the day of her execution she is given a dress smeared with sulphur so she "would go up like a torch." That's when I broke down. I haven't cried over a book since *Lassie, Come Home*, but now I started sobbing as my mind swirled with rescue fantasies. I saw myself on a Rouen rooftop with a rifle, putting a bullet through her head before the flames reached her. Then, somehow, I brought her home alive, proud that my perfectly ordinary apartment could offer her more comforts than the Dauphin's chateau on the Loire. I washed her poor feet, showed her how the shower and toilet worked, and took her shopping, enjoying the look on her face when she discovered that women's exercise tights look exactly like medieval men's hose. I bought her a pair in every color, then we had dinner and talked: "I saw that statue of you in Paris—you looked fabulous!"

I would not be her first American. During her trial she has a vision in which the monkish stenographers taking down her testimony are replaced by writers yet unborn who will champion her cause. One in particular intrigues her:

> He was dressed all in white, in a rumpled coat that buttoned down the front, its wide, bizarre flaps resting upon his chest, a stringlike tie around his neck. His hair, as snowy as his clothes, was wild and unruly, and beneath the large nose a bushy white mustache hid his mouth. A righteous yet humorous light burned like a hearth beneath his considerable eyebrows.

It's Mark Twain, who called her "the noble child, the most innocent, the most lovely, the most adorable the ages have produced." He obviously had a rescue fantasy of his own, and so, I suspect, did Miss Marcantel. *An Army of Angels* is surely a labor of love, but it is also high drama on a par with Victor Hugo and classical tragedy, laid out with the precision timing of seasoned stagecraft, graced throughout by a command of the English language that brings me to my knees.

The American Spectator, October 1997
Book Review

"Goldminer's Daughter"

Rage for Fame: The Ascent of Clare Boothe Luce
by Sylvia Jukes Morris (Random House, 561 pages, $30)

For years biographies of women hewed strictly to the feminist formula: "rediscover" an obscure female writer or artist, call her a genius, portray her as a helpless victim of misogynistic men, and blame phallocentric society for denying her the success she so clearly deserved.

There is reason to believe that these paranoid sagas are on the way out. A new trend in distaff lives suggests that we are poised at the dawn of a Neo-Broad Age wherein biographers defy political correctness to celebrate a different kind of woman, the kind of woman who takes it for granted that the best guarantee of success is not a phallus but something rather more hollow, like a gold mine, and that she is sitting on one.

Last year the Neo-Broad Biography Prize went to Sally Bedell Smith's *Reflected Glory*, an unflinching account of the none-too-bright but horizontally unchallenged Pamela Churchill Harriman, who proved that the unexamined life is well worth living. This year's prize will surely go to *Rage for Fame* by Sylvia Jukes Morris, a riveting biography of the brilliant and talented Clare Boothe Luce. Both women employed the same means to achieve different ends. Pam, a full-time courtesan, did not want a career. Clare did, but in her rise from editor to playwright to congresswoman she never forgot that it was a man's world out there, and that some jobs were what she called "jungle jobs—the kind you hang on to with your tail."

She was born in 1903 in what is today Spanish Harlem, the illegitimate daughter of a German-American adventuress named Anna Clara Schneider who anglicized her name to Ann Snyder. Her father, William Franklin Boothe, was still married to his first wife when he began living with Ann. Their irregular arrangement also produced an illegitimate son, Clare's brother David, but it was a female-centered household. Clare's mother was the strong one, a fact that seemed to drain William Boothe of the energy that had made him a prosperous salesman (Clare would have a similar effect on her future husband, *Time* publisher Henry Luce), until he slid into failure and became a free-lance violinist.

The pair never married, but Ann Snyder Boothe had a knack for falsifying public documents. Money-mad to a pathological degree, she seems to have been a textbook case of the rarely seen "Pompadour complex": compulsive prostitution. As the family moved around the country she may have worked in a Memphis brothel; she definitely was a call girl after she left William Boothe and moved back to New York in 1912. Her life's ambition, she frequently told her daughter, was "small hips, large pearls."

A beautiful woman who was as dark and sultry as Clare was ethereal and blonde, Ann snagged a series of rich "protectors," one of whom took her and Clare to Europe in 1914. She hit pay dirt in Joel Jacobs, a rich Jewish bachelor who kept her in grand style and wanted to marry her, but she turned him down for fear that having a Jewish stepfather would hurt her children's social chances. Knowing she felt this way, Jacobs still supported her, sent Clare and David to the best schools, and bought her a house in Greenwich, Connecticut. There, amid the *creme de la creme*, Ann took up with a socially prominent WASP doctor, but incredibly, the adoring Jacobs continued to put his fortune at her disposal.

It was a lesson in what a woman with "it" can pull off, and it did Clare no good. Endowed with a brain and drawn to books, she was torn between a life of the mind and the life of a social butterfly that her mother urged on her. She compromised by exchanging intellect for cleverness and began to do everything with her fingertips, never giving her all to any task lest hard work and dedication mar the feminine charms that opened social doors. "When the choice came between self-cultivation and the cultivation of the rich, Clare usually opted for the latter," writes Morris. "Yet as soon as she yielded, she disliked herself for doing so."

She worked for ten days at the Washington headquarters of the newly victorious Suffragettes. Having just won the right to vote, they were now pushing for an Equal Rights Amendment, but 17-year-old Clare confessed that she "could not get greatly stirred up over the tragedies of the Double Standard," nor did she like the monotony of fundraising and canvassing; "I wanted to be famous but I didn't want to be a martyr." One Suffragette ideal did impress her, however: their motto, "Failure is Impossible."

Her mother brought the same spirit to the task of finding Clare a rich husband. Learning that the Prince of Wales was stopping at White Sulphur Springs, Ann made reservations and dragged Clare down to West Virginia, but the Prince had already left. Her scheme was less overreaching than it sounds. The unmarried Clare was free of the constitutional impediments that sank the twice-divorced Wallis Simpson, so she could have become Queen. (Years later she met the Duchess of Windsor, and though both disliked women, they clicked as only kindred spirits can.)

In 1923 Clare married George Tuttle Brokaw, a 43-year-old New York bachelor with $2 million. The wedding was set for August 10 but on July 7 George added a codicil to his Will stipulating that if he died before the wedding, Clare would inherit as if she were already his wife. One senses the codicil was Mother Ann's idea in view of the advice she gave Clare when George turned out to be an alcoholic: "Wait it out until he drinks himself to death; a widow's portion is larger than alimony."

Clare had her mother's venality, but she tempered it with wit. Life with George wasn't all bad; at least he was good-natured, or as Clare put it: "He wouldn't hurt a fly unless he got so drunk he fell on it." She enjoyed being a rich socialite, though other socialites found her a little odd. Said one: "Clare Brokaw has a room off her bedroom just filled with books, and she *reads* them." She would savage such airhead females in her play, *The Women*, but meanwhile she was having fun—and a baby; daughter Ann, her only child, was born in 1926. The marriage lasted until 1929, when she divorced George ($30,000 annual alimony) and opted for a career in publishing.

Condé Nast, whom she met at a party, promised her a job at *Vogue* just before he sailed for Europe. She went for an interview with the managing editor, but he, too, was getting ready to sail for Europe and forgot to phone her as promised. She waited for two months, then she simply went to the office, sat down at a desk, and began reading manuscripts. It worked; when Nast and the managing editor returned and saw her, each thought the other had hired her.

She soon tired of writing captions for *Vogue* and moved on to *Vanity Fair*, where she wrote brittle, urbane essays and had an affair with editor Donald Freeman, whose job she wanted. She never slept where she could not do herself some good. Her other lovers included Morrow editor Thayer Hobson, journalist Mark Sullivan, columnist Paul Gallico, and financier Bernard Baruch.

Then 61, the still-virile Baruch also activated her political juices. Although she was a solid Republican who called Franklin D. Roosevelt "a regurgitator of the pabulum of nursery liberalism," she rejoiced when Baruch agreed to advise FDR in 1932, concocting a pipe dream wherein he would be named Secretary of the Treasury and persuade FDR to appoint her to some important government post so that she could take Washington by storm as she had New York. But Baruch was not offered Treasury, and Roosevelt invariably referred to Clare, with a knowing male chuckle, as "Barney's girl."

Meanwhile, her earlier dream came true when Donald Freeman died in a car wreck and she got his job. As editor of *Vanity Fair* she interviewed male writers while lying on her office chaise longue—a blonde, blue-eyed, all-American Odalisque to some. To others, such as French artist Raymond Bret-Koch, she was "a beautiful, well-constructed facade without central heating"; to Irwin Shaw she was "as feminine as a meat ax," and to James Agee she was "a walking c--t with stockings by Van Raalte."

She spent less and less time in the office, preferring to work at home or in some fashionable retreat, until even the smitten Condé Nast complained of her absenteeism. It was her old conflict: being famous as the editor of *Vanity Fair* was more fun than editing *Vanity Fair*. She quit and immediately got a syndicated newspaper column, but the same thing happened. At first, says Morris, her columns were models of the personal-essay form—arresting opening paragraphs, strict adherence to a single topic, closely reasoned arguments leading to neatly turned conclusions—but after a while she began resorting to lists, wordy padding, and long quotations to fill her space, "as if the idea itself, fully worked out in her own lightning-quick head, is intellectual satisfaction enough, executing it a chore."

The syndicate dropped her but it didn't matter: she had met Henry Robinson Luce and he had fallen in love with her at first sight. Ever the publisher, he gave her a deadline: she had a year to fall in love with him, at which time he would divorce his wife and marry her.

Here was a job Clare could apply herself to. She adored her "China Boy" (Luce, the son of Presbyterian missionaries, was born in Tengchow), writing to him on a plane at sunset: "The fiery clouds have turned the silver wings into sheets of red gold . . . You are not here. Widowed, my spirit commits suttee in the sky's pyre." It's doubtful that Luce recognized this as overwritten prose; the editor-in-chief of *Time* was a tin-eared malapropist whose own letters contained such gems as: "Your breasts were uproarious in their unsolemn love."

Though only 38, Luce had trouble consummating the marriage, but sex was not uppermost in Clare's mind. What she wanted was the editorship of his new magazine, *Life*, which she had named, but his all-male staff rebelled and Luce gave in to them. Furious, Clare stormed off to her favorite five-star resort hotel and wrote *The Women* in three days.

It was a smash hit. An unrelieved cat fight with an all-female cast (a gimmick that digs at Luce's all-male staff) and a limitless supply of facile wisecracks, the play and the movie that followed made Clare

a household name and justified the compromise she had made with
her talents. Artistic what-might-have-beens were no longer an arena
of subconscious conflict; she had proved that fingertip cleverness
was the route to fame and fortune.

That settled, she concentrated on being Mrs. Henry R. Luce.
"That yellow-haired bitch is spending his money like water," raged
Time's managing editor. She bought an island off South Carolina and
turned it into a Southern plantation, dressing in hoop skirts for her
gala dinner parties. China Boy no likee. As her Babylonian lifestyle
ate into Luce's Calvinist soul and her stiletto wit went over his
humorless head, what remained of his virility left him and he became
completely impotent.

Their one bond was conservative politics. When they could not
find enough black servants for their plantation, Luce wired FDR that
his "relief legislation" was to blame. Clare, of course, came up with
a much better jab: "Let Roosevelt destroy the American Constitution;
he can't destroy mine." They also hated the New Deal social worker,
Harry Hopkins. Clare faulted *Time* for describing his dandruff—that,
she said, was "hitting above the collar"—but she spoke for all conservatives when she asked: "What is it in this twisted humanitarian
that holds such power over the President?"

In 1939 she went to Europe to test the winds of war. The trip
resulted in an anti-fascist book, *Europe in the Spring*, that won her
the approval of the intelligentsia for the first and only time in her life.
While in England she also won the approval of the American ambassador, who was languishing in bachelor solitude after shipping his
huge family home. "JPK in bedroom all morning," reads her diary.

Her decision to run for Congress in 1942 won the approval of the
man who disapproved of everything. "A really tremendous contrast,
both in manner and appearance, to the average female politico,"
effused H.L. Mencken. The *Time-Life* staff also backed her candidacy as a way to get rid of her. The only tepid response came from
China Boy, who by now was on the verge of a nervous breakdown.

Clare's Connecticut district included a horsey set who were in her
pocket, but to get blue-collar votes she had to pretend to an interest
in the underprivileged and display the union label in her clothes.

Everyone expected a memorable campaign and she did not disappoint. The first incident came about when, sick of mouthing banal clichés about democracy, she let loose with a trademark wisecrack: "Every citizen deserves a minimum wage, a minimum diet, and a minimum set of teeth to eat it with." A conventional politician never could have gotten away with it but the author of *The Women* could and did.

The second incident arose when she called her opponent "one of the men in Washington without faces." Unknown to her, the man had had plastic surgery for facial burns suffered in World War I. She got out of it by ignoring all spin doctors save Immanuel Kant, whose maxim, "Never apologize, never explain," had proved useful many times. Her silence stunted the growth of the faux pas and she won election by a narrow margin.

Rage for Fame is the first volume of the author's projected two-volume biography of Clare Boothe Luce. It deserves high praise on literary and historical fronts, but perhaps its greatest value is psychological comfort. Both for women of my vintage who remember Clare and men who came of age in the feminist era, reading about a woman who never obsessed over sexual harassment and the "hostile workplace" is sheer, blessed relief.

The American Spectator, November 1997
Book Review

"Kitty's Crowning Work"

The Royals by Kitty Kelley
(Warner Books, 547 pages, $27)

W hen Edward VIII abdicated in 1936 he was succeeded by his brother, the Duke of York, a consummate family man who had married Lady Elizabeth Bowes-Lyon in 1923 and produced two daughters, Princess Elizabeth, now Elizabeth II, born in 1926, and Princess Margaret Rose, born in 1930.

According to an old rumor that Kitty Kelley recycles in *The Royals*, the princesses were conceived by artificial insemination, but the way Kelley tells the story makes it difficult to figure out the exact nature of the problem. In one place she writes that the Duchess of York could not "conceive," and in another that her husband could not "impregnate" her. Low sperm count and impotence are two different things, so which was it?

Enter the primary source, identified only as "a royal family friend whose mother was a goddaughter of Queen Victoria," who told Kelley that "the Duke had a slight problem with his 'willy.'" That would seem to settle the matter, but then Kelley's second source, identified only as "a relative of the Earl of Arran," assures her that the princesses "were born by artificial means," but says nothing about the willy. Kelley herself calls it a "fertility problem," which seems to absolve the willy, but then she quotes a cryptic pun by the childless Duchess of Windsor, who said that her own Duke was not "heir-conditioned." We never do find out whether it was willy or nilly, but we are off to a wonderful start.

Elizabeth II prizes order above all else. As a child she got out of bed several times a night to make sure her shoes were lined up exactly even. The same dedication to conformity emerged when she became Queen in 1952. Editorial writers were churning out ecstatic paeans to a "New Elizabethan Age," but she quickly dampened errant visions of Merrie England and aligned herself with the bland fifties: "I do not myself feel at all like my Tudor forebear, who was blessed with neither husband nor children, who ruled as a despot and was never able to leave her shores."

Her first family crisis erupted the following year when Princess Margaret announced that she wanted to marry Peter Townsend. A handsome, well-bred RAF hero and former Palace equerry, Townsend was eligible in every way but one: He was divorced. Margaret pleaded but the Queen was adamant. The specter of divorce had haunted the royal family ever since the Abdication. If Margaret married Townsend she would lose her title, her allowance, and her place in the succession (third at this time); the wedding could not take place in England, and the couple would have to live abroad—exiled like the Duke and Duchess of Windsor.

Margaret gave Townsend up, which cleared the way for Antony Armstrong-Jones, an arty photographer who was rumored to be gay until a friend explained helpfully, "Oh, no, he's bi. He'd never limit himself." Tony's delight in dressing up in Margaret's clothes shocked her footman, who quit and wrote a book that was published in Paris after the Palace warned British publishers that they would never get a knighthood if they touched it.

There were no constitutional impediments to the marriage. Tony was only a "Mister," but any hint that he was not good enough to marry royalty would have damaged the monarchy. In any case, the Queen could hardly object to his having no title when the power to bestow one was hers. Nor could she say no to Margaret, now 30, a second time; that would damage the monarchy too. The only valid objection to Tony was the one that dared not speak its name for fear of damaging the monarchy, so the Queen Mum announced the engagement.

Tony's first choice for best man had been convicted of homosexual offenses eight years earlier. Prince Philip exploded. Tony chose another, but Scotland Yard advised that the second man was susceptible to blackmail. Unable to think of anyone else, he let the Palace choose for him and ended up with a best man he hardly knew: the son of the Queen's gynecologist.

The Westminster Abbey wedding was attended by a host of Tony's friends—fashion designers, hairdressers, interior decorators—as well as his divorced parents and both of his father's former wives and their husbands, but the Duke and Duchess of Windsor were not invited because they had damaged the monarchy.

The marriage produced two children, lots of partying, cross-dressing, and kinky sex, but then the fun stopped. Tony did a striptease on the table at Sandringham, put a bag over his head at dinner so he would not have to look at Margaret, and left a list on her dresser: "Twenty Reasons Why I Hate You." Asked by a hostess how the Queen was, Margaret said, "Which Queen? My sister, my mother, or my husband?"

They were divorced in 1976. By refusing to let Margaret marry a divorced man, the Windsors brought about the first royal divorce since Henry VIII shed Anne of Cleves in 1540. They had gagged on a gnat and swallowed an elephant, and they would do it again in 1981 when they rejected girls with a past and chose a virgin without a brain.

Kelley has come under fire for bringing out *The Royals* two weeks after Diana's death, but she may have solved the mystery of who was at fault. Her description of an Austrian ski trip is electrifying:

> Photographs of the sulking Princess and her forlorn husband appeared in the British press with daily stories about the commotion she was causing: there were reports of one-hundred-mile-an-hour car chases of the Princess trying to dodge photographers and blond decoys she sent out to distract photographers; barricades thrown up and borders closed to the press; reporters roughed up and photographers driven off the road.

Diana had trouble learning to read but she did well enough to send her stepmother poison-pen letters. Countess Spencer doubted her stepdaughter's much-touted virginity, suspecting an affair in 1978 with gin scion James Gilbey, whose clothes Diana had washed and ironed. She had also done the laundry of another beau, Rory Scott, a Scots Guards officer. Countess Spencer was sufficiently worried about rumors that nude photos from this period would appear in the tabloids that she consulted a lawyer at the time of the royal wedding preparations.

In a footnote, Kelley states: "The nude photos of Diana were offered for sale in 1993 by a German magazine but were withdrawn and given to her." Does "her" refer to Diana or the stepmother? Who is the German source? She doesn't say.

She provides some documentation for the most serious question she raises: the paternity of Prince Harry, born in 1984. After Diana's affair with James Hewitt was revealed, "some royal biographers noticed a startling resemblance between the copper-haired Hewitt and rusty-haired Prince Harry. But Hewitt denied he was the father and staunchly maintained he did not meet Diana until two years after the birth of her second son."

But, she adds: "*Private Eye* stated that Hewitt met her at a polo match in 1981 before her marriage."

In a related story she addresses Diana's concern for Harry's financial future. Kelley claims she asked her father to help, and describes his response in this dramatized paragraph:

> "I have given Diana a hell of a lot of money—between $750,000 and $1.5 million—to invest for Harry," he said, and disclosed Diana's concern about her second son's future. Her firstborn, William, destined to become Prince of Wales and eventually King, was guaranteed immense wealth. But not Harry.

Surely Spencer spoke of pounds, not dollars, but we can allow that Kelley converted for American readers. Otherwise, the passage is written like a scene in a novel and we cannot tell from her brief cluster of unnumbered notes where she got her information. All in all, an eminently suspect story—except for two things: the fact that Diana's concern for Harry's financial future was widely reported in the American media, and the sentence "But not Harry."

Why not Harry? His future wealth may not equal William's but his Civil List income and his private inheritance from Charles and the Queen will leave him far from poor. Is it possible that Diana knew he was not Charles's son and feared he would be cut off?

Documented or not, Kelley's Diana stories are a welcome antidote to the lachrymose news coverage of her death and funeral, as refreshing as sherbet between heavy courses. Choose your flavor.

Diana the Clotheshorse: It took six rooms in Kensington Palace to hold her wardrobe, with one room reserved for 320 pairs of shoes. She shopped to take her mind off her bulimic hunger. Whenever Charles saw her eat he would ask, "Is that going to reappear later?" After they separated she got rid of all the low-heeled shoes she had worn to keep from towering over him, saying, "You can throw out those dwarfers, I won't be needing them anymore." Thereafter she wore what she called "tart trotters"—spike heels with ankle straps and open toes. Charles celebrated the separation by giving the newspapers an annual accounting of what he called her "grooming expenses": $25,000 in manicures and pedicures; $24,000 hair; $4,300 colonic irrigation; $2,000 hypnotisms; $4,290 reflexology; $3,800 aromatherapy; $65,000 astrologers and psychics; and $20,000 psychotherapy.

Diana the Humanitarian: When Earl Spencer died and his widow had to vacate Althorp to make way for the new earl, Diana and her brother accused their stepmother of packing her things in Vuitton luggage that did not belong to her. They ordered her maid to unpack everything and put it in plastic garbage bags, then Charles Spencer kicked the bags down the stairs.

Diana demanded that Prince Charles fire the homosexuals on his staff whom she called the "pink mafia," saying she didn't want them around her sons. During an intense discussion of inner-city problems between Charles and a South African philosopher, she broke in and said, "What's the definition of mass confusion? Answer: Father's Day in Brixton." (Brixton is a heavily black London district.)

Diana the Nut Case: Convinced that Palace courtiers were out to get her, she bought a portable shredder and took it everywhere. She tried to push her stepmother down the stairs at Althorp and told the Bishop of Norwich that she was a reincarnated spirit who was gifted with a healing touch. When her bodyguard was killed in a motorcycle accident she accused Prince Charles of ordering his assassination. During discussions of the divorce settlement she asked that any future children she might have by another man be given hereditary titles.

Kelley does a boffo job on Sarah Ferguson, ex-wife of Prince Andrew. Fergie's father was a major in the elite Life Guards cavalry, and the Fergusons, who are landed gentry, are direct descendants of the sixth Duke of Buccleugh, but blood doesn't always tell. Fergie, says Kelley, "acted like the only dame dealt into the poker game."

She was the first member of the royal family to say "prick" on television. Asked what she had for breakfast, she said, "Sausages and a migraine," adding that the migraines came from falling off horses. A member of the Dangerous Sports Club, she competed in a midnight steeplechase and won the DSC's Golden Crutches badge. Her boast, "I'd rather ride than read," explains why the Queen initially liked her.

Fergie's parents were divorced. Her mother is thought to have had an affair with Prince Philip, who was with her at her polo pony farm in Argentina while the Queen was helping the fire brigade run pails at Windsor Castle.

Diana and Fergie met at a polo match and became instant soul mates. Both were into astrologers, clairvoyants, and tarot cards, and Fergie was a regular client of Madame Vasso, a faith healer who placed her under a blue plastic pyramid and chanted.

Diana thought Fergie and Andy would hit it off and she was right. Both loved burping contests and any witticism involving bowels. "She whooped and hollered at all his fart jokes," said a waiter at Windsor Castle. They also enjoyed food fights; to Fergie, throwing rolls at each other in public was what "humanizing the monarchy" meant.

Every time Fergie visited the royal household she brought all her dirty laundry for the palace staff to do. At first the royal family liked her, probably because she enjoyed the charades and parlor games beloved by non-readers like the Queen Mum. The Queen's only advice to her was to wave more slowly, a style Fergie described as "screwing in lightbulbs."

On her wedding day, finding herself suddenly immobilized as she mounted the steps of Westminster Abbey, she turned around and yelled, "Who the hell is standing on my train?" Going up the aisle, she made faces at guests and gave the thumbs-up sign. "All that ghastly winking," said the wife of the Queen's cousin, "so common."

In another attempt to humanize the monarchy she announced on television that "My knickers are from Marks and Sparks"—Marks & Spencer, the middle-class store. Tearing through Harrod's, the upper-class store, she saw a biscuit tin with the Queen Mum's picture on it, knocked on the lid and sang out, "Are you in there, dear?" Bored by her public engagements, she told a Palace staffer, "Maybe the Queen Mum will die and we'll have to cancel everything for the mourning." Meanwhile, Major Ferguson was arrested in a massage parlor.

Fergie "mirrored modern Britain, its gaudiness, its bounciness, its rumbustious lack of mystery," wrote the *Sunday Times*. Offended by the unflattering reflection she presented, the country turned on her with a vengeance. "We wanted a silk purse and we got a sow's ear," wrote one London journalist. "A figure like a Jurassic monster," "the Duchess of Pork," "a royal bike—ridden by everyone."

She was hurt when she saw London street vendors selling chocolate toes, but worse was to come. The *Sun* ran a poll asking "Who would you rather date—Fergie or a goat?" and the goat won.

Kelley's favorite Windsor is the Queen's only daughter, Princess Anne—"blunt as a bullet"—who was the first member of the family to see through Diana. "Too gooey about children," Anne averred, sounding just like her father.

Prince Philip's is the mouth that roars once too often in the opinion of Kelley's most livid critics, who are incensed over her "Insatiable Liz" quotation. During the first year of his marriage to the Queen, Philip supposedly told the Duke of Leeds, "I can't get her out of my bed. She's always there. She's driving me mad."

Kelley got this from the late Duke's son-in-law, Nigel Dempster, the *Daily Mail* gossip columnist. Not exactly in the pristine footnote league, perhaps, but the story rings true when weighed against some of Philip's public gaffes. To a Cairo official on the city's traffic jams: "The trouble with you Egyptians is that you breed too much." To a Scottish driving instructor: "How do you keep the natives off the booze long enough to get them to pass the test?" To British exchange students in China: "If you stay here much longer, you'll get slitty eyes."

Only once does Kelley go too far. Her story about Princess Margaret, Ann Landers, the mayor of Chicago, and *Schindler's List* is unbelievable at any speed, but other than that she has written an irresistible book. True, she dishes up a lot of third-hand dirt, but so did Pepys and Saint-Simon. Kelley shares their unerring instinct for history with its pomp down, and she turns out some of the wittiest one-liners in the business. Her description of the Duke of Windsor "looking like a forlorn little man who had fallen off a charm bracelet" is worthy of Noel Coward.

The American Spectator, January 1998
Book Review

"A Thinking Man's President"

John Quincy Adams: A Public Life, A Private Life
by Paul C. Nagel (Knopf, 432 pages, $30)

O ur sixth President has long been a favorite of quiz shows and Trivial Pursuit junkies: the only son to follow his father to the White House, the last President to be elected by the House of Representatives, the only candidate to win the Presidency while losing both the popular and the electoral vote, and the only President to serve as a member of Congress after leaving office.

All of these events could happen again, but it's doubtful if anyone will ever match John Quincy Adams's greatest "only." It happened after a boating accident on the Potomac where he took his morning swims. He always swam in his drawers and shirt but his aide stripped to the buff. They piled their clothes in the boat and set off, but midway across the river the boat sank, taking all the clothes with it. The pair then swam back to the bank, where Adams removed his remaining garments and gave them to the naked aide so he could return to the White House for help. After he left, the naked Adams sat down on a rock and waited—the only President to do an imitation of Rodin's "The Thinker" in public.

Another singularity has been unfairly attributed to John Quincy Adams: the only President to be called a "misanthrope." Described by most historians as an irritable, gloomy, solitary, rude, icy aristocrat, this complex man has found the perceptive biographer he deserves in Paul C. Nagel, emeritus professor of history and contributing editor of *American Heritage*, whose splendidly researched and engagingly written *John Quincy Adams: A Public Life, A Private Life* gives us a President we didn't know we had.

JQA, as Nagel calls him, was born in 1767 and grew into a charming boy who found it easy to adore a father who was a hero of the Revolution. John Adams and his son shared a rare intellectual compatibility, reading Cicero together and parsing Latin sentences at breakfast. An amazingly gifted linguist from boyhood, JQA learned to read Thucydides' *History of the Peloponnesian War* in the original Greek, which the elder Adams considered "the most perfect of all human languages."

His relationship with his mother was something else. Abigail Adams, canonized by feminists who have spent three decades quoting her marching orders to her husband ("Remember the ladies") during the Constitutional Convention, was America's founding scold who "made no effort to hide her condescending attitude toward males."

Abigail merits her place in the American pantheon, says Nagel. "But while the American feminist movement does well to claim her as its archetype, history should be mindful that her strengths caused her downfall in one respect. As the life of John Quincy Adams discloses, Abigail Adams was a calamity as a mother."

Her specialty was long-distance nagging. In 1778 when John Adams was sent to Paris as a commissioner to promote the American cause, he took 11-year-old JQA with him. The boy learned French in record time and soon was savoring the neoclassical dramas of Corneille and Racine at the Comédie Française. The two Adamses enjoyed "the sort of male rapport that comes when father and son must get on without a wife and mother," writes Nagel, so of course Abigail had to spoil it with an endless stream of reproving letters about the dangers of a sophisticated life.

"For dear as you are to me," she wrote her son, "I had much rather you should have found your grave in the ocean you have crossed, or any untimely death crop you in your infant years, rather than see you an immoral profligate . . ." Vice—by which she meant Paris—was hideous and he must never forget it. "You must keep a strict guard upon yourself, or the odious monster will soon lose its terror by becoming familiar to you."

There was no let-up in her epistolary assault. When John Adams took his son along on a mission to The Hague, Abigail's letters followed him, this time urging him to model his personal habits on "the universal neatness and cleanliness of the Dutch." He preferred the scholarly models at the University of Leyden, where he was admitted as a special student at 13.

Abigail wanted him schooled in America and raised under her watchful eye, but when John Adams was appointed Minister to France, she suddenly changed her mind. Worried now that her husband would be exposed to the seductive charms of the noble ladies of Versailles, she allowed the boy to stay in Paris with his father in the evident hope that having a son in tow would cramp John Adams's style.

Back in Paris, JQA concentrated on perfecting his French. In 1782 the boy of 15 accompanied Francis Dana on a diplomatic mission to Russia, serving as Dana's interpreter in Catherine the Great's French-speaking court. On the return trip they were stranded for five weeks in Stockholm while they waited for a sail wind. Nagel deduces that something significant happened during this delay that caused an uncharacteristic gap in the voluminous diary (340 reels of microfilm) that JQA kept up religiously from childhood until his death at 81. When the entries resume after the Stockholm interlude they reveal an indefinable but intriguing aspect of greater maturity. JQA never spoke of these five weeks, but once, many years later, he called Sweden "the land of lovely dames."

When Abigail joined her husband and son in Paris in 1784, she was taken aback by the discovery that 17-year-old JQA had become a European cosmopolite. Amid much carping about the perils of indolence and the "warm blood that riots in young men's veins," she packed him back to Quincy to live with his aunt and attend Harvard.

It was nothing less than culture shock. The budding young man of the world who had mingled easily with polished statesmen and bons vivants, the joyful scholar who had translated La Fontaine and longed to be "one who can invent, who can create," the lover of great cities who recoiled from the Jeffersonian doctrine of the good earth, was crammed suddenly into the narrow end of a New England funnel where pleasure and stimulation consisted of rustic dances, conversations about the weather, Aunt Elizabeth, and tutoring for Harvard with a country parson.

He sank into what today would be called a clinical depression that worsened when he began his study of law. Blessed—and cursed—with a mind that could not endure tedium, he loathed every aspect of the legal life and lost his first case. His only respite was writing political essays for a Boston newspaper. As it happened, it was his salvation. The essays were brought to the attention of President George Washington (probably by Vice President John Adams), who was so impressed by their astuteness that he appointed JQA Minister to the Netherlands in 1794.

The diplomatic post meant he could give up the law, but it also presaged a life of public service, and he wanted a literary career. Further complications arose when he stopped off in London and met Louisa Johnson. She was the daughter of the American consul, Joshua Johnson, a Maryland tobacco trader who was said to be very rich and to own vast acreage in Georgia. JQA set off for The Hague with fleeting visions of retiring to a Southern plantation to spend the rest of his life writing.

He was able to put Louisa out of his mind once he discovered that diplomacy left ample time for his literary pursuits. Savoring his bachelor freedom, he read and wrote and translated Tacitus, but Fate put Louisa in his path again when he was ordered to London to exchange formal ratifications of Jay's Treaty. The mission dragged on for months, leaving JQA ample time to fall in love.

Abigail got wind of it and wrote carping letters, calling Louisa a "half-blood" (her mother was English) and warning him that a wife raised in Europe would take lovers. JQA replied testily that if he waited until she approved of a girl "I would certainly be doomed to celibacy." Meanwhile, Joshua Johnson confessed that he was bankrupt. JQA's vision of himself as a planter-*littérateur* turned into a vision of a lawyer supporting his in-laws.

Fortunately, he had pull. His perceptive reports on Jay's Treaty had impressed outgoing President Washington and convinced the new President John Adams to name him Minister to Prussia. Better yet, Adams *père* appointed the ruined Joshua Johnson postmaster of the District of Columbia. Ambivalent about the nepotism but vastly relieved, JQA left for Berlin with his new bride.

As his responsibilities increased, the duty of being his father's son joined forces with a subconscious mind haunted by his mother's criticism, turning him into an overanxious workhorse. It was as if he had to read every book, learn every language, to atone for the pleasurable round of balls and receptions that comprised the diplomatic life. Rapidly mastering German, he translated the long narrative poem *Oberon*. (Published in America in 1940, it was deemed "of unusual scholarly and literary merit, remarkable for its fidelity to the original and its genuine artistry.")

Industry became his god and his goad, thoroughness his ruling passion, absorption its own reward. The voluminous letters he wrote his brother while in Germany were later published as a book, *Letters on Silesia*. JQA was, said Tom Adams, "the most exhaustless writer I ever knew."

When John Adams lost his re-election bid in 1800 he recalled his son himself rather than let the victorious Jefferson do it. A devastated JQA returned to Massachusetts, wondering if the literary career he wanted would ever be his. Willing to do anything to avoid practicing law, he accepted the Federalist nomination for the U.S. Senate and was elected by the state legislature in 1802.

His Senate career is a clinical study of psychological conflict. His ulterior motive for taking the job was the Senate's light schedule—noon to three—which would give him time for reading and writing. To prepare for the job, however, he felt it his duty to master American history, but soon tiring of it, he turned to translating his beloved Plautus and Juvenal, which made him feel guilty for shirking his duty.

The strange votes he cast in the Senate have been attributed to simple contrariness, but a closer look reveals a compulsive need to combat his mother's contempt for Europe and her fear of cosmopolitan influences. To understand what drove him we must examine the conditions of life in Washington at this time. It was a mudhole; sans theater, sans opera, sans even a dignified home for the Supreme Court, which sat in Long's Tavern on Capitol Hill. Homesick for the great capitals of Europe, JQA unconsciously tried to bring the mountain to Mohammed by making America a world power.

His pro-expansionist vote on the Louisiana Purchase stunned New England Federalists intent on clinging to their regional dominance. He defied them again when he voted to deny a seat to a senator who had supported Aaron Burr's attempt to take lower Louisiana out of the Union; many New Englanders had supported Burr's scheme as a way to reduce Southern and western influence.

The showdown came when JQA announced his support for the Embargo Act. Designed to stop British and French incursions on American shipping, it threatened to close down New England ports and leave the seagoing region to starve. Incensed, the Massachusetts legislature adopted a resolution ordering him to vote to repeal the embargo, but he refused and resigned his seat.

His voting record screams hatred of provincialism, but he loftily insisted that he simply followed his conscience and put country over region and party. Whether he hoped that a grateful James Madison would reward him with a foreign posting is, writes Nagel, impossible to say. However, that's exactly what happened: He was named Minister to Russia in 1809. His mother refused to bid him farewell, saying, "A man of his worth ought not be permitted to leave the country."

He was an unqualified success in St. Petersburg. The diplomatic set considered him a brilliant conversationalist, President Madison found his reports on Napoleon invaluable, and he hit it off famously with Tsar Alexander I, who played piggyback with the three Adams sons. It was out of personal friendship that Alexander offered to mediate peace between the U.S. and England after the War of 1812, with JQA acting as chief negotiator of the Treaty of Ghent.

Now came the pinnacle of diplomacy: Minister to the Court of St. James's. Never had he been so happy and relaxed as he was in London, but it did not last. When James Monroe named him Secretary of State in 1817, Louisa girded herself for a return of the grim intensity and melancholia that invariably emerged in the politician in his native land.

Back in Mudtown, JQA fought with Speaker Henry Clay, who wanted to direct foreign policy, and became obsessed with the meter. *The Report of the Secretary of State Upon Weights and Measures* is "the finest scholarly evaluation of the subject ever written," says Nagel, but it was supposed to be a pamphlet; JQA in overdrive produced a tome gravid with philosophical digressions, including a prediction that a universal metric system would bring world peace.

Abigail Adams died in 1818 but he did not attend her funeral. Never a neat man, he now became notorious for his unkempt appearance. It was, says Nagel, "an easy and lifelong form of rebellion against his otherwise compulsive reverence for duty." It was also a slap at Abigail's instructions to acquire the scrubbed Dutch look.

He was a superb Secretary of State, getting the Spanish out of Florida, the Russians out of the Pacific Northwest, settling the Canadian border dispute, and ghostwriting what became known as the Monroe Doctrine, but a cloud hung over his entire eight-year tenure: the election of 1824. Jefferson, Madison, and Monroe had all been Secretary of State before becoming President, so JQA was the man to beat.

Andrew Jackson was the man who beat him, winning 152,901 popular votes and 99 electoral votes to JQA's 114,023 and 84. The four-way race also included William H. Crawford, who came in third with 46,979 and 41; and Henry Clay with 47,217 and 37. Since no one had a majority in the Electoral College, the House of Representatives chose the President from among the top three candidates, with each state delegation casting one vote. The result was Adams 13, Jackson 7, and Crawford 4.

His administration was a debacle, beginning with his first State of the Union address. His support for federal internal improvements—roads, canals, and bridges—was already well-known, but now he proclaimed government responsible for culture, science, and the promotion of knowledge, and called for a national university and a national observatory. This, after all, was how the great cities of Europe became the great cities of Europe, but several American senators introduced a resolution to indict him for usurpation of powers.

All his projects were blocked and he accomplished nothing, but duty demanded that he run for re-election in 1828. Not surprisingly, Andrew Jackson won by a landslide.

He returned to Massachusetts in defeat but his most successful public service was still to come, though it began as a trick. Fearing that his sense of duty would make him seek the presidency yet again, a pro-Henry Clay contingent in Boston proposed him for Congress to keep him out of Clay's way. Interpreting the ploy as "vindication," he ran for the seat in 1830 and won.

He spent the last eighteen years of his life in Congress, winning re-election eight times and furnishing the House with some of its most memorable moments. Drawing a bead on slavery, he called states' rights a "hallucination" and fought the "gag rule" devised by Southern members to set aside anti-slavery petitions. Declaring that it violated the constitutional guarantee of a citizen's right to petition the government, he brought stacks of petitions on various and sundry subjects to the chamber and read them out one after another—including one to gag *him*.

Was the Yankee congressman who once dreamed of being a literary gentleman of leisure on a Georgia plantation really so passionately opposed to slavery, or was the cultivated dévoté of European cities subconsciously doing battle with the rural parochialism that the South represented?

We'll never know, but at least he was consistent. He called the annexation of Texas as a slave state "apoplexity of the Constitution," said the Mexican War was nothing but an excuse to spread bondage, and literally used his last breath to vote against commending its veterans. Half-rising from his seat, he whispered a hoarse "No," then collapsed of a stroke. They carried him to a couch in the Speaker's chamber where he died two days later on February 23, 1848.

Several reviewers of *John Quincy Adams: A Public Life, A Private Life* have faulted the author for emphasizing the private over the public, but that is exactly what Adams needed someone to do for him. By showing us the puritan who yearned to be a boulevardier and the lawyer who ached to be a writer, Paul C. Nagel succeeds in making John Quincy Adams, of all people, sympathetic and even lovable.

National Review, February 9, 1998
Book Review

"Air Farce"

Proud to Be: My Life, the Air Force, the Controversy,
by Kelly Flinn
(Random House, 259 pp., $23)

MOST of Kelly Flinn's book reads like an adolescent adventure series, "The Cosmo Girls Go to War," but one passage stands out as a brilliant, if unintentional, example of satirical parody:

> I arrived in Minot in early October: Winter had already begun. . . .
> To my right, to my left, for miles, I could see only farmland. It was
> flat. Extremely flat. No hills, no mountains; just plains. The ground
> was yellow and brown and the crops looked dead. The main road
> through town was only five miles long. . . . I saw a small college, a
> big red brick factory called the Sweetheart Bakery, and a large
> number of railroad tracks. . . . The city still had the feeling of some-
> thing half-finished. Despite all the wide-open spaces around it, it
> felt very claustrophobic.

This is Carol Kennicott of *Main Street* arriving in Gopher Prairie, determined to change hearts and minds and anything else that gets in her way to realize her dream of bringing culture and refinement to Midwestern boosters. That Carol was destined to get into a great deal of trouble was obvious to everyone but Carol, and so it was with the equally obtuse Kelly Flinn. If only she had been able to appreciate her resemblance to her literary predecessor she might have done things differently, but her DNA is missing an irony gene and she doesn't seem to have read anything except manuals.

Flinn, the baby of her family, has four much older siblings; her two brothers were 14 and 8 when she was born and her two sisters 10 and 11. Apparently she was what is tactfully called a "surprise," but she is blind to the connection between being an unwanted child and her need to push herself into places where she is not wanted. Of the circumstances of her birth she says only, "My role in the family was to be cute."

Anxious to establish her tomboy credentials, she dwells on her days as the pride of the monkey bars and the only girl on the soccer team. In high school she compromised with femininity by being "well-rounded," i.e., majoring in extracurricular activities while still keeping up her grades, though she never tells us what the latter were. Like all Great Girl types she used overscheduled joinerism to simulate popularity; finding herself with no date for the senior prom, she had to ask a boy she met at Space Camp.

The first thing she saw when she entered the Air Force Academy was a wall inscribed "Bring Me Men." The second was the marble statue of Pegasus, which, male cadets prophesy, will fly off its pedestal when a female cadet graduates a virgin. Flinn was a virgin and wanted to remain one, but she would awaken at night to find her roommate having sex, and once, two men entered their unlocked room and fondled them as they lay in bed. She wanted to file a complaint but her roommate, sounding as complaisant as a tired old streetwalker, said, "It really wasn't so bad."

Flinn went into gender shock. "I so wished that I didn't have to be around men: since my world was 90 per cent male, I was in a state of anxiety all the time." Even worse than the constant sexual tension were the "gross-out contests" in which, to use the only printable example, male cadets drank to get sick and then ate each other's vomit.

Her feminine side wanted to quit but her tomboy side feared the stigma of not being able to take it "like a man." After the fondling incident, a female counselor told her she would lose her fear of men once she learned how to control a sexual situation. She took this to mean she must initiate sex to prove she was aggressive, so she picked a cadet she calls a "male friend" and told him what the counselor had said. He was silent for a moment, then: "Would you like to go out?" On that drab note she was deflowered. Afterward, instead of feeling the usual female regret, she told herself that "by having meaningless, casual sex without a relationship, I'd just, once and for all, become one of the boys."

She spent a summer at Kunsan AFB in South Korea where, desperately seeking that elusive camaraderie (her favorite word), she tagged along on sprees with F-16 pilots. "Every night we went to bars where women danced naked and swung from poles," and got falling-down drunk on *soju*, or Korean moonshine. This time she did not flinch from the gross-out contests.

> Basically, the men vomited and blew chunks off the second-floor balcony of a restaurant. Since I enjoyed going out and drinking hard with the boys, I was quickly integrated into the group and given a nickname of my own, although I did not get sick. Joining comrades named Chunk Nose, Chunk Lips, and Chunk Face, I was called Chunk Tits.

Her Class of '93 had a high female attrition rate due to a gang rape on the athletic field, several "forced sex" incidents, and indecent exposure in parachuting class, but Flinn, taking strength, she says, from Anita Hill, hung on and graduated.

Next came flight school, where she alienated her male classmates. A highlight of the bonding process was choosing the shoulder patch that would identify them as comrades. The men wanted a naked girl with planes flying through her spread legs, but Flinn, taking strength now from castratrix Lorena Bobbitt, suggested "a knife and a cucumber." The Anita Hill case had made the Air Force nervous about obscenity, so the men had to choose an innocuous patch.

Having signaled her womanly delicacy, Flinn now switched signals and played the consummate tomboy. "I picked up a male pilot's jaunty way of walking, talking . . . I talked fast and low. I kept my intonation flat . . . I never wore makeup in uniform; it made me look too much of a woman."

She was ready for combat, so sunk in unintrospective self-absorption that she assumed everyone else agreed with her: "Faced with growing numbers of women in all areas of professional life, Americans were slowly coming to grips with the idea of seeing their daughters held as prisoners of war and young mothers coming home in body bags."

When her request to fly B-52s was granted, she was heralded as the first female bomber pilot and sent to Minot AFB, home of the B-52, to be the official poster girl for the feminist-hounded Air Force. At last her conflicted family dynamic was resolved: now she could be unwanted *and* cute.

North Dakota should call itself the "Aphrodisiac State." Sex was rife at Minot, Flinn says, because there was nothing else to do. As the bleak vastness settled over her, she caught the spirit of prairie bacchanalia and began to realize what she had been missing.

Her first tumble in the tundra was with an enlisted man, Colin Ferguson, whom she met when she gave what she calls a wine-tasting party. "People were staggering around the house drunk and flopped out all over the lawn." She didn't think she was fraternizing with Ferguson because "I didn't use rank to get him into bed. He was so drunk he just sort of oozed in."

The rest of the book consists of a retelling of her well-publicized downfall. The familiar details need not concern us but her thought processes are not to be missed: "True, women do pose a problem for the Air Force brass. But that problem isn't rooted in the fact that we are women per se. Rather, we're a problem because, in the Air Force's collective imagination, we're identified with sex."

The Air Force is stuck, she believes, in a 1950s morality that makes it associate sex—i.e., women—solely with marriage and brothels.

> But when the objects of their affections started accompanying them into battle, the whole system seemed to fall apart. . . . For if the men of the Air Force are no longer traditional macho warriors, upholding God and country by day and whoring at night, who are they? Sentimental soldiers who risk *falling in love* with their crew? . . . The fear isn't just of women distracting men in the Air Force from

their work. It's of women feminizing men *altogether*.

That's an argument against women in the military if I've ever read one, but for the life of me I don't think she realized it.

A psychologist who examined Flinn said she has "the social skills of a 12-year-old." While this seems to be true, I see something else. She's a type America turns out in droves: the "natural leader," student-council junkies who lead where everyone else is already going, bowing to every cultural ukase along the way while cherishing a fantasy of independence instilled in them by half-baked teachers who hate original thinkers.

Happily for Flinn, America reserves a special niche for natural leaders. "I've been asked," she writes, "to run for Congress."

National Review, February 23, 1998
Book Review

"Mrs. Eaton's Knocker"

The Petticoat Affair: Manners, Mutiny, and Sex in Andrew Jackson's White House, by John F. Marszalek
(Simon & Schuster, 296 pp., $25)

G o back before Monica Lewinsky, before JFK's harem, before Nan Britton and Warren Harding, and you will find a woman named Peggy Eaton. There the comparison ends, for the tarnished escutcheon in her case was not that of a President recumbent but a President rampant.

It took very little to make Andrew Jackson fly into a rage, but chief among his many sore points was the sanctity of womanhood. As a young frontier lawyer he settled his obsessive chivalry on Rachel Donelson Robards, the estranged wife of the pathologically jealous Lewis Robards, whose mother ran the boardinghouse where Jackson lived. Rachel helped her sympathetic mother-in-law with the work, but her friendly, outgoing manner with the boarders so enraged her unstable husband that he deserted her. He claimed that he had gotten a divorce, but in fact he had only petitioned the legislature. The decree did not become final until Rachel and Andrew Jackson had been married for two years.

They went through a second ceremony but Jackson's political enemies never forgot. He fought two duels over Rachel's honor, killing one man, and tried futilely to shield her against the slurs of adulteress and prostitute heaped on her in the vicious presidential election of 1828. He won the election, but a month later Rachel had a fatal heart attack, leaving this most uxorious of men to be inaugurated as a widower seething with unspent rage at scandalmongers.

The epitaph on Rachel's tomb, "A being so gentle and virtuous that slander might wound but could not dishonor," was written by Jackson's political ally and surrogate son, Sen. John Henry Eaton, slated to be his Secretary of War, who had just married a pretty young Washington widow named Margaret O'Neale Timberlake.

Peggy O'Neale had started life sitting on the laps of the politicians who lived at her family's boardinghouse and drank at their adjacent tavern. The proverbial cute kid who sings and dances for guests, she liked being the center of male attention and by 14 had broken her first heart: a nephew of the Secretary of the Navy attempted suicide out of unrequited love for her. After causing a couple of fights between young officers she tried to elope with an aide to Gen. Winfield Scott, but her father caught her as she climbed out the window. At 16 she enchanted a naval purser, John Timberlake, who proposed the day he met her. Anxious by now to get her safely married, her parents agreed to the match and the young couple wed in 1816.

Buxom and russet-haired, Peggy helped out at the boardinghouse and tavern, joining in the political talk with the ease of a woman used to large numbers of men. Her open manner made her a special favorite of Sen. Andrew Jackson, who boarded at O'Neale's, as did Tennessee's other senator, John Eaton, a friend of Timberlake's who had promised to look after her while her husband was at sea. He kept his word; they were seen together socially.

In April 1828 Timberlake died suddenly aboard ship off the coast of Spain. The first vague reports said he was felled by a "fever" but it soon came out that he had cut his own throat. Rumors flew, gathering steam when Eaton and the inconsolable widow of eight months were married with Jackson's blessing on New Year's Day, 1829.

The scandal became official when Peggy called on the Vice President's wife and Mrs. John Calhoun did not return the call. All of the other Washington ladies followed suit, including the other

Cabinet wives, and even Jackson's niece and official hostess, Emily Donelson, who snubbed Mrs. Secretary of War Eaton at the Inaugural Ball.

Next, an unctuous Presbyterian minister, the Rev. Ezra Stiles Ely, wrote Jackson that Peggy's two daughters had been fathered by Eaton, not Timberlake, and that she had had a miscarriage while Timberlake was at sea. Rising to the bait, Jackson demanded to know the source of the miscarriage rumor. He had heard it, Ely said, from another Presbyterian minister, the Rev. John Campbell. Jackson summoned Campbell to the White House and grilled him until he confessed that he had heard the story from a Dr. Elijah Craven, who had since died. Fleeing Jackson's presence, Campbell hired a lawyer—Francis Scott Key—to depose Dr. Craven's widow. Meanwhile, some old lady told him that *she* had heard that Peggy delivered twins during Timberlake's absence.

Morphing this new, faux Rachel onto the image of his beloved wife, Jackson bombarded the Navy with demands for records and affidavits on the dates of Timberlake's voyages. Worried by the way affairs of state were being ignored, Alexander Hamilton's son told Martin Van Buren, "We did not make him President to work the miracle of making Mrs. Eaton an honest woman."

With the Timberlake file in hand, a now-molten Jackson ordered his Cabinet and both Presbyterian divines to the White House where they sat in terrified silence as he roared: "She is as chaste as a virgin!"

Far from settling matters, the unprecedented Cabinet meeting only made them worse. Henry Clay quipped: "Age cannot wither her nor custom stale her infinite virginity." The number of Peggy's alleged lovers rose to two dozen. John Eaton challenged Campbell to a duel. Postmaster General Ingham accused Eaton's aides of plotting to assassinate him. Jackson threatened the Dutch ambassador after a perceived snub of Peggy by his wife. Mrs. Stephen Decatur, widow of the naval hero, received an anonymous letter. The Navy investigated Timberlake's handling of government funds and found a scapegoat in another purser, who committed the first assault on a President when he twisted Jackson's nose.

L'Affaire Eaton ended with the resignation of the entire Cabinet in 1831. The uproar had consumed the first two years of Jackson's Administration, during which time the Nat Turner rebellion and the birth of the abolitionist movement had gone unnoticed by all save John Calhoun, whose break with Jackson was also a break with nationalism. Resigning the Vice Presidency and returning to the Senate freed him to develop his secessionist doctrines of Nullification and States Rights, lending dark irony to the sobriquet of "Peggy of Troy."

The Petticoat Affair is one of those books that irritates even as it engrosses. The author, John F. Marszalek, a history professor at Mississippi State, is so bent on improving Peggy's image that he insists upon calling her "Margaret." Peggy, he decided, "played into the preconceptions"—i.e., it sounds like a hussy—but Margaret "gives readers a chance to look at her from a fresh point of view so they can evaluate the information about her more objectively." Thoughtful, perhaps, but too close to the current practice of renaming schools for my taste.

He also makes too many solemn pronouncements in praise of her liberated instincts—"daring to live her life as she pleased in ways considered improper," etc. This is probably a wise move for a male in today's feminist-dominated academia but it skirts the obvious: Peggy was a narcissist who made herself the center of male attention with woman's time-honored ploy of "Let's you and him fight."

Marszalek redeems himself, however, in a passage about the importance of returning social calls when he quotes the priceless double entendre by the nineteenth-century historian James Parton, who wrote in 1861: "The political history of the United States for the last thirty years dates from the moment when the soft hand of Mr. Van Buren touched Mrs. Eaton's knocker."

The American Spectator, April 1998
Book Review

"Take Me Out of this Ballgame"

Wait Till Next Year: A Memoir
by Doris Kearns Goodwin
(Simon & Schuster, 261 pages, $25)

D oris Kearns Goodwin is the orange-haired lady who wears two hats. The first, tilted well to the left, is a chic thirties number that identifies her as the author of *No Ordinary Time*, a view of the New Deal through a spotted veil that won the Pulitzer Prize and abetted Hillary Clinton's search for the spirit of Eleanor Roosevelt.

Goodwin's other hat, worn rakishly, is Dodger Blue with a big white B-for-Brooklyn, her hometown, identifying her as the designated tomboy in Ken Burns's *Baseball* who regaled us with her childhood memories of da Bums in the 1940's and 50's, when each heartbreaking pennant or World Series loss prompted the devastated faithful to assure each other, "Wait till next year."

Now she has recycled her baseball material, added a family story, and tossed in some political coming-of-age to produce a memoir, *Wait Till Next Year*—a title that, given her literary style, comes across as a threat to publish a second volume.

Memoirs, as opposed to autobiographies, derive their charm from the memoirist's flawed or deliberately incomplete recollections. The best practitioners heed Emily Dickinson's maxim, "Tell the truth, but tell it slant," creating the shadings, gaps, departures, telescoped time, white lies, and rationalizations that give memoirs their piquant complexity and ultimately reveal more about the writer than the stark truth ever could.

Unfortunately, Goodwin was raised on truth at its starkest: the inexorable long black lines of a filled-in baseball scorecard. Her father taught her how to mark them and she got so good at it that she could run her finger along her penciled hieroglyphics and tell him exactly what had happened in every moment of every game she listened to on the radio while he was at work. Not just batters and runs, but "whether a strikeout was called or swinging, whether the double play was around the horn, whether the single that won the game was hit to left or right. If I had scored carefully, using the elaborate system he had taught me, I would know the answers."

She not only scored carefully but saved all her old cards. She claims they helped her find her inner historian and polish her narrative powers, but that doesn't prevent her from writing passage after passage like this:

> The Phillies took a 6-1 lead in the third, due in part to an error by Robinson, who had struck out and hit into a double play in his first two trips at bat. In the fifth inning, it was Robinson again, this time as hero. He sent a triple to the wall which drove in one run, and then he scored a second run himself a few minutes later. In the eighth, the Dodgers scored three more runs, and the ninth inning ended with the game tied.

Other than being a baseball expert who saw some of the legendary greats play, Goodwin the memoirist does not have a very interesting story to tell. When she was still a child her family moved from Brooklyn to Rockville Centre, Long Island, where they settled contentedly into typical fifties suburban life. Only a writer with brilliant insights and a dazzling command of language can successfully tackle conformity and blandness, but Goodwin brings nothing to the task except the maniacal thoroughness of her scorecard technique. What she does with it proves that the play-by-play life is not worth living.

Working in the drugstore:

I pulled the long handle that drew the carbonated water, pushed the short one to add the syrup, and mixed in the cold milk. Finally, with a metal scoop dipped in steamy hot water to soften the hard ice cream, I added two scoops of vanilla or chocolate ice cream and a dab of fresh whipped cream.

How early television affected suburban family life:

For days, our parents discussed the dramatic reaction of Elaine's seventy-five-year-old grandmother, Amelia, to the kidnapping of the little girl, Patti, on *Search for Tomorrow*. Patti was the six-year-old daughter of Joanne Barron, a young widow whose rich in-laws had kidnapped the child after losing a custody battle. A desperate week-long chase ended as police helped Joanne pursue the child's kidnappers through woods, which, in the early days of live television, consisted simply of a dark area filled with a maze of music stands affixed with branches to represent trees. Finding Patti's shoes near a pond, the searchers feared she had drowned, though viewers knew she was still alive in the hands of her evil grandmother.

Inventing and playing a game called "McCarthyism" to learn first-hand about the dangers of unsubstantiated accusations:

When I was on the stand, Eileen Rust charged me with pretending that she and I were best friends while Elaine was away on vacation. She claimed that, within minutes after Elaine had departed for Crescent Lake, Maine, in the Friedles' packed Hudson, with their bird in a covered cage on the back seat, I had raced over to Eileen's house and told her that she was my best friend. For two weeks, she said, we had played together every day. But as soon as Elaine returned, I had lost interest in her. What Eileen said was true. "I didn't mean to hurt you," I cried, as I burst into tears.

Like many aging Democrats, Goodwin tends to wax nostalgic about the things that liberalism has ruined. Growing up a devout

Catholic, she thrilled to "the sounds of the Latin ritual. . . . I developed a lasting appreciation of the role that pageantry, ritual, and symbolism play in tying together the past and the present. . . . The Catholic world was a stable place with an unambiguous line of authority and an absolute knowledge of right and wrong."

Memories of what it was like to be a free-ranging hoyden on a bicycle in an all-white world bring her close to boastfulness. "If we never thought of our neighborhood as safe, that was because it never occurred to us that it could be otherwise. . . ." Further on she repeats herself: "It never occurred to us that something might happen to the bikes we left behind, even less that anything might happen to us. There was simply nothing to fear. No one in our town could remember the last time there had been a murder or even a violent crime."

She is careful never to dwell too long on the way things were. Loath to let anything, even baseball, overshadow her liberal bona fides, she periodically skids to a stop and issues oddly flat, politically correct statements that sound like canned PR: "Only later would I come to understand the true significance of Robinson's achievement: the pioneering role he played in the struggle for civil rights, the fact that, after his breakthrough, nothing would ever be the same—in baseball, in sports, or in the country itself."

Political considerations are only partly to blame for these sudden stops, however. She has trouble making graceful transitions from one subject to another and has to stick her arm out the window to signal her turns.

Her most abrupt switch comes when she is reading *David Copperfield* to her sick mother. Suddenly, out of the blue, the next paragraph begins: "As much as I loved Dickens, however, there was nothing in his vivid portrayals of nineteenth-century London to prepare my mind for the disturbing events of mid-century America."

This is how she gets to the integration battle at Little Rock Central High in 1957, but her stretch is enough to make Willie Mays say hey.

For all the perky good nature and freckle-faced smiles Goodwin projects on TV, *Wait Till Next Year* is notable for its utter lack of humor, unless we count her pubescent infraction of calling up the corner store and saying, "Do you have Prince Albert in a can? Better let him out."

Nor does she seem to have much confidence. In an Acknowledgments section worthy of a small book on the War of the Spanish Succession, she reveals that she researched her own memoir and spends three pages thanking all the people she consulted: schoolmates she had not seen in forty years whom she tracked down and interviewed; the current proprietor of the Rockville Centre delicatessen, the actress who played the beset heroine in *Search for Tomorrow*; the Sisters of St. Dominic, the Rockville Centre Historical Society, the Long Island Studies Institute; her regular research assistant; two old friends to help the assistant; and the son of one of the friends.

It's her scorecard syndrome again, but for all the maniacal research that went into this ostensibly personal book, it contains one big mistake. Listening to adults talking about President Truman and the war in Korea bored seven-year-old Doris because "the 1950 season was about to begin."

The baseball season starts in April; the Korean War started on June 24, 1950.

National Review, April 6, 1998
Book Review

"Hail to the Duds"

Star-Spangled Men: America's Ten Worst Presidents,
by Nathan Miller Scribner, 272 pp., $23)

A SK not what a book about failed Presidents is doing with a title like *Star-Spangled Men*. Did the author mean "star-crossed"? We shall never know. It's as big a mystery as the true story of James Buchanan's broken engagement written by the bachelor Buchanan and sealed for posterity until he changed his mind and ordered it destroyed on his death.

Nathan Miller, a former journalist and U.S. Senate staffer turned historian, presents his highly subjective picks "in order of their worstness, from the poor to the horrid," beginning with Jimmy Carter and ending with Richard Nixon.

Eight of Miller's picks made the cut for something they did, two for doing nothing. Of the latter, Calvin Coolidge was a whirling dervish compared to Benjamin Harrison (1889-93), the little sliver of a man who was the filling between the two administrations of Grover Cleveland.

He was the grandson of our ninth President, William Henry Harrison, who died a month after his inauguration. Benjamin might as well have. Since he believed in the supremacy of Congress he had no agenda. After filling his Cabinet with tycoons he sat back and placidly oversaw the Gilded Age while Speaker Thomas "Czar" Reed ran the country from the House.

He won the Electoral College but lost the popular vote, and it's easy to see why. Standing a pot-bellied five-foot-six on spindly legs, "he resembled nothing so much as a medieval gnome." Teddy Roosevelt called him "a cold-blooded, narrow-minded, prejudiced, obstinate, timid old psalm-singing Indianapolis politician."

Calvin Coolidge won people's affection for being a "character" but Harrison lacked even an offbeat humanity. He had what one wag called "a handshake like a wilted petunia" that caused severe problems on the campaign trail. His speeches were good and aroused enthusiasm, but "people came away silent and downcast after shaking hands with him." He received Oval Office visitors while standing up with his watch in his hand, presenting such a fishlike demeanor that aides cautioned, "Don't think he means to insult you. It's just his way."

His administration saw the passage of the Sherman Silver Purchase Act, the Sherman Anti-Trust Act, and the McKinley Tariff, and was the leading cause of the Panic of 1893 and the Populist movement, but Harrison himself was such a cipher that historians regularly write about these events without mentioning him. Nevins and Commager, the author reminds us, wrote a 685-page history of the United States in which his name never appears.

Franklin Pierce, a handsome, alcoholic mediocrity, did not, to put it mildly, inspire confidence. When the Democrats nominated him in 1852, his wife fainted and his 11-year-old son, Bennie, wrote from school, "I hope he won't get elected." Richard Henry Dana exclaimed, "My God! A third-rate county politician." Nathaniel Hawthorne wrote, "Frank, I pity you—indeed I do, from the bottom of my heart," and a Yankeefied Greek chorus of New Hampshire neighbors cackled, "Frank Pierce is goin' to be spread durned thin."

The gregarious, backslapping Pierce had served in the House and Senate without distinction, making him an ideal presidential candidate at a time when the nation was unraveling over a single issue. Slavery, writes Miller, had destroyed all possibility of consensus, so that anyone strong enough to deal with it would only make things worse. "Only nonentities who angered no one could attract enough votes to win." That meant Pierce, an unknown Northern Democrat with Southern sympathies, or as Nathaniel Hawthorne put it in a campaign biography: "He is deep, deep, deep."

His Whig opponent was Gen. Winfield Scott, hero of the

Mexican War, in which Pierce had disgraced himself by passing out in the saddle. Actually he had struck his groin on the pommel and fainted from pain but the Whigs taunted him as "the hero of many a well-fought *bottle.*"

Two months before his inauguration. Pierce and his wife saw their only son crushed to death in a train derailment. Always emotionally fragile, Jane Pierce now went off the deep end. God had taken Bennie, she told her husband, so that he would have no family cares to distract him from his political responsibilities. As First Lady she stayed in her room writing letters to the dead Bennie, leaving shallow, shallow, shallow Pierce to spread sweet reason over a nation that was reading the just-published *Uncle Tom's Cabin.*

The unsteady drinker was confronted by the high-wire acts of the slavery question. The Missouri Compromise and the Compromise of 1850 had each created one free state and one slave state to maintain an exact representational balance. Now came the Kansas–Nebraska Act with a "popular sovereignty" provision that promised to topple the earlier compromises. Pierce signed the Act, which alienated the North and led a grateful South to abandon him because he could not now get enough Northern votes to win re-election.

The only President to be denied renomination by his party was followed by another Northern Democrat with Southern sympathies, James Buchanan, who performed the ultimate balancing act: the states, he said, had no constitutional right to secede, and the Federal Government bad no constitutional right to stop them. Then he suppressed a Mormon insurrection in Utah, which must have come as a relief.

Miller's opinions are as slanted as those in that great apocryphal work, *An Unbiased Account of the Civil War from the Southern Point of View*. His go in the other direction.

Andrew Johnson, rated a great President by Harry Truman, risked impeachment for a lenient version of Reconstruction, arguing that black suffrage should be left to the states, which alone had the right to establish voter qualifications. Insisting, "I am right. I know I am right, I am damned if I do not adhere to it," he vetoed Radical Republican attempts to extend federal power and urged Southern states to reject the Fourteenth Amendment.

Johnson asked to be buried wrapped in an American flag with a copy of the Constitution for a pillow, but Miller never misses a chance to emphasize his only sin. He tells us that Frederick Douglass detected in Johnson "a bitter contempt" for blacks, quotes his many racial slurs, and offers his own supercilious explanation: "Johnson held the deep-seated antipathy to blacks common to most Southern poor whites."

Johnson's reputation has fluctuated, Miller notes. Formerly revered as a healer and a strict constructionist,

> in the wake of the civil-rights revolution of the 1960s—called the Second Reconstruction—the pendulum has swung the other way. Now, Johnson is viewed as a white supremacist whose attempts to preserve the South as a "white man's country'" undermined Reconstruction and condemned black Americans to a century of racism and repression. Because of this he belongs on my list of America's worst Presidents.

Because of this? Is Miller agreeing with the revised assessment or the pendulum? Hard to say in view of the odd outcroppings of political correctness found elsewhere: "Grant's greatest failure, however, was in protecting the rights of the former slaves, who had voted for him in overwhelming numbers." His *greatest* failure? Grant?

Furthermore, Coolidge's "record on control of the Ku Klux Klan and the appointment of blacks to office was bleak." Silent Cal had "strong views on race," Miller announces, and digs up an obscure Coolidge quote to prove it: "Biological laws show us that Nordics deteriorate when mixed with other races."

Non-racial quotes don't matter. He has Coolidge saying, "I do not care to run for President in 1928," instead of "I do not choose." And Jimmy Carter's "I'll never lie to you" becomes "I'll never tell a lie," He also contradicts himself, stating that Coolidge lacked "a wide-ranging mind," then revealing a few pages later that he translated Dante.

Finally, be ignores a solid achievement: the superb literary style of Grant's unghosted memoirs. Grant was such a born writer that his Gerald Ford–ish remark, "Venice would be a fine city if it were drained," had to be tongue-in-cheek.

The American Spectator, May 1998
Book Review

"Accidental and Forgotten"

Agent of Destiny: The Life and Times of
General Winfield Scott by John S.D. Eisenhower
(The Free Press, 464 pages, $27.50)

America has virtually forgotten General Winfield Scott. He was played once, for laughs, by Sidney Greenstreet in the 1940 movie, *They Died With Their Boots On*, but otherwise he has been relegated to the cutting-room floor of our national consciousness. We tend to have trouble getting interested in historical figures unless we can connect them to the Civil War, yet Scott commanded the future heroes of the Confederacy in the war with Mexico, winning territory that aggravated the debate over the expansion of slavery, and in his last years literally rose from his sickbed to organize the Army of the Potomac for Abraham Lincoln.

John Eisenhower, son of the thirty-fourth president, rescues our forgotten general from an undeserved obscurity in *Agent of Destiny*, a brilliantly conceived and executed study combining an affectionate biography of a complex man with military history so well-written that even the most detailed battle scenes are as vivid as a bang-up miniseries.

Winfield Scott was born in Virginia in 1786 to a comfortably-off family and educated at the College of William and Mary, but he was not a member of the planter class. America's first military hero to spend his entire life in the army began that life as a lawyer, which turned out to be a very wise mistake. Knowing his way around a cross-examination would come in handy whenever he was hauled up before a court-martial or board of inquiry to explain something that had issued from his baroque pen or his opera-buffa mouth—such as announcing publicly his intention to frag his commanding officer.

The officer in question was none other than Brigadier General James Wilkinson, betrayer of Aaron Burr and widely suspected of being Burr's co-conspirator. Scott, who as a lawyer had attended Burr's treason trial in Richmond, had developed a visceral aversion to Wilkinson that reawakened two years later when, as a 22-year-old army captain, he was assigned to Wilkinson's command at New Orleans. En route to his posting he stopped off in Natchez, where he blithely told a group of strangers at an inn that Wilkinson was a "liar and a scoundrel," and promised to "blow him up" if he ever served under him in combat. One of the strangers happened to be a friend of Wilkinson's and reported the incident. Scott served as his own lawyer at his court-martial, which luckily was composed of like-minded officers. The whole army detested Wilkinson, whose misdeeds ran the gamut from attempted treason to taking kickbacks from food contractors, but "the army being the army," they had to find Scott guilty of something, so they invented the crime of "unofficer-like behavior" to avoid the fatal "conduct unbecoming," and suspended him for a year.

Scott had entered the army on the spur of the moment in 1807 after a British warship fired on and boarded the American vessel *Chesapeake* to look for British deserters. President Jefferson called on the states to supply militiamen in case of war, and the patriotic Scott, still angry over Aaron Burr, volunteered. At this time the United States did not have a standing army, just volunteers that were called up and disbanded as needed, but with Britain making trouble again Jefferson decided to establish a permanent force. Liking military life and sensing his true destiny lay with it, Scott applied for and got a captain's commission. His first act as an officer was to visit a tailor. He loved uniforms and spent much time before the mirror admiring the swath he cut. Six-foot-five and ruggedly handsome, in uniform he was a beplumed, begilded "personification of Mars." Between patriotism and vanity he was happy to give up law for soldiering.

It was an ideal time to start a military career. With the British stirring up the Indians on the northern frontier, Scott could look forward to plenty of action and rapid promotions in what would become known as the War of 1812. When William Henry Harrison defeated several tribes at the Battle of Tippecanoe in 1811, James Madison and the "War Hawks" in Congress—Henry Clay and John Calhoun—decided to invade Canada and eliminate the British from North America.

Twenty-five-year-old Winfield Scott was promoted to lieutenant colonel. Able to read French, he studied Napoleonic artillery manuals and adopted the "flying artillery," a light gun that could be moved wherever it was needed. By 1813 he was a full colonel. When the British raided Buffalo the following year he cleared the Niagara frontier of British and Canadian troops, enabling Commodore Oliver Hazard Perry ("We have met the enemy and they are ours") to move his ships into Lake Erie.

Scott inspired another famous remark when he won the battle of Chippewa in 1814. As his troops stood their ground under fire, the British commander, used to facing our poorly trained volunteers, exclaimed: "Those are regulars, by God!" It was the first time American professional soldiers had defeated their British equivalents.

The Canadian invasion failed once the British had exiled Napoleon to Elba and could concentrate all their firepower on America. Attention shifted south when "Wellington's Invincibles" were sent to Maryland, whence they marched on Washington and burned the White House and Capitol.

The War of 1812 was diplomatically inconclusive—the Treaty of Ghent restored the status quo ante—but it enabled James Madison to rid the army of its Revolutionary War relics and raise young men to high command. Winfield Scott emerged a brigadier general and national hero at the age of 28.

He was married that year to a wealthy belle, Maria Mayo, the toast of Richmond, and started a custom that would last over a century when he took her on a honeymoon to Niagara Falls, "showing her the scenes of his former triumphs—no doubt in excruciating detail," writes Eisenhower. Given command of the Army's Third Department (northeast), he settled in New York and cultivated valuable friendships with Martin Van Buren and Governor De Witt Clinton. Life was perfect until Andrew Jackson challenged him to a duel. The trouble started when the touchy Jackson, who was commander of the Western Department, took umbrage at the Secretary of War for ordering one of his officers to Washington without sending Jackson a copy of the order. Overreacting as always, Jackson ordered his subordinates not to obey any War Department order unless it came through him.

Scott and De Witt Clinton were discussing Jackson's brouhaha at a dinner party when the word "mutinous" cropped up. No one was sure which man used it, but a guest who claimed he had overheard them wrote an anonymous letter to the newspaper saying that Scott had used it, and sent a copy of the letter to Jackson.

Scott was fearless but he lacked what Eisenhower aptly calls Jackson's "personal savagery." Accepting Jackson's challenge meant he would either be killed or kill a national hero, so he penned what started out as a timid withdrawal. First he claimed that dueling was against his religion. Next he invoked one of the florid classical allusions he could never resist, saying he did not want to be "an Erostratus, the killer of a defender of his country." Then, having lured Jackson into a bully's smirk, he did an abrupt about-face:

> "I should think it would be very easy to console yourself under this refusal by the application of a few epithets, such as coward, etc., to the object of your resentment, and I here promise to leave you until the next war to persuade yourself of their truth."

Jackson threatened to cut off his ears if they ever met, then let the matter drop. Later, as president, he grudgingly admired Scott for the way he handled the Nullification Crisis of 1832, which erupted when South Carolina challenged the legality of what the South called the

"Tariff of Abominations." Led by John Calhoun, a state convention nullified the tariff, ordered the Port of Charleston to cease collecting it, and threatened to secede if the federal government interfered.

Jackson sent Scott to reinforce the federal garrisons at Charleston, then stirred the pot in his typical fiery fashion, calling secession treason, mocking Calhoun's nullification theory as an "impractical absurdity incompatible with the existence of the Union," and sending Congress the "Force Bill" authorizing him to use troops to collect the tariff. Senator John Tyler delivered an impassioned speech in defense of states' rights and looked upon Scott, his fellow Virginian, as a traitorous Hun.

Scott, meanwhile, took the PR route. A natural schmoozer, he stroked the local officials, ordered his troops to use meticulous courtesy in dealings with citizens, and invited Charlestonians to visit Fort Moultrie for what today would be called an open house. Finally, a local sugar mill caught fire and Scott sent 300 unarmed troops to put out the blaze. Conquered by his charm and mesmerized by his godlike figure dripping gold braid, a grateful Charleston simmered down.

He had an unerring instinct for knowing when to get tough. In 1838, his friend, President Van Buren, sent him to Buffalo to prevent anti-British Americans from getting involved in the Canadian independence movement called the Patriots. Confronting an angry crowd in his full-dress uniform, he said:

> "I stand before you without troops and without arms, save the blade by my side. I am, therefore, within your power. Some of you have known me in other scenes, and all of you know that I am ready to do what my country and what duty demands. I tell you, then, except it be over my body, you shall not pass this line—you shall not embark."

Bitten by the presidential bug, he tried and failed to get the Whig nomination in 1840 and 1844, but both losses turned out to be providential. In 1840 the Whig candidate, William Henry Harrison, won the election but died after a month in office, creating so much upheaval and confusion in the government that the bill naming Scott General-in-Chief sailed through the Senate and was signed by his enemy, the dazed new president John Tyler, almost as an after-thought.

The election of 1844 led to the event that made Scott a legend. Henry Clay, the Whig candidate, was defeated by James Polk, an unbending advocate of the annexation of Texas whose victory was a virtual declaration of war on Mexico. Polk, a Democrat, saw Scott as a potential Whig challenger in 1848. To prevent him from achieving the battlefield glory that would appeal to voters, Polk kept him in Washington and put General Zachary Taylor in command of the Mexican expedition. Taylor went on to win the battles of Buena Vista and Monterrey while Scott in Washington was left to design the medal struck in Old Rough and Ready's honor.

The cold Polk, unmoved by martial glory, wanted only to gain the most territory with the least trouble. To this end he conceived a plan he called "masterful inactivity" in which American troops would simply occupy large areas of Mexico and wait for the Mexicans to offer peace.

A thunderstruck Senator Thomas Hart Benton reminded him that sedentary occupation, while inimical to the American temperament, was ideally suited to the Spanish, who "loved procrastination." Since they had outwaited the Visigoths for 300 years and the Moors for 700 years, said Benton, the only course was to capture the port of Veracruz and march on to Mexico City. Seeing his chance, Scott drew up a plan based on the conquest by Hernando Cortès, and Polk, knowing that no one else could pull it off, gave him command.

Always loath to risk lives unnecessarily, Scott rejected a frontal attack of Veracruz for an "active siege"—first cutting the city off and then bombarding it. Once he had a truce in place the Protestant Scott joined local officials for Catholic mass at Veracruz Cathedral and ordered his occupying troops to salute priests. It was a replay of his Charleston PR; insuring the rights of the Church would win the good-will of the Mexican people, and more important, isolate Santa Anna, who regularly robbed Church coffers.

American efforts to bribe Santa Anna into making peace went awry when he cheated Polk's representative out of $10,000, and so the war went on. At the battles of Contreras and Churubusco, Scott's forces under Lee and Beauregard captured seventy "Patricios," a band of Irishmen and Irish-Americans who had deserted the U.S. Army to fight for Mexico. Scott the lawyer weighed each case and decided to hang fifty of them. It was done immediately after Scott's men and forty Marines captured the fortress of Chapultepec. The moment the hangman saw the American flag rise over these ancient halls of Montezuma, he released the traps.

Scott's nickname, "Old Fuss and Feathers," was never more apt than when he made his triumphal entry into Mexico City. Riding at the head of his army to "Yankee Doodle," he was so resplendent in his gold epaulets and snowy plumes that even some Mexicans applauded him. A deputation of Mexican leaders did more, asking him to take over as dictator until order was restored. Being Scott, he was shocked; and being Scott, he was flattered.

Martial glory made him a presidential contender as Polk had feared, but the Whigs, finding more of the common touch in Zachary Taylor than in the imperious Scott, chose Old Rough and Ready over Old Fuss and Feathers in 1848.

Scott finally got the Whig nomination in 1852 but his campaign was a disaster, his first faux pas coming in his acceptance speech. To win Southern votes, the Whigs had included a platform plank pledging support for the Fugitive Slave Law. Scott, whose military mind equated the platform with an order, thought he had to obey all of it. Abandoning the careful statement Horace Greeley had written for him, he promised to do so, which promptly alienated Northern Whigs, who shouted, "We accept the candidate but we spit on the platform." Hanging the Patricios lost him the Irish vote, and his tendency to preen was exploited by the opposition, who recycled some of his bombastic gems, such as his famous order to "fire upon my rear." Democrat Franklin Pierce, who had served under him in Mexico, won by a landslide.

He was still General-in-Chief on the eve of the Civil War. Seventy-five years old, he had dropsy, vertigo, and a huge belly from a lifetime of gourmandizing, but the citizens of Washington, expecting invasion at any moment, were reassured by his mere presence despite his age and infirmities.

A deputation from Virginia tried to enlist his services for the Confederacy but he told them: "I have served my country under the flag of the Union for more than fifty years, and as long as God permits me to live I will defend that flag with my sword, even if my own native State assails it."

He was burned in effigy at the University of Virginia and denounced as a "free-state pimp" for arranging the guard detail that protected members of the Electoral College when they met in Washington in February 1861 to make Lincoln's victory official. He was also assigned to protect Lincoln at the Inaugural, but the president-elect, knowing him to be a Southerner, sent an aide to check him out. Sick in bed when the aide arrived, Scott struggled up and said: "If necessary, I shall plant cannon at both ends of Pennsylvania Avenue, and if any of the Maryland or Virginia gentlemen who have become so threatening and troublesome show their heads or even venture to raise a finger, I shall blow them to hell."

No one else in the army had the experience and know-how to do all the things that needed to be done. The biggest problem once Lincoln had called for volunteers was getting troop trains from the North through secessionist-minded Baltimore. Scott devised a system of spur lines to Washington and organized the recruits into an army, but in his heart he did not believe in the war.

"*Cui bono?*" asked the lawyer-soldier. "Fifteen devastated Provinces . . . to be held for generations by heavy garrisons, at an expense quadruple the net duties or taxes which it would be possible to extort from them, followed by a Protectorate or an Emperor."

Winfield Scott resigned from the Army in October 1861 and died in the hotel at West Point on June 1, 1866. He served fourteen presidents, thirteen of them as a general officer. A man who carried out the dreams and plans of other men, his legacy, writes John Eisenhower, lay in being the chief agent of Manifest Destiny whose victories made national expansion possible. When he was born the country consisted of thirteen states; when he died it filled the continent. "Yet he became a soldier almost by chance."

National Review, May 4, 1998
Book Review

"The Sucker Gene"

*Other Powers: The Age of Suffrage, Spiritualism, and the
Scandalous Victoria Woodhull*, by Barbara Goldsmith
(Knopf, 531 pp., $30)

W OMEN'S studies is truly phenomenal, something like
parthenogenesis. In 1957 *The Lunatic Fringe* by Gerald
W. Johnson contained a chapter about Victoria Woodhull,
but now she gets regular full-length biographies. I reviewed one three
years ago, and two more have been published so far this year.

Instead of a life-of, Barbara Goldsmith's *Other Powers* is a life-
and-times. She expanded it, she explains, because not placing
Victoria Woodhull in historical context would make her seem "merely eccentric and even aberrant." Sorry, but Victoria Woodhull is
eccentric and aberrant any way you slice her. What makes this book
work is the way it places *us* in historical context. From the nineteenth
century's version of the Psychic Network to the sexual predations of
the Rev. Henry Ward Beecher, the story of Victoria Woodhull is the
story of Bill Clinton's America.

Victoria Claflin was born in Homer, Ohio, in 1838 to a mother
who fell into trances and a father who brewed "Life Elixir" from
corn whisky, laudanum, and molasses and sold it to the yokels. A
deep vein of con artistry ran in the family. Deciding that Victoria and
her sister Tennie were clairvoyant, Buck Claflin took them on the
road, billing five-year-old Tennie as "The Wonderful Child." Soon
she was the golden goose; when word spread that she had correctly
predicted a fire and told a farmer where to find his lost calf, people

flocked to her to have their fortunes told and their futures predicted.

Victoria, who had real intelligence as well as street smarts, was harder to handle. All Buck wanted was a carnival performance but she went into deep trances and transfixed customers with riveting stares from her oddly slanted pale blue eyes. She predicted a shipwreck to the exact moment but she was far more interested in predictions about herself, as when her favorite spirit, Demosthenes, told her, "Your work is about to begin."

At 15 she married a drunk, Dr. Canning Woodhull, who moved to California for the Gold Rush; when that didn't pan out the resourceful Victoria took to the stage and part-time prostitution in San Francisco until her spirits told her to go home. Back in Ohio, she found that Buck's miracle cancer cure—mutton fat and lye—had burned off a woman's breast and Tennie had been indicted for manslaughter. Another sister, Utica, had become addicted to the Life Elixir she had helped brew and was now a nymphomaniac.

The family fled to Chicago where Buck ran a brothel for his younger daughters, blackmailing their clients by pretending to be the distraught father of a ruined virgin. Victoria set up shop as "Madame Holland," curing female complaint with mesmerism. Colonel James Blood brought his wife to be cured, only to fall under Victoria's spell himself. They ran away together and were soon joined by Tennie in New York, where they went after America's richest mark: Commodore Cornelius Vanderbilt, who believed in spiritualism.

The spiritualist craze had begun when the invention of the telegraph in 1842 made invisible energy commonplace and respectable. Civil War deaths provided a lot of spirits to contact, and disfranchised women embraced spiritualism as their only source of power: suffragist Elizabeth Cady Stanton, who wrote the Declaration of Women's Rights on a séance table used by the Fox sisters, was a believer; so were Mark Twain and Mrs. Horace Greeley.

Bamboozled by Victoria, who massaged his psyche, and Tennie, who aimed lower, Vanderbilt staked them to a brokerage for women investors. Aided by his stock tips, they made a fortune and attracted Susan B. Anthony, who persuaded Victoria to join the woman's suffrage movement. It wasn't hard to do: convinced that this was the work the spirit of Demosthenes had meant, she started a newspaper, *Woodhull & Claflin's Weekly*, to promote the cause—i.e., herself. It was through her contacts with suffragists, especially her starstruck admirer Isabella Beecher Hooker, that Victoria heard the rumors about Henry Ward Beecher, pastor of Brooklyn's Plymouth Church.

Beecher craved "unconditional approbation" but he had a mean streak. Given a fine pair of bays by a rich parishioner, he raced them for forty miles, until one horse dropped dead and the other was lame. Rejecting harsh Calvinism, he concocted a "feminized, romantic conception" of religion as a warm, indiscriminate bath of love. To be truly religious, he told his flock, you must sin, since Christ can't very well save you if you don't. There was no such thing as orthodoxy, he said; "Orthodoxy is my doxy and heterodoxy is your doxy."

Beecher's doxies were in the amen corner every Sunday, gazing up at him adoringly as he championed women's rights and called God "Mother." One of his mistresses made a deathbed confession to her husband that she had gone regularly to Beecher's study, letting herself in with the key he gave her, until she saw another woman entering with a key. She died and her husband kept quiet out of pride, but then Lib Tilton confessed *her* affair to her editor-husband Theodore, a political activist known to the suffragists, and Victoria Woodhull found out about it.

By now her megalomania was full-blown. Lionized as suffragism's most electrifying speaker, she called herself "the evangel" and claimed her spirits had told her she was destined to rule the world. In 1872 she was nominated for President by the far-out Equal Rights Party and advocated free love, calling marriage "the most terrible curse from which humanity now suffers." The radical suffragists ate it up but the moderates recoiled, especially Catherine Beecher. "You speak of free love with derision while your own brother practices it," Victoria accused. "I do not condemn him, I applaud him!"

Convinced that she could make Beecher come out publicly for free love, she dropped hints of the Tilton affair in her weekly. She was riding for a fall, and it came. Her reprobate family, which now included both husbands—Colonel Blood, whom she had married, and Dr. Woodhull, whom she had not divorced—as well as her utopian socialist lover, Stephen Pearl Andrews, exploded in a bloody brawl and ended up in police court.

The press had a field day with this Grant-era version of trailer-park trash. They had made Victoria an overnight celebrity and now they made her an overnight laughingstock. This was the same week that a beaming, teary-eyed Beecher celebrated his 25th anniversary as pastor amid flower-tossing children. Determined to bring the hyp-ocrite down with her, Victoria published "The Beecher–Tilton Scandal" on the front page of her weekly, sparing no salacious detail and "defending" the preacher with the doctrines of free love.

"Every great man of Mr. Beecher's type has had in the past and will ever have, the need for and the right to the loving manifestations of many women," she wrote. "With his demanding physical nature, passional starvation, enforced on a nature so richly endowed, is a hor-rid cruelty."

Victoria was arrested by Anthony Comstock for sending obscen-ity through the mails and spent Election Day in jail. The only person to stand by her was Isabella Beecher Hooker, but when Isabella tried to speak on free love from her brother's pulpit he got a doctor friend to say that the "satanic influence" of Mrs. Woodhull had made her temporarily insane, and committed her to an asylum.

The church held an examination of the Beecher affair. Lib Tilton was found guilty of plaguing the preacher with "inordinate affec-tion," and Beecher was reprimanded for allowing his "great generos-ity" to blind him to the perfidy of such women.

Elizabeth Cady Stanton called it "a holocaust of womanhood," but the best spin came in Theodore Tilton's unsuccessful civil suit against Beecher.

Eunice Beecher stood by her man. Her husband had been taken advantage of, she testified, because "it is hard to convince the dear, guiltless, simple-hearted man that such baseness and treachery could exist."

If you want to know what happened to Victoria and Tennie, read the book. In addition to being a brilliant evocation of the Gilded Age, it's the best analysis I have ever read of the sucker gene in the American DNA.

National Review, May 18, 1998
Book Review

"Gay Rites"

*A Pilgrim's Way: The Personal Story of the Episcopal Bishop
Charged with Heresy for Ordaining a Gay Man
Who Was in a Committed Relationship*, by
Walter C. Righter (Knopf, 192 pp., $22)

BACK in the Cold War, whenever I had to review an unreadable book, I always comforted myself with the thought, "Maybe the Russians will drop the Bomb and I won't have to finish reading this." Those were the days. This time, stuck with *A Pilgrim's Way: The Personal Story of the Episcopal Bishop Charged with Heresy for Ordaining a Gay Man Who Was in a Committed Relationship*, by the Rt. Rev. Walter C. Righter, author of the longest subtitle in publishing history, all I could hope for was an asteroid.

There's no real way to review it so I'll just tell you what, to the best of my knowledge, are the bare bones of the story and then I'll tell you why I had so much trouble pulling them together.

Righter's troubles with the traditional wing of the Episcopal Church began in 1972 when, as Bishop of Iowa, he broke a tie at the Diocesan Convention with a vote favoring the ordination of women. Soon after, he was asked to issue a statement on homosexuality. At this time the American Psychiatric Association held that homosexuality was treatable, and so he recommended that the church stick to redemption and leave therapy to the shrinks. When his stance drew praise from a conservative churchman, he says, "I recognized my error at once."

Thereafter he became a champion of gay rights, aligning himself with the liberal wing as the church moved inexorably toward the question of gay ordination. The problem was that there were no unequivocal rules to go by. The canon on ordination contained a "conscience clause" allowing bishops to refuse to ordain women if they could not bring themselves to do it, so the question of gay ordination was a collision waiting to happen.

After Bishop Paul Moore of New York ordained an out but unpartnered lesbian in 1977, conservatives, sensing the drift, pushed through a resolution stating that gay ordinations were "not appropriate" if the candidate was living with someone, and "recommended" that they not be done. This mealymouthed wording was all it took to activate the Emma Goldman streak in certain Anglican divines, namely Newark's Bishop John Spong, who ordained Robert Williams in 1989.

Williams, who stated publicly that Mother Teresa's life would be enhanced "if she got laid," was soon forced to resign. The House of Bishops voted to dissociate themselves from Spong's action, but Bishop Righter, by then retired and filling in as Spong's assistant bishop in the Newark Diocese, followed Spong's lead and ordained Barry Stopfel, who lived with his "life partner," as a deacon. The next year Bishop Spong ordained Stopfel as a priest. He was assisted by a proud Bishop Righter, who wore a rhinestone-studded red stole belonging to his new gay protégé, afterward laughing when someone asked him if he always consecrated in drag.

In 1994 Righter signed Spong's statement that homosexuality was "morally neutral." The following year he was accused of heresy by a small right-wing conspiracy—ten bishops, seven of them "from the South and Southwest" and four violently opposed to ordaining women. "There it was, the clear link between misogyny and homophobia," Righter mourns. His accusers, "not understanding the tides of history and focusing only on their fears, were attempting to stop the efforts of the church at inclusivity."

On a more hardball level they were trying, he thinks, to get at Bishop Spong through him. Spong was their real target but they were afraid to go after him first because of his media savvy and withering wit. To "get Spong but deny him the spotlight" they used Righter as a stalking horse.

Righter beat the heresy rap and made a triumphant appearance at last year's church convention with his wife, both of them sporting crosses beside the pink triangles on their name tags, and Mrs. Righter proudly driving around with her HRETIC vanity plates. The gay Barry Stopfel is now rector of St. George's in Maplewood, New Jersey, which has grown 30 per cent since he took over, thanks not only to gay and lesbian communicants but also to "young couples with small children who want an inclusive experience for themselves and their children."

Nobody got burned at the stake but you'll get burned if you shell out 22 bucks for this book. First, there's the literary style:

> I left him and walked outside, bumping into the Presiding Bishop as I went out the door. He stopped and said, "Are you all right?" I guess I must have come out of the door rather abruptly, with an angry look on my face. I nodded and said, "Yes, I came outside because I wasn't going to listen to any more of that bulls—." Sensing my anger and frustration, Ed said, "I'm glad you walked away." I deeply appreciated his compassionate response.

Second, there's that dreadful liberal earnestness. People who lack a sense of humor always tell a funny story by announcing how funny it is. Of Righter's wife, Nancy, we learn: "She took great delight in embarrassing friends by giving them condoms from GMHC (Gay Men's Health Crisis, a dynamic leader in AIDS-related work). We all laugh about the story, and it became a part of our family history."

Third, there's his teasing. Told as a boy about his aunt's gay husband, he says: "There was nothing judgmental in what I was told . . . later on in life I was to discover more about that story." What was he told? What did he discover? While awaiting trial he received a check from Bishop Desmond Tutu, who "stated clearly his convictions about homosexuality." What were they? Waiting to go on *Nightline*, he was so grateful for Ted Koppel's kindness that he vowed to remember him in a prayer from the new 1979 prayer book, "For Those Who Influence Public Opinion." I would dearly love to hear this invocation, wouldn't you? But he doesn't quote it.

Not only does he fail to finish what he starts, sometimes he doesn't even start it. What was life like in the Newark Diocese with the withering Bishop Spong? "For a variety of reasons, too complex to describe here, the cathedral people were out of synch with their bishop." IF NOT HERE, WHERE?!

Finally, there's the vortex that comes from not knowing how to put a book together. Reading this clotty, repetitive, subject-hopping mess is like trying to clear a jungle with a Dustbuster. Righter handles chronology like someone playing with the rewind and fast-forward buttons of a tape recorder. In the first chapter he tells us he got divorced without mentioning having got married, then waits eight chapters to reveal that he's been married not twice but three times, holding forth meanwhile on the Episcopal practice of forcing divorced priests to resign without making it clear that the canon was changed before he shed his wives.

The real definition of heresy can be found in his Acknowledgments when he thanks eight people at Knopf "who gave form and order to my work." This book was a trial by publishing and everyone involved sank like a stone.

National Review, June 1, 1998
Book Review

"Nice Jewish Girl"

Bitch: In Praise of Difficult Women, by Elizabeth Wurtzel
(Doubleday, 432 pp., $32.95)

ELIZABETH Wurtzel is a good girl who wants to go bad. In a way she already has; her first book, *Prozac Nation*, was an addiction memoir about her misadventures as a souped-up depressive, but hers was a passive kind of badness that involved letting trouble happen to her instead of actively causing it—i.e., nice badness.

Deciding that female assertiveness is the only way to go, she pulled herself together and vowed to be "one of the women who write their own operating manuals," only to discover that legions of feminist-fatigued women are reading *The Rules* to bone up on passivity. That did it. Now she's mad as hell and she's not going to take it any more, so she has gone whole hog and written an operating manual called . . . well, *Bitch*.

The trouble with women, she believes, is that we never go whole hog, but persist in our self-defeating struggle to combine female sexual power with niceness. In the Fifties we drenched ourselves in "Tabu" and "My Sin" and made nice. In the Nineties perfumes are named "Opium" and "Poison" but we're still making nice. Seeing a woman wearing today's black lipstick and nail polish, you'd expect to find her exsanguinating men; instead you find her in the self-help section of the bookstore looking for the latest volume on how to make your relationship work. It's no coincidence that the coping

genre is marketed exclusively to women; "Men don't need relation-
ship books because women will learn to behave," says Miss Wurtzel.
"If we're from Venus and they're from Mars, we'll learn to speak
Martian. We'll be good."

What keeps women toeing the line is fear of being called a bitch,
which the author defines as "anyone who decides that what she wants
and needs and believes and must do is more important than being
nice." Society now permits a woman to have a career and a sex life
but "as soon as she lays down the option of my way or the highway,
it's amazing how quickly everyone finds her difficult, crazy, a nightmare: a bitch."

The epithet—or accolade—is so easy to come by that even
humanitarians can qualify. "Anytime a woman projects an intense
personality, she is *somebody's* idea of a bitch," though not necessari-
ly Miss Wurtzel's. She maintains that a bona-fide bitch must also be
sexy, which lets out the intense Eleanor Roosevelt (true: bitch is the
one thing I never heard her called) as well as the pseudo-intense Janet
Reno and Donna Shalala, who are ponderous and meddlesome,
respectively. As long as Clinton's Cabinet contains women like these,
she says, "then as far as I'm concerned it's still half-empty."

Wearers of the Scarlet B run the gamut from Madonna and
Courtney Love to "icy young blondes of the Grand Old Party" such
as Laura Ingraham. Their common ancestress is Delilah, "the first
woman to be blamed simply for being sexy" and the most interest-
ingly presented woman in this book. Miss Wurtzel, educated at an
Orthodox Jewish high school, really knows the Old Testament.
Legend holds that Delilah was a prostitute hired to frame Samson, but
"the Bible is fast to identify women who ply their wares in the sex
trade," and Delilah is not so identified. Moreover, she is introduced
with the words, "Her name was Delilah," instead of "Delilah was her
name," the former being the Hebraic structure that indicates a
respectable person.

Comparing them to a modern-day Israeli-Palestinian couple, the
author believes Samson and Delilah were married and that she was
fed up with trying to make their relationship work. "She was in love
with a deadly weapon and got tired of competing with his solo

intifaddeh." Jealous of his outlet for rage while she could only worry and seethe, she turned him over to the Philistines to end the tension and exchange passivity for power: "She destroyed him to create herself," and posterity, unable to tolerate such ruthless autonomy in a woman, punished her by making her a symbol of female evil.

Miss Wurtzel is devastating on the First Lady. "Hillary Clinton truly did choose marriage *über alles*. That she has come to stand for hardheaded, hardhat feminism is just ridiculous" in view of the fact that "she's just some guy's loudmouthed wife." She's "like a parent living through a child . . . a power sneak-binger . . . a female eunuch—possibly in Hillary's case, even minding the harem." What makes people think of her as a bitch "is not that she's a nontraditional First Lady, but that she's so utterly traditional"—yet steely. In sum, her bitchiness consists of one thing: "She has the smugness of the one he comes home to."

As for Just My Bill, Miss Wurtzel socks him with the two best lines in the book:

"Clinton . . . has made being full of s— not just a mere peccadillo, but in fact the greater part of his personality."

"At the moment we live in a mea culpa hell. Any idiot can say I'm sorry, but it takes a real mensch to say I'm not sorry, or better still, to just shut up."

The last thing the world needed was one more word on Sylvia Plath and Zelda Fitzgerald, but Miss Wurtzel supplies about 25,000. Brilliant and funny, she is also the most undisciplined writer since Thomas Wolfe, more exhausting even than Camille Paglia, a diamond in the rough who frequently stops writing and simply talks on paper:

> Now, me, I'm not a femme fatale. Like Delilah I think I just cart too much, I fall in love and I get stupid as bubble bath. Or perhaps my emotional involvement is just overdetermined: I get obsessed and overwrought about whatever man comes along because I don't know what to do with myself, with the excess of self I drag around like a hundred and twenty pounds of dead weight. Whether the emotion is true or truly wished for, anytime anything resembling love comes my way, it makes a fool of me.

Churning out landslides of prose leads her into serious errors, like "balling out" for "bawling out" and her claim that Mary Queen of Scots was not beheaded. She is prone to non-stop sentences—the longest one in the book weighs in at 124 words—and garrulous asides in parentheses: "(Chaplin's second wife, whom he wed when she was fifteen and knocked up, was actually named Lilita, a fact not unknown to Nabokov, whose literary legacy was just a vowel away; by the time Chaplin married his last wife, Oona O'Neill, he was 54 and the bride was his oldest yet—at seventeen.)"

She also plunks a 245-word parenthetical disquisition on O.J.'s poor spelling in the middle of her Nicole-as-bitch analysis; asks five or six rhetorical questions in a row (a device of women writers who are still afraid of "unfeminine" declarative sentences); double-emphasizes her opinions with "Look," and "See," and "I mean"; and sums up an obvious line of argument by writing "Blah, blah, blah." She indulges in the Bijou syndrome, dragging us through one movie synopsis after another to illustrate her point; and the Tin Pan Alley syndrome, quoting miles and miles of rock lyrics that mean nothing to anyone over thirty unless you happen to work in ASCAP's permissions department, in which case you're still counting up what she owes.

But her worst excess comes at the very end of her tightly printed 432-page opus. In an Acknowledgments section worthy of a modest work on the War of the Spanish Succession, she thanks 58 people and the staffs of three hotels. What kind of bitch would do that?

The American Spectator, July 1998
Book Review

"Long Live *Punctilio*!"

*Empire by Default: The Spanish-American War and
the Dawn of the American Century* by Ivan Musicant
(Henry Holt, 740 pages, $35)

C uba was a gleam in presidential eyes long before nearsighted
Teddy Roosevelt packed six extra pairs of spectacles to make
sure he could see San Juan Hill. Thomas Jefferson wrote, "I
have ever looked on Cuba as the most interesting addition which
could ever be made to our system of states," a sentiment echoed by
John Quincy Adams, who regarded the annexation of the island as a
natural follow-up to our acquisition of Spanish Florida and a necessary step in establishing the newly proclaimed Monroe Doctrine.

Franklin Pierce nearly went to war to acquire Cuba and even considered buying it from Spain to placate the South, whose long-stand-
ing dream of annexing it as a slave state remained alive through most
of the Civil War. It was not until 1865 that all talk of Cuba finally
ceased, leading the anti-expansionist reformer, Carl Schurz, to say
with evident relief, "One South was enough."

But Souths have a way of rising again. By the second administration of Grover Cleveland, Cuba was exciting new attention. A revolution broke out that quickly degenerated into a Pink Panther movie
after the death of Jose Marti in 1895 left it without a sane leader.
Under the outlandish "General" Gomez, the freedom fighters sought
to make Cuba worthless to Spain by seeing to it that there was nothing to export. To this end they burned the big sugar, tobacco, and cof-

fee plantations, and shut down the factories by proclaiming that anyone who went to work would be shot.

Spain responded by sending General Valeriano Weyler y Nicolau, son of a German father and a Spanish mother, dubbed "Butcher" Weyler by William Randolph Hearst's *New York Journal* after he instituted his "reconcentration" policy of moving the entire rural population into the cities, burning their fields and killing their animals so that the rebels would not be able to live off the land. Now there was not only nothing to export, but nothing to eat.

Meanwhile, in the Philippines, another revolution was in progress. Led by Emilio Aguinaldo, the Filipinos did not rebel against Spain per se but against the Catholic monastic orders who ran the islands like medieval Inquisitors. The monks had virtually enslaved the natives, forcing them to work on church lands and hanging them by their thumbs or crushing their bones if they disobeyed. In retaliation the freedom fighters captured the monks and boiled them in oil or roasted them on spits.

It was "Spanish colonialism at its repulsive worst," writes naval historian Ivan Musicant, "a combination of brutality, beneficence, and ineptitude" that was lumbering to a halt after four hundred years, but Spain would not and could not admit it. Her blind spot grew out of two unique attitudes. Her "*punctilio*," that native blend of fierce pride, unbending honor, and supercilious inertia that comprised the Spanish psyche would not permit her to consider granting independence or even dominion status to her few remaining colonies. Moreover, any change in their status would have amounted to blasphemy: "It was an enduring part of Spanish mythology that the empire had been bestowed by God as a reward for the liberation of the Iberian peninsula in 1492 from Islam."

When the sui generis United States, part fresh kid and part gentle giant, comes up against iron tradition and anachronistic mayhem of this magnitude a memorable story is sure to result. It is told by Ivan Musicant in *Empire by Default*, a soup-to-nuts account of the Spanish-American War that captures the texture of 1890's life so well and presents the players so vividly that readers can produce their own mental movie.

Scene: The "Star-Spangled Banner" is played at the end of every vaudeville show to the cheers of Hearst-hyped patrons who see the Spirit of '76 in every independence movement, no matter how chaotic or far-flung. Cut to Congressman "Uncle Joe" Cannon, later Speaker of the House, bemoaning a weak president's slavish devotion to public opinion: "McKinley's ear is so close to the ground it's full of grasshoppers." Cut to the insomniac William McKinley, Civil War veteran, praying and weeping and taking his epileptic wife's sedatives to silence the voice-overs: Minister to Madrid James Russell Lowell intoning poetically, "The gravity of the Cuban situation is hardly yet understood in Spain," and U.S. Consul Fitzhugh Lee, nephew of the Confederate general, urging him to send a battleship to Havana to rescue American citizens in case the insurgent riots grow worse.

The arrival of the *Maine* was billed as a diplomatic gesture symbolizing a new era of understanding. For this reason her skipper, Capt. Charles Sigsbee, could not drag the harbor bottom or use picket boats as he wanted, but he did mount a nighttime quarter watch instead of the usual anchor watch after reading the violently anti-American handbills circulating in the city.

Shortly after nine on the night of February 15, 1898, as the last notes from the Marine bugler's taps faded away, Sigsbee heard what sounded like a rifle shot, followed by a metallic roar. Of the 355 officers and men on board, 96 survived, thanks in large part to Spanish naval vessels that sped to the scene and showed the wounded every courtesy and solicitude. Sigsbee, who believed then and ever afterwards that his ship had been sunk by a mine, telegraphed the War Department, "Public opinion should be suspended until further report," but it did no good. Hearst's banner headline read: "Remember the Maine, to Hell with Spain!"

Diving teams from both nations inspected the wreck. Spanish divers reported that the hull plates forward of the boilers were bent outward, indicating an internal explosion, but said nothing about the damage to the keel: It was bent into an inverted V, the apex thrusting upward through the deck, indicating an external explosion. A Washington newspaper poll of naval officers found a majority believed it had been an accidental internal explosion. An American torpedo officer said it was spontaneous combustion, citing the position of the powder magazine next to the coal bunkers. "He was absolutely right," says the author, "but would anyone of consequence listen?"

Eyewitnesses were heard from. A Spanish naval officer saw a "brilliant illumination of colored gases" consistent with an exploding powder magazine; the *Maine*'s watch officer saw no gas bubble or water column consistent with a mine, nor did anyone see the surest evidence of a mine: dead fish on the surface. No one but the American public believed that Spain had officially sanctioned the placement of a mine, and the possibility that a few freewheeling Spaniards had taken it upon themselves to plant one was genetically unthinkable: There were no freewheeling Spaniards; rogue patriots are not consistent with *punctilio*.

The possibility that the noble Cuban freedom-fighters had planted a mine to start a war between the U.S. and Spain, and that it had set off a second explosion in the powder magazines, was inconsistent with American public opinion (and perhaps the author's; he doesn't mention it). No American politician would have dared cast suspicion on the freedom-fighters, but the Court of Inquiry hinted as much in its verdict: The explosion was caused by a mine "planted by persons or agencies unknown," but Spain was held responsible only because it had occurred in a Spanish harbor; she was never officially accused of planting it.

As war fever mounted, McKinley made one last peace effort, consulting secretly with Archbishop John Ireland in hopes of getting Pope Leo XIII to wield his unparalleled influence over Spain, all the while worrying that his Protestant midwestern constituency would find out about it. The Vatican plan fell through when Congress passed and McKinley signed a Joint Resolution authorizing U.S. intervention.

The author's account of the land war has its moments, but much of it seems merely dutiful and sometimes it slips into a drone. There's a logical explanation for this. Musicant, winner of the Samuel Eliot Morrison Award for Distinguished Naval History, is a blue-water man whose heart is clearly in his magnificent account of the war at sea.

Anyone who is disgusted with Pat Schroeder's politically correct navy will get a thrill up the spine and a lump in the throat reading these descriptions of a time when America's sailing men were wind-whipped, not pussy-whipped, and morale was in the stratosphere. Be prepared to wipe away a few tears.

At Manila Bay, the moment Commodore George Dewey's immortal order, "You may fire when you are ready, Gridley," was passed to the fleet, "bands in the *Olympia* and *Baltimore* began playing "The Star-Spangled Banner." At the last note the men gave a rousing cheer and firing commenced."

It was not the only music heard that day. Aboard the *Raleigh* a young lieutenant went below deck to check on the crew in the powder division and found them singing a new popular song. He had never heard it before but his instincts told him it would do for this war what the rebel yell had done for the last one:

> "Men, we've got 'em on the run. I don't know what that tune is you were singing but it's a corker; keep it up. I want the music to reach the upper deck." And through the rest of the battle, the strains of "There'll Be a Hot Time in the Old Town Tonight" rolled up through the ammunition hoists and cheered the men at the guns.

When plans were being made to blockade Santiago, Lt. Richmond P. Hobson conceived a plan to block up the harbor by sinking a collier containing 2,000 tons of coal, "corking the Spanish like a bug in a bottle." The mission, which involved setting off explosives with split-second timing, would be carried out today by Navy Seals, but Hobson had to do it with seven volunteers:

> The signal had gone from the flagship seeking volunteers "for a desperate and perhaps fatal expedition." From the *Iowa* came the reply, "Every man on this ship wants to go"; the *Texas* responded with, "Two-thirds of the . . . crew are fighting for first place." Hobson was besieged with junior officers begging for a chance at death or glory.

By contrast the Spanish navy was the mouse that roared punctiliously. Said Capt. Charles Sigsbee, "In everything they did, except in respect to etiquette, the practiced nautical eye could not fail to note their inferiority." One battleship sailed without guns because the engineers had not finished fitting her out. Another had no hoisted coaling baskets; someone forgot to load them so the men had to carry coal on board in sacks, which took days instead of hours. When a cruiser was found to be admitting water through her propeller shaft the crew plugged it with cement, making it impossible to use her engines; she had to be towed to the Philippines.

The sorriest vessel was the *Vizcaya*, whose bottom had not been scraped. A blanket of barnacles and a full lawn of sea grass as thick as a vegetable garden cut her speed in half and used up so much coal that she, too, had to be towed, but she was carrying the wrong type of towing equipment so she yawed her way across the Atlantic in a tangle of parting lines. She was, said Vice Admiral Pascual Cervera, good for "nothing but a buoy."

The author's portrait of the Spanish is a fascinating study of the reactionary mind. Cervera's orders, "cooked up in the fantasy world of ministerial chambers" in Madrid, were to "destroy Key West and blockade the entire east coast of the United States." The Minister of the Admiralty was certain of victory because, he said, the Spanish navy was made up of proud Spaniards while the American navy consisted of "immigrants without a past." (This has echoes of "One Southerner can lick twenty Yankees" and "Gentlemen always fight better than rabble.") Cervera, a rare realist, shook his head. "It is fruitless and useless. It is Don Quixote. We go to a Trafalgar." "God bless you," the minister said serenely.

Nonetheless, the reader of *Empire by Default* comes to admire Spanish *punctilio*, recognizing it as the "civility" we crave today, an antidote to our spiritual grunge. As American sailors of 1898 discovered after the United States inflicted a crushing defeat on Spain at Santiago Bay, *punctilio* arouses a universal emotion: When a good loser makes a grand gesture the humanity of every man is exalted.

Seeing a badly wounded Spanish captain in a shattered lifeboat, Capt. "Fighting Bob" Evans of the *Iowa* hoisted a canvas chair into the boat to bring him up. When he stepped on deck "he slowly straightened himself up, and with an effort unbuckled his sword belt, kissed the hilt of his sword, and with a graceful bow presented it to Evans, who refused it to the cheers of his battleship's crew."

That day Adm. William T. Sampson cabled Washington: "The fleet under my command offers the nation as a Fourth of July present the whole of Cervera's fleet." The world marveled over the casualty figures. Spain lost 323 men; the United States—exactly one.

"It hardly mattered that the Spanish still held out in Santiago, or in Havana for that matter," writes Musicant. "The battle had wrested for the U.S. Navy total control of the sea, and thus, according to Mahanian doctrine, had won the war in an afternoon."

National Review, August 17, 1998
Book Review

"Hot for Coolidge"

Coolidge: An American Enigma, by Robert Sobel
(Regnery, 462 pp., $34.95)

F INDING that elusive last piece of the puzzle that was Calvin
Coolidge has frustrated historians for 75 years. Robert Sobel
fares no better than the rest, but he has a knack for digging up
obscure quotes that illustrate the unusual scope of the frustration. The
best of these comes from a now-forgotten journalist who called
Coolidge "one of the two great enigmas of the first third of the twentieth century, the other being the popularity of the play *Abie's Irish
Rose.*"

Sobel, a professor of business history at Hofstra University, has
put together a book that, like Coolidge himself, makes no claim to be
other than what it is. He readily admits that he did no original
research and has no new revelations to offer, but his familiarity with
secondary sources and his expertise in mining them for their most
trenchant contributions make *Coolidge: An American Enigma* both
an informative text and a consistently readable story.

He likes Coolidge, both the man and the President, and defends
him with conviction. The most widespread libel he demolishes, committed by hostile Wilsonian historians eager to paint Coolidge as a
philistine, are the words, "The business of America is business." This
statement has taken root in quotation dictionaries and been enshrined
in *A Pocket History of the United States* by the exalted duo of Nevins
and Commager, but it's wrong.

The words were taken out of context from a speech entitled "The Press under a Free Government" that Coolidge delivered to the American Society of Newspaper Editors on January 17, 1925. Considering the question of whether the dual role of a newspaper as both a purveyor of information and a profit-making business present-ed a conflict, Coolidge opined that it did not. On the contrary, the duality was representative of national life as everyone understood it. "After all," he said, "the chief business of the American people is business," and "the chief ideal of the American people is idealism."

The next day the *New York Times* headline read, "Coolidge Declares Press Must Foster America's Idealism." The subhead read: "Financially Strong Journalism, He Says, Is Not Likely to Betray the Nation." No newspaper quoted him as saying, "The business of America is business." The distortion, says Sobel, is the work of histo-rians, "who dropped 'chief' to make it sound even more pro-business."

Historians who relish the picture of Coolidge as a cold fish never mention that he always kissed his father on arrival and departure, even when trailed by the White House press corps. Throughout his life his wrote his father long intimate letters, including one when he was a struggling young lawyer that contains the much-quoted line, "I see no need of a wife so long as I have my health." This has been offered as proof of his bleak nature but it was probably one of his deadpan quips. He expected people to be clever enough to supply the requisite mental picture of the Invalid on His Honeymoon, but like all dry wits he expected too much.

At 33 he married a woman who would one day be called the most charming First Lady since Dolley Madison. Grace Goodhue was a scintillating brunette with a big sweet smile who loved people. They met in Northampton, Massachusetts, where he practiced law and pol-itics and she taught at a school for deaf-mutes, which led to some confusion when Coolidge was mistaken for one of her students.

The legend of Silent Cal has not been exaggerated but neither has it been explained. Here was a man who never went out of his way to ingratiate himself with voters, who never slapped a back or flashed a smile, who never pressed the flesh except with the greatest reluctance and never gave any outward indication that he felt anyone's pain but his own at being forced to stand in receiving lines, yet he won election after election. What was his secret?

Sobel considers the familiar theories—the famous "Coolidge luck" that put him in the right place at the right time, such as the Massachusetts governor's chair during the Boston police strike; the isolationism of a war-weary electorate who found symbolic justification in his withdrawn personality—but the most intriguing speculations center on Coolidge's origins.

At the time of his birth in 1872, Plymouth Notch, Vermont, consisted of three public buildings—a church, a school, and a general store run by his father—and three private dwellings, one of which housed the Coolidges. Untouched by post–Civil War social changes such as European immigration, its inhabitants were all descended from seventeenth-century colonists, but to say that the hamlet was cut off from America is to ignore the fact that it was also cut off from Vermont, a "notch" in the most literal sense that was virtually inaccessible.

In short, Coolidge was from Brigadoon. "There was nothing to suggest to a boy that conditions would change violently," he wrote in his autobiography. "I never mistrusted that history was not all made. . . ." These are the words of a crustaceous provincial but they are also the words of a man immune to the guilt and self-doubt that produce the smarmy politician driven by a need to be loved. Perhaps, for one brief shining moment, American voters caught on.

Coolidge: An American Enigma suffers from an embarrassment of enigmas. Sobel does not know what to make of Coolidge's devoted aide, the remarkably self-effacing Frank Stearns, who vanished immediately after Coolidge's death in 1933 and, shunning countless chances to ride his White House experience to success in his own right, died six years later in the obscurity he sought.

Coolidge himself was puzzled by Stearns, writing his father, "I do not know why he has been so interested in my success but he has been very much so." Sobel states that Stearns "would have fallen on his sword for Coolidge," but he is unable to explain why except to say that both were Amherst men: "In that time, the loyalties graduates felt for their colleges and fraternities ran deep. Stearns's dedication to Coolidge may have derived, in part at least, from his passion for his school." Then, seeming to realize this won't do, he throws in the towel: "Suffice it to say, Frank Stearns was an enigma, much like the man to whom he was devoted."

It does not suffice. Stearns provided a clue to his own psychology in his description of his early dealings with Coolidge: "The entire absence of effort to impress me was different from the action of any politician that I had ever met, and it finally interested me so much that I began to look him up." This sounds like someone who craves punishment seeking out someone capable of supplying it. Sobel missed an opportunity to analyze an early exemplar of a type our era has come to know all too well: the slavish political acolyte.

Sobel's other unnecessary enigma is the extroverted Mrs. Coolidge. "What a lively, inquisitive person like Grace Goodhue saw in Coolidge is difficult to imagine," he writes, making no effort to imagine beyond listing Coolidge's virtues—hardworking, honest, decent, trustworthy, and "difficult to imagine as a philanderer"—and concluding, "Coolidge unquestionably loved her deeply."

All this is true, but Sobel overlooks the illusion cherished by all extroverts, the challenge they can never resist, the bet they constantly make with themselves: that they can bring an introvert "out of his shell." If Grace ever admitted this to Coolidge he no doubt told her what he told the woman who bet that she could make him say more than two words: "You lose."

The American Spectator, September 1998
Book Review

"House Mothers"

*24 Years of House Work . . . and the Place Is Still a Mess:
My Life in Politics* by Pat Schroeder
(Andrews McMeel, 244 pages, $24.95)

*Representative Mom: Balancing Budgets, Bill, and Baby in the
U.S. Congress* by Susan Molinari with Elinor Burkett
(Doubleday, 291 pages, $23.95)

Retiring congresswomen Pat Schroeder and Susan Molinari have come out with Beltway memoirs under two separate titles, but they could just as well have been published as one book called *Declining and Falling Made Easy*.

It matters not at all that Schroeder is a Colorado Democrat and Molinari a New York Republican. Such distinctions have no meaning on the barren heath of the mediocre female mind, and that is the terrain we are asked to traverse. Nothing soars here, nothing. Both books writhe and heave with that terrible earthbound ordinariness of women that Nietzsche deplored when he said, "Wives and children have destroyed more artists than the cholera."

The authors have such similar stories to tell and so many attitudes in common that it's hard to remember which book you're reading. Both are beset by men behaving cluelessly, men who don't take them seriously, and men who are "threatened by strong women," a category in which they persist in placing themselves thanks to a shared inability to grasp the definition of *nerve-wracking*.

Their most interesting common ground is their loathing of Newt Gingrich. To Schroeder he's merely a neurotic prone to projection ("If he accused someone of a certain behavior it usually meant he was doing it himself"), but Molinari strongly suggests that he's insane, citing his identification with Napoleon, his excited claim that Mongolians in yurts are reading the Contract With America, and those times when "He'd call Bill and other members of the leadership and weep openly while talking about resigning because saving the world was simply too heavy a burden for him to manage."

Both brag about being terrible cooks and housekeepers and take pains to make themselves sound like Oscar Madison. Molinari leans heavily on the phrase "total chaos" and defines dinner at home as Chinese take-out eaten straight from the cartons. Schroeder, who reheats a lot of leftover one-liners, claims that "My children thought a balanced meal was holding a hamburger with both hands," and excuses her messy housekeeping with her tiresome pun, "I was doing House work elsewhere."

Since both are officially liberated they don't bother to watch their language, but their vulgarity is uninspired and their scatologisms clichéd. Both are "pissed off" a lot. Schroeder uses "scumbags" and "rat's ass" but retreats into a version of ladylike restraint in a chapter entitled "Congressional Bulls--t." Molinari comes right out with the S-word and also uses an expression that, while not obscene, is nonetheless jarring coming from a woman: Instead of going somewhere, she "drags ass." This idiom, like "chow down," is customarily used only by teenage boys and young enlisted men traveling in packs.

The most oppressive similarity between their books is the smug satisfaction they take in having created a Congress that is sinking helplessly into the muck of "women's issues" in the most literal sense. There are children, children everywhere—seen, heard, nasty, brutish, and short. From Pat Schroeder wiping apple juice off herself at her swearing-in to Susan Molinari's baby crawling down the House aisle, the storied chamber now resembles the women's restroom at a Greyhound bus station.

The atmosphere is humid—and in Molinari's case, fetid. During a debate on funding the National Endowment for the Arts, Molinari's daughter Susan Ruby escaped from the GOP side and crawled over to the Democrat side. When she realized her baby was missing, Molinari panicked and went looking for her in defiance of the time-honored rule that representatives never cross the aisle in the middle of a debate. Meanwhile, Rep. Nita Lowey (D-N.Y.) waylaid the errant baby and, also ignoring the rule, crossed the chamber to return her to her mother. They met in the middle.

"We shared a hug," Molinari gushes, "then looked at each other and laughed. Ideology, even party loyalty, became irrelevant. A really important and pressing matter was at hand: Susan Ruby needed her diaper changed."

That's the general idea, now to the nuts and bolts. Both women are nutty and both bolted, but Schroeder is by far the more obnoxious. Her book is one long, snide wisecrack, except that it's not very long: The print is primer-size in keeping with her intellectual level. She has the worldview of a teenage diarist, unblessed by analytical thinking or even simple staying power. Except when she discusses her obstetrical history—unabridged evocations of pain, blood, and suffering at the hands of medical misogynists—she skimps on details and avoids dwelling too long or too deeply on anything. The struggle over the Equal Rights Amendment that consumed the seventies gets about two pages, but hey, it lost, so what can you say?

More to her taste is the flippant anecdote: "I did have great neighbors in Virginia I could call on if my housekeeper collapsed. I never knew how to thank them, so I would send flowers. One day the florist asked why I was always sending flowers to women!"

All of her anecdotes are crafted around her self-image as a feminist Scourge of God with a cute sense of humor. When Colorado's Cherry Blossom Princess needed a male escort for the festival, Schroeder donned a bunny suit and did the honors as Peter Rabbit. Later she wore the suit for Chinese children at the U.S. embassy's Easter egg hunt in Peking, answering her critics with the observation that the U.S. Congress would be a better place if members wore bunny suits instead of power suits.

She has the bumptious egotism of the *miles gloriosus*, the stock character of the braggart soldier in Renaissance literature. Soon after her arrival in Congress in 1973, a group of conservative Southern Democrats invited her to a prayer breakfast, "perhaps thinking it would tame me." Asked to say a few words, she proposed an Eleventh Commandment: "Thou shalt not bulls--t thy colleagues." The conservatives sat stock-still, pale and shocked, she notes proudly, and later complained to the media that she had violated their sensibilities.

Her trademark is a condescending, heavy-handed sarcasm that she mistakes for slashing wit. Recalling the time Oliver North named her one of the 25 most dangerous people in America, she says: "I like to imagine this brave marine sleeping with a nightlight because I'm on the prowl."

When she emerged as a fierce opponent of the Vietnam war, John Wayne paid her a visit to keep her on track. "Imagine," she carols, "this little gnat, me, was such a worry to the hawks that they sent John Wayne after me!" She claims he offered her a cigarette lighter inscribed "F--k Communism—John Wayne" that she declined to accept, much to the disappointment of her husband, who pointed out how valuable it would be someday as a celebrity artifact. It would also be valuable as proof of this story.

Equally suspect is her claim that at a victory party after her initial election to Congress in 1972, a reporter she fails to name asked her daughter, then two, what she wanted to be when she grew up. The child piped, "I want to be a congresswoman like my mother so I can say 'f--k' and 's--t' and not get in trouble," then turned to Schroeder and said, "I told you I didn't want to come." Forgive a spinster's ignorance, but do two-year-olds speak in such complete sentences? Schroeder is careful to note that her daughter was "a very precocious age two," but that means nothing coming from an American mother.

The kind of mother Schroeder is comes through loud and clear in a blithe confession about the problems of juggling career and homemaking. A less dense woman would have kept it to herself, but her eagerness to display her great sense of humor blinds her to the petty cruelty of her admission: "If our kids grumbled about doing their own laundry, I had a lowly trick: I'd ruin one of their favorite items with a little bleach in the wash."

Everything is played for laughs. The eighties: "No one knows how many minks gave their lives for Ronald Reagan's inauguration." The Bush-Quayle ticket: "What the two of them had in common was their trust funds—they were both members of what I call the lucky sperm club." Closing the gender gap: "Maybe in the year 2000 male politicians soliciting the female vote will wear 'I feel your pain' high heels and empathetic pregnancy pillows in their trousers."

Schroeder's humor is celebrated in feminist circles but it's the kind of humor that, were she a man, would result in vacation post-cards that say, "The scenery is beautiful, wish you were her. Ha-ha."

If Schroeder is a *miles gloriosus*, Susan Molinari's desperate need to please and placate is reminiscent of Chaucer's Patient Griselda. It began with her overbearing father, Guy Molinari, former Staten Island congressman and New York GOP powerhouse, who has done everything possible to test and torment her and keep her coming back for more, and extends in a twisted way to her husband, Rep. Bill Paxon, who, she complains at one point, is "too nice."

The high point of Susan Molinari's life was keynoting the 1996 Republican National Convention while her husband and father sat in the gallery taking turns holding her now-famous baby, Susan Ruby. The low point came less than a year later when she suddenly quit Congress before her term was up to anchor "CBS News Saturday Morning."

She was no sooner settled in her new job than two more low points came her way: Bill Paxon's ostracism from the House GOP power structure after his part in the failed coup to topple Newt Gingrich, followed by his sudden announcement that he, too, was quitting Congress—not to take a new job, but to spend more time with Susan Ruby.

Blinking back tears, he told astounded reporters that he was through with politics, finished! Never again would he run for office because the time and travel demands interfered with the free exercise of his paternal instinct.

"It's out of pure joy that I'm doing this," he said in a choking voice. "This is not a fall, this is a rise. I'd rather be home. This horse wants to be in the stable with the colt."

That, in a nutshell, is the sad tale of Susan Molinari, once a comer but now a goner, stuck with a husband who thinks he's Stella Dallas. She tries to explain how it all came to this, but her tangled account of political infighting makes as much sense as the annexation of Schleswig-Holstein. She refers to Dick Armey as a "chainsmoker" so presumably he's the villain of the piece, but it doesn't matter because the jaw-dropping part of her book is her story of life with father.

She begins by apologizing for not being an interesting abused daughter in the dramatic Christina Crawford mold, but "nothing much happened to me that was neurosis-provoking." This is the most unintrospective claim since Nero called himself a great artist. The only child of a semi-invalid mother who was unable to have more children, Susan was taken over by Guy Molinari and made to guess what he expected of her while he played both roles in a good cop-bad cop head game. He kept her constantly off-balance and unsure of herself, refusing to utter one word of praise when she brought home straight A's, yet encouraging her to follow his footsteps into politics, "although I suspect he wouldn't have done so if he'd had a male heir to his mantle."

Short and blond, she worried constantly that people did not take her seriously, yet in a self-thwarting move that seems unconsciously designed to court an unserious image, she became a high-school cheerleader. After attending college close to home she worked for the Republican National Committee until her father urged her to run for the Staten Island seat on the New York City Council in 1985. The 27-year-old Susan won the election—and the sobriquet of "Guy's Doll" from the New York media.

Her first husband was John Lucchesi, a Staten Island limo service operator, whom she married when she was 30 after having a panic attack on the eve of the wedding. The ceremony was spoiled by her father's incredible *faux pas*. She was walking up the aisle on his arm when suddenly he stopped. She thought he was overcome by the thought of losing her, but then she saw Robert and Elizabeth Dole seated among the guests. He had stopped beside their pew to greet them because "he couldn't resist being Guy Molinari."

Her wedding story belongs in a Miss Manners column, but her

Lincoln Bedroom story provides new material for Aeschylus. Four days after George Bush was inaugurated he invited twenty couples to a dinner and a tour of the White House private quarters. "My father asked me to go with him as his 'date.' When we got to the Lincoln Bedroom, the President showed us in and offered to take photographs of the couples on Lincoln's bed. He actually pulled out a Polaroid camera and, two by two, we paired off for our special photographic session."

Re-elected to the City Council, she was just beginning to enjoy her job when "my father threw a monkey wrench into it all by announcing that he was considering giving up the congressional seat he'd held for almost a decade." He did just that, deciding to run for the gritty job of Staten Island borough president so that Susan could run for his vacated seat. It was quite a come-down for him; the good cop had sacrificed his career for his daughter, or so it seemed.

Susan won the seat and basked briefly in the knowledge that "my father's friends, men who had patted me on the head and indulged me as a teenager, were suddenly my peers," but then the bad cop struck again. Daddy Dearest invaded her first press conference and took it over, upstaging her entirely. "Competition for media attention was already a tradition between us," she chirps uninsightfully, "and he got plenty that day complaining about my crazy sneakers, unconventional coats, and 'superior jogging prowess.'"

Now divorced, she invited her female roommate to be her date the first time she was invited to the White House as a member of Congress. She began seeing Bill Paxon but when he started getting serious "I panicked and broke up with him." Well she might, for he got his kicks from planning her future, "a future he was sure would include the presidency."

Once they were married he began urging her to run for governor of New York. She rather liked the idea, but so did her father, who told the press, "Molinari and Molinari would make a good ticket, but we can't agree on which of us would be which." Asked what she thought about the idea of a father-daughter ticket, she quipped luridly, "If Bill and Hillary can be President, why can't Guy and Susan be governor?" Electra rides again, but not for long. Shortly afterward she and

Paxon had a drunken fight in a Staten Island bar and she began screaming, "Forget it! I'm not running for governor! Forget it!"

Susan Molinari is so bereft of self-knowledge and introspective power that one is tempted to read this book through spread fingers like a queasy juror looking at autopsy photos. Just when you think she can't possibly get any blinder, she does. Here is her ultimate rationalization of life with Daddy Dearest.

> If I came up with a good line about an issue, he'd steal it and make it his own. . . . Or we'd agree not to tell reporters something and, suddenly, the information would appear in the *New York Post*. . . . Later I'd find out that he had actually sent out a press release. . . . But every time my dad stole a line from me, he was acknowledging how clever I was. Every time he beat me to the punch with the media, he taught me to mover quicker. Our rivalry was a game of pride, our private game, an affirmation of love and respect that only a daughter who goes into the family business can enjoy.

Molinari's labored explanation of why she suddenly quit Congress to take a job in televison is a study in truth through denial. Ws she driven out by GOP conservatives who had had enough of her pro-abortion, anti-gun "moderate" stances? Of course not. Strong women can't be driven out, and she's a strong woman. Did she step aside to give her husband center stage as the politician of the family? Of course not. Everybody knows that Bill saw *her* as a future president. Was she burned out? Of course not. Cheerleaders don't get burned out, and she's a little bundle of pep who "jumps into my sweats" when the jogging hour strikes.

She never really nails down her reason. Her need to be upbeat leads her into clichés about "making choices" and "controlling my life," her need to be trendy sends her off on obsessive tangents about career versus motherhood ("I just lay there looking at Susan Ruby with utter wonder"), and her need to come across as average and uncomplicated produces a self-portrait for the record books: "Growing old in Congress, being one of those wizened veterans who practically dies on the House floor, would never have fit my temperament. I'm a baby boomer raised on television. My attention span simply isn't that long." Just as well—CBS fired her in June.

Molinari is an exposed nerve, but Pat Schroeder is a slick babe with a spin. She alludes to burn-out but quickly establishes herself as an elder stateswoman in the making, teaching at Princeton, serving as president of the Association of American Publishers, and thinktanking at the Institute for a Civil Society. We can see the handwriting on the wall, except that it's on letterheads. Lots of them, each with Schroeder's name on the left-hand side—the board members' side, the Vernon Jordan side, reserved for those who get paid huge sums for being listed on the left-hand side of letters.

So concludes this assessment of *Declining and Falling Made Easy*. In the interests of what is lately called full disclosure I should state that I'm getting a procurement bonus from the French Foreign Legion for every man who reads it.

National Review, September 1, 1998
Book Review

"Daddy Dearest"

Will This Do?: An Autobiography, by Auberon Waugh
(Carroll & Graf, 288 pp., $24)

C HILDRAISING in the English upper class violates every principle of what Americans used to call "togetherness" and now call "parenting skills." Exchanging affection and attention for alchemy, the happy few combine a perpetually choleric father and a mother detached to the point of somnambulism, add a sadistic headmaster, shake vigorously, and pour. To the horrified incredulity and cloaked envy of their American cousins, out comes a Winston Churchill.

Now they've done it again, probably for the last time. Post–World War II egalitarianism and post-Diana emotionalism have conspired to turn the green and pleasant land into one big slippery slope, but Auberon Waugh, born in 1939, is pure unhugged gold.

His father, Evelyn Waugh, modern England's most savage wit as well as her most devout Catholic convert, combined his two cachets by hating children and having six. Regarding them "as part of the cross which every Christian must bear," he ran them down in letters to friends and in his own diary, predicting they would become "defective adults: feckless, destructive, frivolous, sensual, humorless." A master of riposte himself, he had no patience with broad childhood humor and grew infuriated when they laughed at pratfalls and sight gags. Their inability to appreciate and practice sophisticated verbal wit proved they were working-class clods at heart and therefore beneath his contempt, and he did not shrink from telling them so to their faces.

The most terrifying aspect of Evelyn Waugh as a parent was that he reserved the right not just to deny affection to his children but to advertise an acute and unqualified dislike of them. This was always conditional on their own behavior up to a point, and seldom entirely unjustified, but it was disconcerting, nevertheless, to be met by cool statements of total repudiation.

Mrs. Waugh had the aristocratic lineage so prized by her class-conscious husband, but unfortunately for the children she also had aristocratic interests. A countrywoman happiest when slogging through her cow pasture in muddy Wellies, she was the last to notice the bald patches in her fur coat but the first to notice mange in her beloved animals. She had nothing against children, it was just that they didn't walk on four legs.

A wife first, a dairymaid second, and a mother last, she played the complaisant zombie to her husband's unspeakable selfishness in the matter of the bananas. Just after the war, the government tried to alleviate five years of harsh food rationing by decreeing that every child in England should be allowed one banana. At this time there were three little Waughs, none of whom had ever tasted a banana.

My mother came home with three bananas. All three were put on my father's plate, and before the anguished eyes of his children, he poured on cream, which was almost unprocurable, and sugar, which was heavily rationed, and ate all three. . . . From that moment, I never treated anything he had to say on faith or morals very seriously.

Coming as a kind of schizoid relief from paternal contumely and maternal detachment was the extreme permissiveness the children enjoyed. When Auberon developed an interest in chemistry at age nine, his parents gave him a back room in the house for a lab and ordered large quantities of sulphur, saltpeter, charcoal, nitric acid, and glycerine for making gunpowder and other explosive materials; glass tubing and spirit lamps and a Wolff jar for distilling alcohol. "Some will decide that this was a deliberate, Charles Addams–like plot to get rid of me," he writes, but his parents were just as indulgent about firearms, which endangered everyone, and bad school reports, "holding all authority in derision until the threat of expulsion brought with it the danger that children might be returned home."

Sent to boarding school at six, he acquired a headmaster only the English could produce: a pedophile who hated children. He was a brilliant classicist who taught Greek so well that Waugh can still conjugate all the irregular verbs, but he refused to enlighten his charges on the facts of life, "which was probably just as well, as he would almost certainly have got them wrong." A fetishist attached to an item known as "the Furry Object," the headmaster liked to watch naked boys being weighed at the annual physical but otherwise "never lifted a finger or touched a boy except to beat him."

Opting to do his national service before entering Oxford, Waugh was commissioned a cornet in the Royal Horse Guards and sent to Cyprus, where he accidentally shot himself with a machine gun. Noticing that it was a little askew on its mounting, he "seized the barrel from in front and gave it a good jiggle." The next thing he knew he was on the ground being comforted by his corporal, who looked so stricken that Waugh could not resist saying, "Kiss me, Chudleigh." His father would have loved it, but the parody of Nelson's last words was lost on the working-class Chudleigh.

Only 19, he lost a lung, his spleen, and several ribs. As he lay in the Cypriot hospital his mother rushed to his side but managed to control her emotions admirably. In a letter to her husband she dutifully reported on their son's injuries before turning to more pressing matters: "If Lucy is still giving 40 lbs. a day of milk she had better be artificially inseminated next time she comes bulling with the Aberdeen Angus bull. If she is not giving as much as 40 lbs. I do not want her served at all."

When Waugh recovered he sold his first novel, *The Foxglove Saga*, and entered Oxford, but quickly left when he realized that "the role of a published novelist among the other undergraduates would be an odious one, requiring endless displays of modesty and self-effacement." In fact his close call with death had given him the kind of maturity that makes college life unbearable. And so, with nothing more than a small disability pension, a first sale, and a name that hurt more than helped in left-wing journalistic circles, he decided to gamble on himself in the uncertain game of freelance writing.

Will This Do? takes its title from the question every journalist asks himself on submitting an article. Auberon Waugh drew a resounding "Yes!" often enough to become one of England's busiest writers, a roving satirist who has had a finger in every Fleet Street pie since 1960: a weekly column for the *Times*, a political column for *Private Eye*, a column on country life for the *Evening Standard*, and even a wine column for *Tatler* in which he compared a cloying bouquet to "a dead chrysanthemum on the grave of a stillborn West Indian baby" and was accused of racism by a Lambeth midwife.

Now editor of *Literary Review* and author of "The Way of the World" column for the *Daily Telegraph*, he is a wordsmith without peer who deplores the encroachment of the tabloids: "It is irritating to those who have spent time and trouble cultivating the vituperative arts to see what passes for vulgar abuse in the proletarian newspapers. Vituperation, in the right hands, is part of life's pageant."

Amen.

National Review, September 28, 1998
Book Review

"The Love Doctor"

The Clinton Syndrome: The President and the Self-Destructive
Nature of Sexual Addiction, by Jerome D. Levin, PhD
(Prima, 272 pp., $24.95)

A T LAST Bill Clinton's elusive legacy has been nailed down and rendered succinct. Like Oedipus, Electra, Napoleon, and those beset Viennese women named "Anna," he will be enshrined in the pages of psychiatric literature as an eponym for what ails us. "Sexual addiction" lacks punch and "Don Juan" rings fewer and fewer bells in our dumbed-down culture, but thanks to this exquisitely well-timed book, compulsive tomcatting will henceforth and forevermore be known as the "Clinton Syndrome."

The author, Jerome D. Levin, is a psychologist in private practice who teaches at Manhattan's New School for Social Research, trains addiction counselors, and voted for his subject twice, but he does not sound like a typical representative of this usually earnest and super-cilious scene. He gives Clinton due credit but no quarter, treats con-servative assessments such as R. Emmett Tyrrell's with seriousness and respect, and exchanges the droning jargon of the helping profes-sions for a refreshing down-to-earth authorial voice ("the guy needs to be liked and loved too much").

Levin introduces his theme, "Sexual addiction is not about sex," by pointing out something so obvious that we are left wondering why no one ever caught it before: Monica Lewinsky looks like Clinton's mother—the same abundant black hair, heavy makeup, and general aura of flashiness. Moreover, she arrived in the White House not long after his mother's death on January 6, 1994, and was there during two other psychologically significant losses: the assassination of Israeli Prime Minister Yitzhak Rabin on November 4, 1995, and the death of Commerce Secretary Ron Brown in a plane crash on April 3, 1996.

The three deaths were a virtual re-enactment of the traumatic events that shaped Clinton's early life. The loss of his mother took him back to the first time he lost her, when she left him with his grandparents while she attended nursing school in Louisiana. Ron Brown's death in a plane crash replicated his biological father's death in a car crash before he was born, and the assassination of Rabin robbed him of an older man he regarded as a surrogate father.

"Anyone watching the video of Clinton at Rabin's funeral would be unable to deny his devastation." The Israeli leader, says Levin, was Clinton's masculine ideal; a heavy drinker who could hold his liquor and still function, not an alcoholic failure like stepfather Roger Clinton. Rabin was also a man's man, a tested warrior whose physical courage had helped establish his nation and whose moral courage had helped sustain it. Rabin's was an unequivocal identity that made Clinton uncomfortably aware of his own reputation as a draft-dodger with his finger in the wind who was ruled by polls and focus groups.

"The sex addict feels unloved and unlovable and so looks obsessively for proof that this is not so." Of the three deaths, Rabin's was the most important in the chronological scheme because Clinton's relationship with Monica began the same month. In need of validation and reassurance after having come face to face with his insecurities, "Clinton had about as much chance of leaving her alone as a cocaine addict has of passing up a line."

The American Psychiatric Association's checklist of the symptoms of sexual addiction fits Clinton like a glove, especially the first three: 1) Sexual activity that interferes with work, 2) Sexual activity in potentially dangerous situations, and 3) Repeated sex-related legal problems.

The key to his behavior—the First Rosebud, so to speak—is his early fear of abandonment that was set in motion by the realization that he was a posthumous child, and by the extended absence of his mother while he was a toddler. When she returned home she made up for lost time by doting on him, much to the resentment of his grandmother, who had enjoyed exclusive doting rights during her daughter's absence and was not about to relinquish them without a fight. And so they fought over him, two painted, dyed-haired dames outdoting each other to see who could shower Billy with the most love and attention, until he soaked up the lesson that women are where it's at; if you want to be adored they're the people to see.

Using promiscuous sex to banish fears of being left alone is a losing proposition. Women who are escorted in by state troopers are invariably escorted out with the same dispatch. Quickies can only rekindle unresolved abandonment anxieties, which must then be tranquilized with more quickies, until the swordsman arrives at 5) Tolerance: needing increased amounts of sexual activity to achieve the high or desired effect. This has been the story of Bill Clinton's life. The only territory he seems not to have marked is 8) An enduring desire to control sexual activity and simultaneous failed attempts to do so.

The author believes the Kathleen Willey incident proves that Clinton's behavior has crossed over into compulsion. Once again he calls our attention to significant dates. The Oval Office groping took place on November 29, 1993. In October, Clinton had learned that his 1984 gubernatorial campaign had been named by the Resolution Trust Corporation as one of nine criminal referrals made as a result of its investigation of Madison Guaranty Savings and Loan. The Whitewater issue was officially out and under investigation, yet Clinton took a chance on getting caught making sexual advances in the White House at this of all times, and, as Mrs. Willey related, seemed to be excited by the risk.

His refusal to settle the Paula Jones case before it reached the damaging discovery phase indicates, says Dr. Levin, that he is so deeply in denial that he might well have lied to his lawyers rather than admit to them, and therefore to himself, that his sex life had been out of control.

Levin does not think Clinton is a sociopath, nor is he self-destructive in the usual meaning of the word, but his addiction has progressed "to the point where the potential to self-destruct is now evident." Levin finds troubling hints in Clinton's reaction to Nixon's death. "Clinton was inexplicably grief-ridden and led an unusually (and some say, inappropriately) prolonged period of public mourning for Nixon." To Levin, Clinton's identification with Nixon, when considered alongside his identification with John F. Kennedy, amounts to a morbid fascination with disaster that bodes ill.

"I cannot help but wonder whether Clinton has hit bottom. As far as we know, Lewinsky is the last name on his doomsday list. However . . . I would speculate that he is currently controlling his behavior because he is too frightened to do otherwise and that he has not really relinquished his denial. If this is the case, he remains vulnerable and might yet take that final and fatal step, get involved with another woman, become mired in yet another scandal, and end his Presidency in disgrace. If he does, his identification with Nixon will be complete."

National Review, November 9, 1998
Book Review

"Out and About"

Empty without You: The Intimate Letters of Eleanor Roosevelt and Lorena Hickok, edited by Rodger Streitmatter
(Free Press, 307 pp., $25)

R EADING other people's love letters is a bummer, especially when one of the parties is a professional writer and the other a commaless wonder. Then you get a choice between parsed sweet nothings and dangling sweet nothings.

Eleanor Roosevelt and Lorena Hickok were polar opposites. Where ER was puritanical and abstemious, "Hick," as she was known to her Associated Press colleagues, was a cussing, drinking, chainsmoking newspaperwoman and a hulking butch lesbian whose sexual proclivities were common knowledge. The daughter of a South Dakota itinerant laborer who disowned her when she was 14, she had pulled herself up by her bootstraps to become one of America's top political reporters.

In 1932 the 40-year-old Hick covered FDR's first presidential campaign and developed a starry-eyed crush on the candidate's 49-year-old wife. For her part Eleanor Roosevelt began to single Hick out of the press pack and show her favoritism. The crop-haired, baggy-suited reporter was invited to breakfast alone with the future First Lady, stay in her Hyde Park cottage, and accompany her on family visits. In return Hick gave Eleanor a diamond-and-sapphire ring that had been presented to her by opera diva Ernestine Schumann-Heink in gratitude for a flattering interview. Eleanor not only accepted it, but wore it.

Hick's editors pressed her for the inside stories and scoops she was in a position to get but she would not risk losing ER's trust. Worse, she committed journalism's unforgivable sin when she let FDR's advisors vet her copy. By the end of the victorious campaign her objectivity, and hence her newspaper career, was gone. Invited to spend Inauguration week in the Mayflower Hotel with the Roosevelt party, she sealed her professional fate when she was shown a final draft of FDR's First Inaugural address and failed to report its contents to her AP boss.

Shortly thereafter she quit the AP and went to work for the New Deal as an inspector of relief programs, driving around the country and writing up reports. Between trips she lived in the White House, sleeping in a room adjoining ER's.

When Hick was on the road she and ER began a correspondence that would continue, with diminishing intensity, for the rest of their lives. The most significant letters were written in 1933-35 when their intimacy was at white heat. These caused a sensation when the collection was made public by the Roosevelt Library in 1978. Since then, Roosevelt scholars with a penchant for Gay Liberation have insisted that ER and Hick had a lesbian affair, while traditional Roosevelt scholars have just as insistently countered that the letters evince nothing but the lavish affection that otherwise repressed Victorian ladies sometimes poured out on their friends.

The Victorian theory does not fit the decidedly unladylike Hick, who, though born in 1892, was not repressed. She had been "out" since girlhood, had lived with a female lover in Minneapolis, and had made a pass at a woman reporter when the two shared a hotel room.

As for ER, she was Victorian, repressed, and a lady, but she was known to hang out with lesbians. In the Twenties she was a regular visitor to the Greenwich Village digs of lawyer Elizabeth Read and her companion Esther Lape; and was fast friends with Nan Cook and Marion Dickerman, who built a cottage on Hyde Park property where Nan made hand-crafted furniture, carving their three monograms, "E.N.M.," in each piece.

Hick's most explicit letter to ER recalls with longing "the feeling of that soft spot just northeast of the corner of your mouth against my lips."

ER's letters typically begin and end with intimate sentiments:

"Hick my dearest, I cannot go to bed tonight without a word to you. I felt a little as though a part of me was leaving tonight, you have grown so much to be a part of my life that it is empty without you even though I'm busy every minute." She then launches into a breathless description of her White House day, closing with a wish "to put my arms around you."

After they had talked on the phone while her son was in the room she wrote: "Jimmy was near & I couldn't say '*je t'aime et je t'adore*' as I longed to do but always remember I am saying it & that I go to sleep thinking of you & repeating our little saying."

The ring: "Hick darling, I want to put my arms around you, I ache to hold you close. Your ring is a great comfort, I look at it & think she does love me, or I wouldn't be wearing it!"

Hick's photo on her mantel: "Oh! how I wanted to put my arms around you in reality instead of in print. I went & kissed your photograph instead & tears were in my eyes. Please keep most of your heart in Washington as long as I'm here for most of mine is with you!"

In 1933 when Eleanor could still move about unrecognized the women motored alone through the remote Adirondacks. In *Reluctant First Lady*, the biography Hick published after ER's death, she describes a revealing incident in a tourist cabin: "Mrs. Roosevelt started thrusting her long, slender fingers in my direction. I was so ticklish that all she had to do to reduce me to a quivering mass of pulp was to point her fingers at me." In no time, she confessed, ER had her "writhing out of control."

Was this highly symbolic language a code for something more? Whatever their relationship was or was not, by 1935 the dew was off the rose. Now we find ER writing: "I know you often have a feeling for me which for one reason or another I may not return in kind but I feel I love you just the same . . ."

As ER pulled back, Hick's letters descended into lovesickness: "At times life becomes just one long, dreary ache for you." Always moody, she now spoke of life not being worth living and hinted of suicide.

Nonetheless, they kept in touch, exchanging some 3,500 letters by the time ER died in 1962. Of these, 300 were chosen for inclusion in

Empty without You by editor Rodger Streitmatter, whose previous books include *Unspeakable: The Rise of the Gay and Lesbian Press in America*. Although his commentaries leave no doubt that he hopes ER and Hick had a full-fledged affair, he believes that the more important question is: "What impact did the relationship have on each woman?"

He credits Hick with inspiring ER's activist First Ladyship and hints that without her ER might have stayed home and baked cookies. This is a stretch; she had taken up socialistic meddling in the Twenties before the two met. He is correct, however, in his claim that Hick made a writer out of her. The former star reporter edited ER's early efforts, teaching her how to organize her feverish thoughts until she was able to write an autobiography and a syndicated column, "My Day," that ran six days a week for 27 years.

Meanwhile, Hick, too old to return to newspapering, was reduced to writing publicity for the World's Fair and books for "young adults." In a supreme twist of irony, this masculine woman was thrust into the feminine role of the supportive wife. Once a respected professional, she had sacrificed her career and identity on ER's altar and wound up in obscurity and genteel poverty. That she regretted her decision is clear from her reaction to a patronizing description of herself in ER's autobiography: "In those days I was somebody in my own right. I was just about the top gal reporter in the country."

Did they or didn't they? I say no, but Streitmatter, like most Eleanor writers, is too respectful of her lauded humanitarianism to see her for what she was: a tease. It's clear to me that a lot of hugging and kissing went on, but when Hick tried to go further ER hit the brakes while at the same time behaving in ways that would encourage Hick to try again. The tickling episode is a case in point: ER employed this horseplay as the repressed often do, as an innocent way of "accidentally" touching forbidden places.

She also dragged the obese Hick along on vigorous hikes, then laughed when she got short of breath and lectured her about her smoking. Here we see the insecure, unattractive woman who at long last has found someone even more insecure and unattractive than herself, calling attention to her companion's gaucherie in order to feel, for once in her life, like the belle of the ball.

National Review, December 21, 1998
Book Review

"A Book for All Readers"

The Life of Thomas More, by Peter Ackroyd
(Doubleday, 447 pp., $30)

E RASMUS addressed him as *mellitissime Thoma* and famously proclaimed that his sweetest Thomas was *omnium
horarum*—a man for all seasons, whose affability remained
constant through fair weather and foul. It's true that Thomas More
joked even on the scaffold, but Erasmus, who liked puns and double
meanings, may also have alluded to the many people who had no idea
what made him tick.

Foremost among them was the upfront Dame Alice More, whose
letter to Henry VIII pleading for her husband's life made it clear that
she considered him a little touched. Even Erasmus, who probably
understood him as much as anyone could, was reduced in the end to
throwing up his hands and crying, "If only he had left theology to the
theologians!"

The philosopher's outburst highlights More's greatest contradiction: he was an ascetic man of the world. Grandson of a rich merchant, son of a King's Bench judge, exposed while a page in the
household of the Archbishop of Canterbury to the highest gloss of
savoir faire, he was the master mold of urbanity and the very glass of
sophisticated social ease, yet underneath his silks and velvets he wore
a hair shirt.

A perplexing duality marked his every thought and deed. He died in defense of papal authority and always bowed to his father, even in adulthood when he outranked him, but he himself was a permissive father who spanked his children with feathers. His attitude toward women was almost schizoid. More the dominant male married his first wife solely to avoid the sin of fornication; when she died giving birth to their fifth child, he remarried a month later solely because he needed a housekeeper. Yet More the feminist was the first Englishman to champion education for women and personally instructed his daughter Margaret in Latin and Greek, fashioning her into the most erudite woman of her time.

The King himself was caught short by his contradictions. More's detached, ironic personality seemed ideally suited to the divorce situation. Surely this easily amused courtier would not scruple to tinker with the law for the sake of Henry's pressing marital needs, nor would the author of *Utopia* be one to object to reforming society along more progressive lines. Yet when Henry made More his Lord Chancellor with this purpose in mind, he found he had acquired a Nathan.

More's latest biographer, Peter Ackroyd, does not fully understand him either—many of his conclusions are prefaced with, "It is possible that . . ."—but he presents More in a way that invites readers, especially conservatives, to identify with him. Born in 1478 as the Middle Ages were turning into the Renaissance, More "embodied the old order of hierarchy and authority at the very moment when it began to collapse." Anxiety is the unavoidable fate of people who bridge two epochs. Those who today live with an ever-present gnawing sense of dislocation brought on by the Sixties' assault on traditional values can easily understand how Thomas More must have felt.

Like today's neo-cons, he was for a time part of what he later fought. His friendship with Erasmus grew out of their mutual enthusiasm for the "new learning," a movement opposed to priestly control over education. For centuries, the medieval church had maintained that the Bible, Aristotle, and the canon law of Justinian comprised the totality of knowledge and obviated the need for more. These three sources being finite, however, learning had turned back in on itself and descended into "Scholasticism," which flirted with lunacy. The famous story of monks debating how many angels can dance on the head of a pin may be apocryphal, but Scholastics did argue the difference between *vinum bibi bis* (wine I drank twice) and *bis vinum bibi* (twice wine I drank).

Thomas More called this *stultissima solertia* (foolish ingenuity) and promoted the teaching of Greek and Roman literature and rhetoric on grounds that the precision logic and lucid eloquence of classicism would infuse piety with clarity and hence strengthen faith.

Because the New Learning extolled human reason over church authority, it was called "Humanism." Erasmus was in the vanguard, writing (in seven days during a stay at More's home) *In Praise of Folly*, a satirical look at greedy churchmen and lazy mendicant friars that became the most famous secular work of the sixteenth century. Thomas More took a leaf from Plato's *Republic* and described a perfect society called "Utopia." The word was his coinage, taken from the Greek elements meaning "no place," but this subtlety was lost on many. Like all liberal movements, Humanism got hijacked and all hell broke loose.

Thomas More and Martin Luther never met, but "the battle between the two men is like an internalized conflict between the warring selves of sixteenth-century civilization." More, now a member of the King's Council, wrote a scathing response to Luther. Luther was a dishonest liar (*improbe mendax*), an ape (*simium*), he deserved to have someone defecate (*incacere*) in his mouth, he celebrated Mass on the toilet (*super foricam*), and he wriggled his bum (*clunem agitat*) when preaching. In his reply, Luther compared the Catholic world to a gigantic anus and himself to an incipient bowel movement and predicted, "We will probably let go of each other soon."

Scatology was in common usage in an age when people lived close to their wastes, but More and Luther crossed the line into what Ackroyd calls "a reverse world of the medieval imagination, filled with frantic symbols of fear and disorder." Their cloacal and bestial imagery makes the same psychological statement found in "babooneries," the dramatic tableaux and puppet shows of the Middle Ages in which the sacred was represented by the profane. It was a battle between control and release: More stood for the one and Luther for the other, but they expressed themselves with the same language.

When Lutheran tracts found their way into England, More took up duties not covered in the two movies about him. He became a heretic hunter, raiding homes and university rooms and sending the guilty to the stake. Ackroyd does not give an exact count but records several of More's satisfied appraisals, e.g., "He was well and worthely burned in Smythfelde."

It was during the heresy crisis that Henry VIII turned into Bill Clinton. The entrance of Ann Boleyn into his life inspired him to read the Bible, specifically Leviticus, where he made an amazing discovery. After 18 years of marriage to his erstwhile sister-in-law, Catherine of Aragon, he suddenly realized that he had uncovered his brother's nakedness and should therefore be granted an annulment.

Obsessed by his idea, he singled out More for intense consultations, even coming to his Chelsea home and walking in the garden with his arm slung around his councilor's neck. Next to the tall, burly Henry, the short More must have looked like Bruce Lindsey in a codpiece.

We can hear Henry–Bill thinking: heretics aren't so bad after all, might in fact be useful. . . . He began secretly to read their confiscated tracts—Ann slipped him one by William Tyndale—looking for a loophole that would get him out of the marriage without risking his new title of *Fidei Defensor*. The situation turned into a Tudor version of the Keystone Kops: More chasing heretics and Henry granting them safe conduct in case he needed them later.

The author fleshes out the familiar story of More's arrest and trial with a wealth of detail that occasionally becomes turgid and redundant, but his attention to cases from More's early legal career makes the crux of the matter clear. The English schism was an inevitable extension of Praemunire, the fourteenth-century statute that maintained the rights of King and Common Law against the Pope and the clerical courts.

The Life of Thomas More is hard going. The Latin is fun and instructive but ye olde Englysshe ys nott. The protagonist's complexity and detachment may wear thin for some—I ultimately found him too much of a Catholic Ashley Wilkes—but the rich background of late-medieval life is superbly done. Ackroyd's evocative accounts of pageants, Corpus Christi plays, maypoles, comets, omens, mad nuns, schoolboys on tall stools reciting declensions, and the bells of St. Mary-le-Bow marking the liturgical day are not to be missed. Whatever your opinion of Thomas More, this is a book for all readers.

National Review, January 25, 1999
Book Review

"In All Modesty"

A Return to Modesty: Discovering the Lost Virtue,
by Wendy Shalit (Free Press, 291 pp., $24)

N o different drummer can keep up with Wendy Shalit. When they drop in their tracks from exhaustion she just gets another one and marches on. She's been her own woman since becoming a sex-ed dropout in fourth grade, and on through her cantankerous four years at Williams College, where she raised a lone voice against coed bathrooms and compounded her political incorrectness by publishing a polemic against the practice in *Commentary* that left her conformist classmates reeling in shock.

Since then her name has become the byline that connoisseurs of well-written unconventional wisdom look for, turning up in *City Journal*, where she is a contributing editor, as well as the *Wall Street Journal* and NATIONAL REVIEW—but not *Cosmopolitan*, for reasons which will shortly become clear.

Now just 23, she has published her first book. *A Return to Modesty* is about women, and so uncompromising in voice and stance that one is tempted to think of its author as Simone de Shalit or Wendy Wollstonecraft, but make no mistake: she imitates nothing and no one, and her roast of the sacred cow of female sexual freedom is going to stampede our nation of sheep and hand liberals their heads on a platter.

She blames the death of modesty on feminists, who claimed that modesty was "invented" by men to enslave and subordinate women.

Show the least sign of modesty, feminists warned, and men will no longer take you seriously. Worse, modesty suppressed female desire. The media latched onto this and a cultural icon was born: the woman without hang-ups who traded being good for being good in bed, and abandoned her search for Mr. Right for what *Cosmo* called "undifferentiated lust" with lots of Mr. Right Nows.

We went from a nation that believed a virtuous woman's price is far above rubies to one that believes a virtuous woman is as sounding brass. Meanwhile, the New Woman went from prize to prey. Without the social conventions of modesty, her prerogative to say no was overridden by men's prerogative to expect sex.

Today's young women are profoundly unhappy, Shalit maintains, so desperate for a revival of modesty that they practice today's ersatz versions of it—sexual-harassment suits, date-rape-awareness vigils, and "No Means No" protest marches to remind men that women don't feel undifferentiated lust.

Another substitute is eating disorders. Since women make up 90 percent of anorexics and bulimics, starving and throwing up are ways to establish a clear difference between the sexes in a culture that insists there aren't any.

Shalit thinks we have arrived at the critical point noted by Rousseau in his warning against women trying to be like men: "The more women want to resemble them, the less women will govern them, and then men will truly be the masters."

The disappearance of modesty has increased misogyny and violence against women. When men were taught that "A woman is more particular" about whom she sleeps with, they could be philosophical about sexual rejection. But now, encouraged by ringing endorsements of undifferentiated lust to think that women are just like them, they are much more likely to be impatient and uncomprehending when a woman says no to sex. "Modesty gave men a frame of reference for a woman's 'no'—without it, the modern man always takes no as a personal rebuke. . . . Failure to sleep with someone is now an act of hostility."

Modesty also improves the quality of life in general. When men believed they had to make themselves worthy of a woman, admonitions such as "Lips that touch liquor shall never touch mine" carried real weight, because "what women will and will not permit does have a profound way of influencing an entire society."

Women can't tell men how to behave—they either inspire or fail to inspire. Today we inspire them by slamming doors on their fingers, pushing them away when they help us with our coats, and then, when they learn their lesson and begin to treat us with equal-opportunity boorishness, we change our minds and seek to enforce by fiat the respect which was once grounded in custom.

Is modesty natural? Shalit contends that it is and offers four proofs.

1) The universal propensity of pubescent girls to be embarrassed by everything under the sun, as witnessed by their constant moans of "I could die! I could just die!"

2) The universal windy-day gesture: Women might wear slit skirts because it's the fashion, but let the slightest breeze come along and they automatically hold the slit closed to cover what it was designed to reveal.

3) The "Not That Way" freeze and sudden retreat: the involuntary prudishness that comes over a woman when an obtuse man, thinking to compliment her, says something like, "You'd make a great porn star."

4) The body-noises divide: Men, the blithe spirits, take them in stride, but to women they are mortifying. (A *Mademoiselle* advice columnist writes that a great many of the letters she gets are some version of "What do I do when my boyfriend starts burping?")

If modesty is natural, then, can it be a virtue? Here Shalit displays her gift for making intellectual points in conversational language by starting—and winning—an argument with Immanuel Kant. The German philosopher believed that since modesty flows from woman's natural circumstances, and is not the result of a rational struggle, it can't qualify as moral. Shalit agrees that the fashion slave who wears a slit skirt and instinctively clutches it against the wind is morally neutral, but what of the woman who refuses to wear slit skirts in the first place? "In Kantian terms, then, a woman who struggles with her culture and opts for modesty would, in fact, seem to be acting virtuously."

Shalit confides that her friends have warned her that when this book comes out she will be mercilessly attacked and mocked by the forces of sexual equality. What will no doubt enrage them the most is her call for a return to the "cartel of virtue"—that time-honored female instinct wherein women made a silent pact to behave themselves in the interests of group and society to ensure that men would have to marry. In other words, cut off the free milk and make him buy the cow.

To help gird her for the coming combat with apoplectic feminists, let me offer that I well remember the heyday of the cartel of virtue in the 1950s. It can be brutal, especially the way it encourages virtuous women to gang up on their erring sisters, but it is far less brutal than turning all women into erring sisters as happens under our present system of sexual mayhem. In any case, the cartel of virtue is the only known way to get women to stick together, so tell the feminists to think of it as sisterhood.

Shalit sees signs that modesty is making a comeback. Antioch College's much-derided guidelines on asking permission to kiss and touch are not very different from *The English Gentlewoman* (1631) and the many Victorian chapbooks about men who "take liberties."

There is movement on the "Quietly Confessed" front—Shalit's name for the paragraph in "balanced" news stories about coed dorms, in which a lone girl who objects to the arrangement is quoted under the attributive, "she quietly confessed." After Shalit's *Commentary* article was reprinted in *Reader's Digest* she was inundated with supportive letters from such girls.

Sexual differences are beginning to be acknowledged in reports of new hormone discoveries (e.g., oxytocin, released by the female during sex and thought to make women cling emotionally to the men they sleep with).

Women have begun to swap stories about the rare man who gave up his seat on a bus or tipped his hat—or as Shalit puts it, in what may be the best line in the book: "Within a certain circle of women, incidents of chivalry are now traded like sightings of aliens or solar eclipses."

The growing interest in rigid social strictures manifested by the

Jane Austen craze tells her that young women are pining for interference as their mothers once pined for liberation, even to the extent of wanting to be nagged and called on the carpet.

Of herself she admits, "I'm always pining for someone to young-lady me," but she doesn't need it, at least from a reviewer's standpoint. Her ability to think things through in her own way and come to her own conclusions makes every page of this book wise, fresh, and funny, sparkling with her special brand of astringent charm. If she can write like this at 23, her future output can only be contemplated with pure joy.

The American Spectator, February 1999
Book Review

"A Date Which Should Live in Irony"

*The Five Weeks of Giuseppe Zangara: The Man
Who Would Assassinate FDR* by Blaise Picchi
(Academy of Chicago, 273 pages, $26.95)

At 9:15 on the evening of February 15, 1933, the greatest "what if" in American history was played out in Miami's Bayfront Park. The attempted assassination of President-elect Franklin D. Roosevelt is almost forgotten today, but for connoisseurs of Fate there is nothing quite like it.

FDR arrived at the political rally tanned and relaxed from a deep-sea fishing trip on Vincent Astor's yacht. Sitting atop the back seat of a convertible, he rode slowly through the packed crowds and stopped in front of a stage full of VIPs, among them the mayor of Chicago, Anton J. Cermak. After making a brief speech from the car, he was talking privately with the dignitaries who came down from the stage to greet him when five shots rang out.

Some 30 feet from the car, a man in the third row of spectators was standing on tiptoe on a rickety chair, his arm stretched over the heads in front of him, firing a .32 revolver at the presidential party. Directly behind him was Thomas Armour, a Miami carpenter. Directly in front of him was Lillian Cross, wife of a Miami doctor, who was also standing on a chair. Either Armour or Mrs. Cross grabbed the gunman's arm to deflect his aim—both so claimed afterwards—or perhaps it was the unsteady chair. Whatever happened, all five shots missed FDR and hit others. Two people were seriously wounded: a Mrs. Mabel Gill and Mayor Cermak.

The crowd and the police pounced on the gunman. The Secret Service ordered FDR's driver to get out of the park but the president-elect countermanded them and went back to pick up the wounded. On the way to the hospital he cradled Anton Cermak's head on his shoulder and kept talking to him—"Tony, keep quiet, don't move, Tony"—a steady murmur of encouragement that doctors later said kept Cermak from going into shock.

FDR stayed four hours at the hospital, showing by his actions what he would soon express in words about the need to banish fear. That his behavior this night was fresh in the minds of the nation that heard his First Inaugural address established his presidential bona fides as no mere speech could:

> The people around FDR were watching him to see how this man who was about to lead a troubled nation would react to the attempt on his life. That February evening he was still an unknown quantity. In the immediate aftermath of the assassination attempt, virtually every word and action of the president-elect was reported to the nation. . . . Was he frightened? Nervous? Relieved that he had escaped unhurt? Was he rattled or petulant? He was none of those things. He appeared unfazed, calm, deliberate, cheerful—throughout the shooting itself as well as during its aftermath. He said and did all the right things at the right times: He stopped the car twice to pick up the wounded; he assured the crowd that he was all right; he calmly talked Cermak out of shock, and he visited the victims that night and returned to the hospital the next day with flowers, cards, and baskets of fruit. He had met his first test under fire, and he had impressed not only his associates, but the press and the nation. It was on this note of personal courage, graciousness, and self-confidence that he was to assume the reins of government seventeen days later.

The gunman was a naturalized Italian bricklayer named Giuseppe

Zangara who stood all of five-foot-one, hence his awkward firing position. He may be our most interesting assassin, if only because he was a registered Republican whose chief motivation seems to have been hypochondria.

Born in 1900 in Calabria, the province at the toe of the boot, he was a sickly child made sicker by a brutal father who beat him, starved him, and put him to work at the age of six, when his chronic stomach pain began. This pain became the central fact of his life. He brought it up constantly during his questioning, interjecting it into his simplistic political views: "I shoot kings and presidents, capitalists got all-a money and I got bellyache all-a time."

He sounded like an anarchist, yet he condemned them along with Communists, socialists, and Fascists, proudly insisting that his views were "nobody but mine," a claim borne out by a search of his room. Unlike the Oswalds of this world he had no taste for turgid political manifestos; the few books he owned were English-language aids.

Walter Winchell, who was in Miami that night, immediately concluded that Zangara was not a presidential assassin but a hit man for the Chicago mob who had been sent to shoot the man he did in fact shoot: Mayor Anton Cermak. Many people agreed; Cermak was a reform mayor and dedicated anti-Prohibitionist who had made enemies in the underworld, but Zangara insisted that he wanted to shoot only "kings and presidents" and disclaimed all ties to all groups except the bricklayers' union, which, he said, he had joined only because he had to. "I don't like no peoples," he explained.

The FBI investigation proved him right: He belonged to nothing and no one. An atheist, he believed only in "what I see. Land, sky, moon," and said he felt no remorse over wounding Cermak and Mrs. Gill, but his rationale was not so much cold and psychopathic as matter-of-fact and practical: "You can't find a king or a president alone. Lots of people stick around him and you got to take chance to kill him. All the chiefs of people, never alone. The chief of government you no see alone. He go all the time with a bunch."

Since Cermak and Mrs. Gill were still alive, Zangara was arraigned on four counts of assault with intent to kill, with a murder charge pending should one or both of them die. He insisted on pleading guilty, saying, "I kill capitalists because they kill me, stomach like drunk man. No point living. Give me electric chair." Sentenced to four terms of 20 years each, he told the judge, "Don't be stingy, give me hundred." He rejected an appeal.

Meanwhile, as the country hung on the fates of the two victims, a wacky controversy heated up. Who saved FDR's life by spoiling Zangara's aim—Mrs. Lillian Cross, the doctor's wife, or Thomas Armour, the trusty carpenter? The Miami police doubted Mrs. Cross's story, as did most Miamians, but the national press wanted the plucky little housewife so that's what America got.

FDR had personally thanked Mrs. Cross and invited her and her family to sit with the Roosevelts at Inauguration, but when Florida Congresswoman Ruth Bryan Owen, daughter of William Jennings Bryan, nominated her for the Medal of Honor, supporters of Thomas Armour began beating the drums for their man.

At first Armour maintained a tight-lipped resignation, but seeing Mrs. Cross basking in undeserved fame eventually made him mad enough to begin lobbying for a Medal of Honor for himself. It went on for six years, peaking when Mrs. Cross appeared as a guest on the popular national radio show "We the People," hosted by the renowned Gabriel Heatter, and Armour bombarded the network executives with affidavits, gaining nothing but a reputation as a crank. History got in the last word: Mrs. Cross's death in the 1950's received national attention while Thomas Armour's 1973 pasing drew only local notice.

The other 15 minutes of fame went to Dade County Sheriff Dan Hardie, a third-grade dropout who emerged as a mellifluous specialist in foreign languages after he claimed to be the only person who could make himself understood to Zangara. All he did was speak to the prisoner in broken English interspersed with a few Spanish words such as "hombre" and "amigo," but an excited reporter fell for it and the rest of the press corps followed suit. In no time Hardie, a typical Southern lawman who split heads and infinitives, was routinely described as "something of a linguist," which was soon expanded to "interpreter."

The whole picture changed for Zangara when Anton Cermak died on March 6, two days after FDR's inauguration. His death came about through a misdiagnosis of his injuries that his doctors tried to cover up by citing a pre-existing condition. This opened a legal door for Zangara to claim that his bullet had not caused Cermak's death, but he insisted on pleading guilty.

He was electrocuted on March 20 in what still stands as the swiftest legal execution in this century. It's a measure of his unknowable personality that he was able to be both stoic and cocky in the death chamber. To the minister intoning sonorous prayers he snapped, "Get to hell out of here, you sonofabitch," and strode toward the chair unassisted, shouting, "I go sit down all by myself." A reporter-witness compared it to a man hopping in to a barber's chair. As they put the hood on him he called out, "Viva Italia! Goodbye to all poor peoples everywhere!" His last words, spoken to Sheriff Hardie at the controls, were "Pusha da button!"

The story of the attempt on FDR's life has never been told except in a few magazine articles, but now Florida criminal lawyer Blaise Picchi has filled the 65-year gap with *The Five Weeks of Guiseppe Zangara*, a book that is impossible to put down. A native Floridian, Picchi paints an evocative picture of a vanished Miami that conveys the texture of a bygone age, interviews the still-living persons who were there on the fatal night, digs up never-published documents, and presents a Zangara who is intriguingly reminiscent of Céline, the French writer who was cleared of charges that he collaborated with the Nazis when the judges agreed that "He was too much of a loner to collaborate with anybody."

The American Spectator, March 1999
Book Review

"Ageless Senator Strom"

Ol' Strom: An Unauthorized Biography of Strom Thurmond
by Jack Bass and Marilyn W. Thompson
(Longstreet, 359 pages, $24)

I n his 1969 book, *Gothic Politics in the Deep South*, Robert Sherrill noted that Strom Thurmond lives in a world of metaphysical absolutes: "It is a world of one Eden, one Hell, one Heaven, one Right, one Wrong, one Strom."

South Carolina's 96-year-old senior Senator is proof of the biblical injunction that the last shall be the first. No matter which way you slice him—powerbroker of both major political parties as well as one of his own, the Lancelot of Southern chivalry who addressed abortion advocates as "lovely ladies," or the teetotaling lecher whose exploits make Bill Clinton look like a celibate—Ol' Strom is a law unto himself.

The same could be said of his birthplace. Edgefield is the county seat of a region that stood out even in the fiery, class-conscious South Carolina of Strom's youth. Charleston had snobbish aristocrats, the "Upcountry" had democratic aristocrats, and Edgefield had "nice people, but they'll shoot you," as one observer put it.

The place had a long, proud history of violence based on metaphysical absolutes. It was Edgefield's congressman, Preston Brooks, who in 1856 beat Massachusetts Sen. Charles Sumner with his cane, nearly killing him. Another fractious native son was Sen. "Pitchfork" Ben Tillman, so called for threatening to stick a pitchfork in Grover Cleveland's ribs, who told the Senate in 1902, the year of Strom's birth: "When the Constitution comes between me and the virtue of the white women of the South, I say to hell with the Constitution."

Strom's father, who was Tillman's personal lawyer and campaign manager, missed out on a political career of his own because, as Strom explains, "One time he had to kill a man." It happened in 1897 when a drunken political enemy confronted him on the street and called him a "low, dirty scoundrel." In reply, young Will Thurmond pulled out a pistol and shot him through the heart. At his trial, which was attended by his fiancée Gertrude Strom, he pleaded self-defense and was acquitted by twelve white male Edgefieldians who did not doubt that self-defense included defending one's honor. Some years later, when Will Thurmond ran for Congress and lost badly (though carrying Edgefield), he used the occasion to instruct his eldest son. "Never kill anybody," he told Strom. "It will hurt you all your life."

The youthful Strom channeled his aggressions into vigorous calisthenics, which he still practices, daredevil motorcycling, and an obsession with control that forged lifelong traits of neatness, efficiency, and punctuality. As a child he liked to stack his family's canned goods by size and became upset if he could not brush his teeth immediately after eating. Today his Senate office runs like a precision instrument, unsurpassed for prompt constituent service; no phone is allowed to ring more than twice and there is a 24-hour turnaround on all mail. He clocks his staff, putting them on a late list if they do not arrive by 9 a.m. sharp—and he still carries a toothbrush in his pocket.

After graduating from Clemson when it was still a military college, he briefly taught school, served as county superintendent of schools, then read law with his father and went into practice with him. Elected to the state senate in 1932, the 30-year-old Strom was a handsome, dimpled bachelor with washboard abs and a "shady reputation" among the young ladies in the Junior League, who had heard about his bevy of "big-busted girlfriends," not in the Junior League and whose company he seemed to prefer.

The shady reputation entered the realm of galactic legend in 1940 when the still-unmarried Strom, by now a circuit court judge, was romantically linked with Sue Logue, the only woman ever sent to the electric chair in South Carolina.

The Logue murder case began when Davis Timmerman's mule kicked J.W. Logue's calf to death. Angry over his failure to get restitution for the calf, Logue confronted Timmerman in the latter's general store. Grabbing a new axe from the shelf, Logue swung it at the merchant with intent to bisect, but Timmerman ducked in time, grabbed his gun, and shot Logue through the head.

After Timmerman's acquittal on self-defense, the Widow Logue persuaded her sharecropper to kill him. But when he shot one of Timmerman's hired hands by mistake, she and her brother-in-law, George Logue, decided to hire an assassin. Summoning their nephew, Joe Frank, a Spartanburg policeman, they gave him $500 and asked him to find somebody.

Joe Frank offered the job to Clarence Bagwell, Spartanburg's town drunk, and drove him to Timmerman's store. Bagwell entered and fired five shots into Timmerman, after which Joe Frank drove him home. The hapless pair were soon caught and Joe Frank confessed that Sue and George Logue had put him up to it. The sheriff and his deputy went to arrest them, but as they approached the house the Logues opened fire, killing the sheriff and fatally wounding the deputy, who managed to kill the Logues' sharecropper before dying.

Ol' Strom heard about the stand-off as he was leaving church and rushed to the Logue place, striding fearlessly onto the porch and calling out to the Logues to surrender. A voice from within replied, "Don't come in, Strom, or we'll have to kill you," but he ignored it, talked his way inside, and persuaded Sue Logue to give herself up.

Sue's uncharacteristic submissiveness lent credence to longstanding rumors that Strom already had had his way with her. As school superintendent he had given her a teaching job despite the rule that married women could not be hired, and it was said that they were caught in flagrante in his office. Moreover, she was reputed to possess an unusual "vaginal muscular dexterity," as the authors delicately phrase it. Add that to her go-for-broke nervous system and you have a woman that Ol' Strom was not likely to overlook.

The Logues and their hired gun were sentenced to the electric chair. They say Strom accompanied Sue when she was taken from the women's prison to the state pen, and according to the driver, the two of them were in the back seat "a-huggin' and a-kissin' the whole way."

The case that began with a stomped calf ended with nine people dead and Strom Thurmond enshrined in good ol' boy hearts as the only man to make love to a woman while she was being transferred to Death Row.

When America entered World War II the 39-year-old judge announced he would "rather be airborne than chairborne" and pulled political strings to get assigned to combat duty. He got his wish when he took part in the D-Day invasion and landed behind the German lines in a towed glider that broke up on contact. He sustained several deep cuts and a sprained knee but refused hospitalization and rejoined his unit under fire. He captured four Germans, saw action in the Battle of the Bulge, rose to the rank of colonel, and won the Bronze Star, the Belgian Order of the Crown, and the Croix de Guerre.

Though he courted danger recklessly, he led an eerily charmed wartime life. Once he was standing beside an officer whose head was blown off; another time, in a French village, he decided for no reason to cross the street moments before a shell landed where he had just been walking. Similar miracles of positioning would mark his political career, which began in 1946 when he ran successfully for governor of South Carolina as a New Deal liberal.

He proved to be such a progressive governor that the Realtors Association called him a Communist when he came out for rent control. He also favored a state minimum wage, an end to the poll tax, workmen's compensation, and better Negro schools, but it was his stand against lynching that won him national attention.

South Carolina had never put night riders on trial, but he insisted on doing just that in his first year in office, with solid support from what he called "good white people." As expected, all 28 defendants were acquitted by a largely redneck jury, but, said the *New York Times*, "A precedent has been set. Members of lynching mobs may now know that they do not bask in universal approval." It was an accurate prediction: No further lynchings occurred in South Carolina.

A year later Strom Thurmond was the Dixiecrat candidate for president, preaching states' rights and vowing, "There's not enough troops in the Army to force the Southern people to break down segregation." What happened? Biographers Bass and Thompson, both South Carolinians, believe he went on automatic pilot; "he began responding from an inner core that had absorbed through osmosis the ethics of the historic crucible of Edgefield, of honor and fighting spirit in defending the white South against those who aroused the region's deep feelings of grievance."

Strom, who is not introspective, expressed the same thoughts in objective terms: "Whenever a great section of this country is regarded as so politically impotent that one major party insults it because it is 'in the bag' and the other party scorns it because there is no chance for victory, then the time has arrived for corrective and concerted action."

What angered him was Harry Truman's decision to ignore the South and push for civil rights legislation to win the urban black vote and lure liberals away from the left-wing Henry Wallace, who was also running for president in 1948. To this day he denies that he was motivated by racism, insisting, "It was a battle of federal power versus state power," but since segregation was the only state right in dispute at the time, the authors contend that his stance was racist by default.

Whatever may have lurked in the gnarled confines of his Edgefield subconscious, by running as a third-party candidate and carrying four Southern states "he broke loose the psychological moorings that tied the Deep South to the Democratic Party."

He was finally married at age 44 to 22-year-old Jean Crouch. Returning to private law practice, he defended a woman who shot her husband three times in the chest and three times in the back, getting her off with Edgefield's favorite plea of self-defense. Itching to get back into politics, he got his chance in 1954 when the Democratic nominee for U.S. senator suddenly died three days before the legal deadline for certifying a candidate. Rather than hold a new primary, the State Democratic Committee hand-picked a replacement, but with no Republican in the race the Democrat was bound to win, which meant that the new Senator had been chosen, in effect, by an oligarchy.

In the ensuing political firestorm, Ol' Strom sprang to the defense of the "people's right" to pick their own man and announced his write-in candidacy. The former Dixiecrat had broad appeal thanks to the Supreme Court's decision on school integration a few months earlier, but the immediate problem was a clerical one: How to prepare a state full of semi-literate voters for the first write-in national election in its history?

The *Charleston News & Courier* obligingly filled its front page with a picture of a giant ballot containing Strom's name inscribed by hand. In case anybody still didn't get it, former Secretary of State Jimmy Byrnes had thousands of pencils imprinted with Strom's name distributed to polling places to forestall possible legal challenges due to misspellings. Even so, some ballots were marked "Storm Thermun" and "Strim Thorman," but there was no point in challenging them because Ol' Strom won by 60,000 votes, becoming the only politician in American history elected to national office by write-in.

It is impossible to decide which incident in Strom Thurmond's life constitutes his finest hour, but this affectionate, unflinching biography is the place to find them all. Is it his 1957 filibuster against a civil rights bill, when he dehydrated himself with steam baths and spoke for 24 hours and 18 minutes—a record that still stands—as an aide waited in the cloakroom with a bucket so that he could relieve himself while keeping one foot in the Senate chamber? (He didn't need to.)

Is it his 1964 announcement that he was switching parties, when his tagline at the bottom of the TV screen changed in mid-speech from "(D-SC)" to "(R-SC)" in a manner reminiscent of the time he crossed the street in the French village just before the shell landed?

Or is it his unabashed answer when asked if he regrets his Dixiecrat candidacy? "I don't have anything to apologize for. I don't have any regrets. . . . The States' Rights Party addressed a legitimate issue in 1948 America—whether our states should surrender power to the federal government."

In our present era of maudlin contrition and non-stop breastbeating, the last may be the first.

National Review, March 22, 1999
Book Review

"Virtuecrats"

George III: A Personal History, by Christopher Hibbert
(Basic, 464 pp., $27)

America's last king was the first national figure we condemned as "out of touch," yet if George III reappeared today he would energize so many focus groups that both parties would draft him for Campaign 2000. He had enough virtues for Bill Bennett, enough family values for Gary Bauer, enough ethnic insecurities for Bob Torricelli, and enough depraved sons to start a new Clinton administration.

His reign of 60 years (1760–1820) was longer than most due to the death of his father, the Prince of Wales, when he was 13. Nine years later his grandfather, George II, died and the stripling prince became George III, the first of the "German Georges" to be born in England instead of their native duchy of Hanover.

Despite his youth he had no interest in sowing wild oats. Legend has it that he had an early affair with a Quaker woman, Hannah Lightfoot, and fathered three children by her, but the letter he wrote to his tutor, Lord Bute, suggests he was still a virgin and wanted to remain one. He confessed to:

a daily increasing admiration of the fair sex which I am attempting with all the philosophy and resolution I am capable of to keep under. . . . How strong a tussle there is between the boiling youth of 21 years and prudence! The last I hope will ever keep the upper hand, indeed, if I can weather it out a few years, marriage will put a stop to this combat in my breast.

The slightly priggish tone of this letter and its undercurrent of self-conscious pride in his own rectitude were typical. One of the first acts of his reign was a proclamation entitled "The Encouragement of Piety and Virtue," in which he vowed to "punish all manner of vice, profaneness, and immorality." As a constitutional monarch he had nothing but the power of example, but he used it, sometimes with comical ineffectualness, as when he made a point of rationing his mourning for the adulterous Horatio Nelson while all of England was awash in grief.

His concern for his image was rooted in insecurity. He longed to be seen as a true Englishman, but the Hanoverian claim to the throne was a stretch, going back to a daughter of Charles I who had married the Elector of Hanover, whereas Bonnie Prince Charlie, who was still alive, was the grandson of the deposed Stuart king, the Catholic James II. The Hanoverians were offered the Crown because they swore to uphold Protestantism, but the Stuarts had the stronger claim.

It may have been a subconscious desire to inject his descendants with some Stuart blood that made George fall in love with Lady Sarah Lennox, great-granddaughter of Charles II by one of his mistresses, and propose to her. As a Protestant she was eligible, but Lord Bute, fearful that an English queen's male relatives would clamor for government posts, insisted that George marry a German princess. Eager to please Bute, whose Scottish accent he imitated, George gave in without a struggle, using the opportunity to issue another virtue bulletin: "The interest of my country shall ever be my first care, my own inclination shall ever submit to it. I am born for the happiness or misery of a great nation, and consequently must often act contrary to my passion."

He took no interest in the choice of a bride. Any Protestant princess would do, and while a pretty one would be nice, it wasn't necessary: Whatever Lord Bute decided was fine by him. Bute, assisted by George's mother, Augusta of Saxe-Gotha, chose Charlotte of Mecklenburg-Strelitz, whose simian features jarred with the freshness of her 17 years. The contrast grew less jarring in middle age, when a Court wag would observe, "The bloom has gone off her ugliness."

They were married the same day they met. Such brutal dynastic arrangements spelled disaster for many another royal couple, but not these two. Charlotte was as pliable, dutiful, and as eager to please as George, so they pooled their virtues and pleased each other.

Though delicately built and small-breasted, Charlotte proved a champion whelper. She had 15 children—eight boys and seven girls—nine of them before she was 30, all of them big and several born so fast that she barely had time to get into bed. George was as devoted to his children as he was faithful to their mother, ever alert to the need to set a good example for them, especially for the two oldest boys, George, Prince of Wales, known as "Prinny," and Frederick, Duke of York.

He set the best of examples, getting up at 5 a.m. and lighting his own fire, writing a précis of every book he read, and demonstrating the pleasures of self-denial with his abstemious dietary habits, such as eating only the fruit filling of pies and leaving the pastry. Charlotte went along with all of it, doing her part by upholding the standards of Court decorum described by novelist Fanny Burney, one of her women-in-waiting.

"If you find a cough tickling your throat you must arrest it from making any sound; if you find yourself choking with forbearance, you must choke—but not cough.

"In the second place, you must not sneeze . . . you must oppose it by keeping your teeth grinding together; if the violence of the repulse break some blood-vessel, you must break the blood-vessel—but not sneeze. . . .

"If, however, the agony is very great, bite the inside of your cheek for a little relief; taking care to make no apparent dent outwardly. If you gnaw a piece out, it will not be minded, only be sure either to swallow it or commit it to a corner of the inside of your mouth, for you must not spit."

The parents whose multitude of virtues concealed a multitude of virtues ended up with a litter from Hell. Prinny and Freddie became so obstreperous that their tutor, to save time, beat them both at once like the Katzenjammer Kids. Prinny became a compulsive eater, drinker, and gambler who brushed off suggestions of constructive activity with, "The day is quite long enough to do nothing." Convinced that his father hated him, he got even by entering into an invalid marriage with a Catholic in a secret ceremony, and later accused his legal, Protestant wife of adultery in the House of Lords. Craving maternal warmth, he sought out mistresses older than himself, often sharing them with his favorite crony and the King's sworn political enemy, Charles James Fox, an atheist who spat on the floor, paddled naked in a giant bowl of cream, and urinated on the dinner roast.

Freddie's mistress, Mary Anne Clarke, was arrested for selling army commissions. The third son, William, Duke of Clarence, lived with the actress Dora Jordan, who had 14 illegitimate children, ten of them his. Edward, Duke of Kent, lived in voluntary exile in Paris with his French mistress. Ernest, Duke of Cumberland, was suspected in the murder of his valet. Augustus, Duke of Sussex, took up radical politics and married his much-older mistress, who tried to shake down the King with threats to publish royal documents in her possession.

By the time this dynastic Jerry Springer show played itself out, virtue junkies George III and Charlotte of Mecklenburg-Strelitz had 56 illegitimate grandchildren, including one by Princess Amelia. Add the King's periods of insanity, his attempt to strangle his heir, and the Queen's terrified flight from his boudoir in her shift and you have another irresistible biography by British writer Christopher Hibbert, peerless master of history with its pomp down.

The American Spectator, April 1999
Book Review

"Like a Brokaw Record: The Most Banal Generalizations"

The Greatest Generation by Tom Brokaw
(Random House, 412 pages, $24.95)

O nce upon a time, the human race was divided into writers and talkers, a sensible arrangement that, like so many other sensible arrangements, America has completely demolished. Having no real grasp of either literary style or brilliant conversation, we assume that introspective writers can yak it up on television, and expect the soundbitten to turn subtle and reflective on paper the moment they are alone with their thoughts.

Tom Brokaw, NBC's boyish basso profundo of the video prompter, has anchored a book. A tribute to the Americans who fought World War II, *The Greatest Generation* is a collection of the wartime experiences of obscure people, famous people, and some big fish in little ponds, chiefly those dappling Brokaw's native South Dakota and Upper Midwest.

Unless you have just returned from a Tibetan retreat you are already familiar with its contents because Brokaw has been telling stories from it, quoting himself in almost word-for-word approximations of the text, on every talk show that will have him—which is to say, all of them. The stories are quite effective in spoken form, but to meet them in print is to know with Socratic certainty that unexamined words are not worth reading.

His inviolable subject goes a long way toward saving Private Brokaw from critical reviews, but in truth *The Greatest Generation* is an overwritten, underanalyzed, frequently obtuse, unintentionally funny, cliché-ridden narrative about common men of uncommon valor winning hearts and minds amid the chilling effect of the cancer of racism.

His explanation of why he was inspired to write it churns with the urgent superlatives and drumbeat repetitions of a Special Report. World War II was "the greatest war the world has seen," brought forth "the greatest national mobilization of resources and spirit the country had ever known," was fought by "the greatest generation any society has ever produced," indeed, by "the greatest generation any society could hope to produce."

But wait, there's more. They were "a generation birthmarked for greatness, a generation of Americans that would take its place in American history with the generations that had converted the North American wilderness into the United States and infused the new nation with self-determination embodied first in the Declaration of Independence and then in the Constitution and the Bill of Rights."

When an author gets this carried away it's a dead cert that an anti-climax is coming, and Brokaw delivers a beaut:

> They became part of the greatest investment in higher education that any society ever made, a generous tribute from a grateful nation. The GI Bill, providing veterans tuition and spending money for education, was a brilliant and enduring commitment to the nation's future. . . . They were a new kind of army now, moving onto the landscapes of industry, science, art, public policy. . . .
>
> They helped convert a wartime economy into the most powerful peacetime economy in history. They made breakthroughs in medicine and other sciences. They gave the world new art and literature. They came to understand the need for federal civil rights legislation. They gave America Medicare.

These overwrought hosannas to the greatest generation are the hallmark of the book and crop up on nearly every page. However sincere his admiration may be, we can't help sensing that Brokaw is obsessed with World War II, and we begin to wonder why. It is fruitless to expect him to tell us because his skill at avoiding insight, which I will come to presently, is another of the book's hallmarks, but we learn enough to guess.

His father went to war, yet didn't. A civilian maintenance worker at an army air base in South Dakota, "Red" Brokaw was drafted, but the base commander pulled strings to get him back, reasoning that Red, a mechanical genius who could fix anything, was more valuable where he was. Brokaw describes his mother bursting into tears of relief at her husband's reprieve, but his early memories of growing up on a stateside army base—"The war effort was all around us"—evoke a picture of a little boy whose father was in the Army, yet wasn't.

There are also hints that he is self-conscious about falling between the generational slats. Born in 1940, too young to be a Depression baby, too old to be a Boomer, a member of a generation with no name, rank, or serial number who was the wrong age for every war of his time, he seems compelled to atone for his ambivalent chronology by identifying with the first generation he can remember.

The identification is total and relentless, a convert's zeal turned on history, replete with comparisons that betray a subconscious fear of falling from grace, as when he venerates the WWII generation as the last to disapprove of divorce. "My age group, which preceded the Baby Boomers, retained that attitude, but it did begin to unravel. At my fortieth high school reunion, second marriages were not unusual and there were a number of third marriages." By contrast, at WWII reunions "almost all the veterans show up with their first wives; if they're with a new mate, it's because the first one died."

Brokaw's historical method is a study in unconscious irony. His passionately stated premise that the WWII generation is the finest America has ever produced begs the question of what has happened to us since and sets up a generational war in the name of the war that "brought us together." Having painted himself into this corner, Brokaw is forced to conclude that if his WWII vets are the heroes, there must be a demographic villain someplace, *ergo* it must be the Baby Boomers. This is the closest he comes to surprising us. Members of the liberal media are not supposed to criticize the sixties, but if Paris was worth a Mass to the theologically flexible Henri IV, WWII is worth a heresy to the generationally obsessed Brokaw. He never actually condemns Boomers outright—that would imply a flaw in their parents—but he never misses a chance to work them into his narrative.

Typical is his chapter on (former) Rep. Sam Gibbons (D-Fla.), a member of the 101st Paratroopers who saw action on D-Day. In 1994, writes Brokaw, "When a well-organized class of GOP Baby Boomers took control of the House, determined to deconstruct many of the policies put in place by Democrats," Gibbons was so incensed when they cut off debate on Medicare reforms that he grabbed a Boomer congressman by the necktie and bellowed, "You're a bunch of dictators! I had to fight you guys fifty years ago!"

At other times he simply hints of something bleak. Describing the family of Lloyd Kilmer, who survived two German POW camps, he tells us: "Their first son, Lloyd Jr., was born in 1950, and Frank followed four years later. Baby Boomers." If that were on a movie sound track we would hear a sonorous gong or an eerie minor chord played on a zither.

Since the Boomers sprang from the loins of the greatest generation that ever lived, it behooves him to explain how the apple came to fall so far from the tree. But waiting for a talker to analyze what he writes is futile: Godot will show up first.

Brokaw, like television, skims the surface but never digs deeply enough to find the conflicts in his statements. Positing that most members of Gen-WWII were born around 1920, he credits them with blanket self-sufficiency and attributes it to their having come of age during the Depression. Accepting hardship and fighting for survival were "just the way they were raised," he writes, ignoring the fact that people who came of age during the Depression also came of age during the New Deal and spent their formative years watching Franklin D. Roosevelt give the store away. That this just might have something to do with "They gave America Medicare" seems not to occur to him.

The dual message of the 1930's also eludes him in his story of Dr. Charles Van Gorder, who liberated a train full of American POWs and operated on the D-Day wounded for 36 straight hours until he collapsed into an opened abdomen. After the war, Van Gorder, wishing to go where he could do the most good, opened a practice in an Appalachian town that had never had its own doctor. Eventually he had so many patients that he decided to build his own hospital. To finance it, he applied for federal Hill-Burton funds and soon found himself spending most of his time filling out forms. Today, writes Brokaw in all innocence, Van Gorder "laments" bureaucratic control of medicine.

Some of Brokaw's veterans turned into the classic absentee father of the 1950's, the emotionally distant, workaholic striver and Organization Man whose children rarely saw him because they were always in bed when he got home. Why did the greatest generation produce this type? Here we have a subject in desperate need of some original thought, but Brokaw gives it only droning boilerplate:

> In the service they had learned the importance of identifying an objective and pursuing it until the mission was accomplished. Also, they felt they had to make up for lost time. These were the children of the Depression, with fresh memories of deprivation, and the postwar years were abundant with opportunities to make real money. They didn't want to miss out.

Describing the writer's instinct, Maupassant spoke of "looking for the underside of things, even if it means turning over a rock." Is it possible that men who have enjoyed four years of freedom from women, children, and the tedium of domesticity would seek in the working world, which was then largely masculine, a replication of the exclusively masculine world of war? Yes, it's entirely possible, but it's not exactly the greatest thing to say, so forget it.

Whether from laziness or lack of imagination, Brokaw does not even try to penetrate the stories he tells. No doubt he calls this "letting them speak for themselves," but it's more a matter of letting them languish on the page while he rounds them off with one of his inanities or goes on to something else.

Hawaii Senator Daniel Inouye worried about racism when he learned that his Japanese-American unit would train at Camp Shelby, Mississippi, but to his surprise, he and his comrades were inundated in Southern hospitality and treated royally. "For the first time in my life," he told Brokaw, "I danced with a white girl."

This, Brokaw intones earnestly, "was a reflection of the racial schizophrenia loose in America. The Magnolia State was the epicenter of discrimination against black citizens, treating them as little more than paid slaves, and yet it made the extra effort for Japanese-American soldiers at the same time the U.S. government was shipping their families off to internment camps."

Period. Paragraph. Over and out. Has life in television left him so overscripted that he can't figure out how much Southerners and Asians have in common? Both put a premium on manners, formality, hierarchy, ritual, custom, and all things old. As the heroine of Hamilton Basso's novel of South Carolina, *The View from Pompey's Head*, put it: "We're like the Japanese. We grow rice and worship our ancestors."

It cannot be said that Brokaw's prose runs the gamut between fallen archness and irony deficiency because he never strives for either. Its usual path is between a network news human-interest feature and a Sunday-supplement advice column.

A former South Dakota governor and Medal of Honor winner: "No one would ever accuse Joe Foss of slowing down. Even now, at the age of eighty-two, he inhales life in big, energetic drafts."

A survivor of Guadalcanal who returned his Sioux foster son to the reservation after the boy tried to burn down the house: "This is not an unusual occurrence when white families try to raise young Indians. The cultural differences often become too great to be successfully managed, but Gordon still feels disappointed that it came to a bad end."

War stories, like childbirth stories, eventually start to sound alike, and even Brokaw seems to realize it. As the book goes on he gives the war shorter and shorter shrift, concentrating on the post-war and present-day activities of his veterans, especially those who went into politics, larding his accounts with turgid interjections on the evils of racism and sexism.

He saves his most unabashed liberal bias for the story of former Oregon Senator Mark Hatfield, who saw action on Okinawa and served with MacArthur in the occupation of Japan. A liberal Republican whose anti-Vietnam stance landed him on Nixon's enemies list, Hatfield was called soft on Communism by GOP regulars, who virtually shunned him when he later came out against the invasion of Grenada and Desert Storm. He retired in 1996, giving Brokaw another crack at the Boomers:

> Some of the newer Republican senators, with their strict conservative dogmas, may never understand a man like Mark Hatfield, but then they've never shuttled Marines ashore under heavy fire at Iwo Jima or Okinawa. They've never looked out on the unworldly landscape of nuclear devastation and shared their lunch with a starving Japanese child.

The most vivid story in the book is Art Buchwald's sojourn in the Marines, but it owes nothing to Brokaw, who put it together from Buchwald's war memoir, *Leaving Home*. A walking disaster who dropped a bomb on the tarmac as he was loading it onto a plane, Buchwald was reunited after the war with his Parris Island drill instructor, Pete Bonardi, who told him: "I was sure you'd get killed. You were a real s--tbird." Buchwald agreed, and gave him an autographed picture: "To Pete Bonardi, who made a man out of me. I'll never forget you." Bonardi kept the picture in his hospital room during his final illness, and at his request it was buried with him.

This story needs nothing else, but unfortunately Brokaw adds a comment: "I confess that I weep almost every time I read that account, for it so encapsulates the bonds within that generation that last a lifetime."

I may have missed the greatest one, but reading this book makes me a veteran of the War of Brokaw's Ear.

The American Spectator, May 1999
Book Review

"The Man Who Defined American Culture"

Noah Webster: The Life and Times of an American Patriot
by Harlow Giles Unger
(John Wiley & Sons, 386 pages, $30)

A s a member of the usage panel of a major American dictionary, I am often struck by the attention given to diversity and multiculturalism in the ballots I am asked to submit. Defining words is coming more and more to be seen as "judgmentalism" by definition, and dictionary editors, once serene pedants, now rate combat pay.

How sweet it is, then, to review this superb biography of Noah Webster and read some of the entries in the first (1828) edition of his magnum opus, *An American Dictionary of the English Language*:

LOVE, v.t...The Christian loves his Bible.
INESTIMABLE, adj...The privileges of American citizens, civil and religious, are inestimable.
INDULGENCE, n...How many children are ruined by indulgence!
MODESTY, n...Unaffected modesty is the sweetest charm of female excellence.

Noah Webster is often confused with his younger distant cousin, Daniel, the senator from Massachusetts who famously proclaimed to Southern separatists, "Liberty and Union, now and forever, one and inseparable." Noah fought for liberty as a member of Yale's class of 1778, marching out with other student Minutemen to meet the red-coats at Saratoga, but he fought for union on the battleground of American culture.

Cultural unity was the defining force in his life from his birth in 1758 in the Connecticut farming village of Hartford. Direct descen-dants of Mayflower leader William Bradford, the Websters were mem-bers of the Congregational church, then Connecticut's established church and still a Puritan theocracy. Separation of church and state was unknown. Property taxes supported the church, the vote was restricted to church members, the temporal offices of sheriff and aldermen were filled by clergymen and deacons, and Sunday morning worship ser-vices merged into afternoon town meetings in the church building: The political elite and the Calvinist Elect were one and the same.

Growing up diversity-deprived gave Noah Webster a rock-solid identity, but the world beyond his homogeneous Eden was fast becoming a multicultural caldron. In religion the Great Awakening was replacing predestination with equality of salvation, while the political situation resembled the Tower of Babel. French was the lan-guage of Vermont and Maine, Dutch was spoken in New York, and the dominant German-speaking farmers of Pennsylvania fired on English-speaking migrants who tried to settle there.

The linguistic conflicts in the Revolutionary Army were even worse and pointed Noah toward his life's work when he observed the troops awaiting mustering-out in Newburgh, New York, after the war:

[H]e heard a dizzying cacophony of languages and accents. . . . He could not understand them, and the sporadic fights he saw told him that many of them could not understand one another, either. Far from producing unity, the independence for which they had fought so long and hard had turned them into a nasty, squalling mob. Webster had come expecting warmth and mutual affection between his countrymen but found only strangers thrashing about in a raging sea of anarchy. . . . [H]e realized that only a uniform method of speaking—a common language—would ever ensure the fraternity Americans needed to remain united in nationhood and govern themselves peacefully.

Giving up law for teaching, he opened an academy and threw himself into the task of imposing order on the chaos of 18th-century American speech. His greatest fear was the social and political divisions that invariably grew out of dialects. The nations of Europe had been rent by them; even in tiny England, Yorkshiremen and Cornishmen could not understand each other. What would happen in spacious America when a steadily growing immigrant population confronted the caprice of *-ough* and the subtly different vowel sounds in rove-move-dove?

Reasoning that no one would say "sparrowgrass" and "chimbley" who learned how to spell "asparagus" and "chimney," he decided to change the traditional alphabetical method of teaching reading to one that emphasized syllables and sounds.

Existing primers grouped words that had no attributes in common except initial letters (age, all, are, ape). As most of them had been published in England they also contained British spellings such as "honour" and "theatre," and worse, word lists composed of English shires and towns exposed American children to the unhelpful news that Pontefract is pronounced "pumfret." The few available American texts followed the British alphabetical method, and terrorized children with practice sentences describing slow pupils being consumed by the fires of Hell. Finally, there being no children's literature, the only available reader was the Bible with its polysyllabic Hebraic names and archaic verbs.

Lacking the materials he needed, Webster had to write his own. The result was *The American Spelling Book*. He grouped words according to sound (bug, dug, tug) to appeal to children's natural love of rhymes, used homophones (bear, bare) to construct jokes and games, and emphasized syllables instead of the sound of each letter so that pupils readily understood that "example" was pronounced "exam-pul" and not "examplee."

To realize his goal of "a national language," the Minuteman-turned-pedant practiced his own version of ethnic cleansing. To sever the cultural ties with the mother country that many Americans, especially former Tories, still clung to, he eliminated all English spellings, dropped double consonants having no effect on pronunciation (traveller, waggon), and ruled that the last letter of the alphabet was "zee," not "zed."

His spelling book proved so popular with his pupils and their parents that he decided to publish it, but authorship was a perilous business under the Articles of Confederation. The first form of government established by the newly independent colonies, the Confederation was a states' rights nightmare under a virtually powerless Congress. There was no national copyright law, nor much of a national anything; states issued their own money, levied customs duties on each other, and flirted with the right to declare war. To copyright his book, Webster would have to petition each of the 13 legislatures separately.

This he did, embarking on America's first book tour, networking and schmoozing his way from Massachusetts to Georgia, introducing himself to printers and schoolmasters and making friends with influential men such as James Madison, who obligingly introduced a copyright law in the Virginia legislature.

His efforts succeeded—he published his copyrighted primer in 1783—but the experience proved that the Articles of Confederation, like multilingualism, invited disunity and eventual anarchy and must be eliminated.

To this end, he wrote four powerful political essays published as *Sketches of American Policy*, in which he outlined a plan for the creation of a strong federal government. The impact of this work, in the opinion of his present biographer, makes him more of a Founding Father than he has been given credit for. "Although ignored by most historians, Webster's *Sketches* preceded by two and a half years the publication of the Federalist essays, which appeared in 1787-88, and both Alexander Hamilton and James Madison borrowed almost all of Webster's concepts for their essays."

It is known that George Washington read the *Sketches* because

James Madison borrowed his copy during a visit to Mount Vernon in 1785. Moreover, during the Constitutional convention of 1787, Webster, who was then teaching in Philadelphia, received visits from Washington and other delegates. "There is no concrete evidence that these visits directly affected deliberations or the Constitution's final form," writes Unger. "It may, however, be more than coincidental that after each such visit to Webster, Washington and the delegates returned to the convention and reached compromises suggested by Webster, or inserted language in the Constitution that was similar to or exactly that found in Webster's *Sketches* or other writings."

At least one part of the Constitution as finally adopted has his fingerprints on it: Article I, Section 8, Paragraph 8, proposed by his old friend James Madison, gives Congress the power to establish national copyright and patent laws.

An ardent Federalist, Webster was incensed by Thomas Jefferson's enthusiastic support of the bloody excesses of the French Revolution and his statement that "France is our true mother country." He suspected Jefferson of complicity with "Citizen Genet," Revolutionary France's minister to the United States, whose fiery speeches accusing Washington's Federalist administration of monarchical aspirations incited pro-Jefferson mobs to riot, nearly destroying Philadelphia. Disgusted by their shouts of "Vive la France!" and bawled renditions of "La Marseillaise," Webster called them "the French Democratic Party consisting of American citizens" and said that Jefferson, who was Washington's secretary of state at the time, should be charged with treason.

He grew increasingly conservative as time went on, coming to regard steadily expanding political freedom on a par with unregulated spelling and pronunciation. To his way of thinking, anarchy was anarchy and he was against it wherever it reared its head. He argued passionately against extending the suffrage to non-property owners, stating unabashedly, "I would definitely prefer a limited monarchy, for I would sooner be subject to the caprice of one man, than to the ignorance and passions of the multitudes."

He expressed his increasingly unpopular views in his capacity as editor of a variety of newspapers and magazines, but all lost money.

Finally, when Jefferson became president, Webster abandoned political writing and returned to his first love.

At this time, Dr. Samuel Johnson's 40,000-word *Dictionary of the English Language* was regarded as a sacred text on both sides of the Atlantic. Several American lexicographers had published dictionaries but they were slim (25,000 words), vague ("bemused" defined as "overcome with musing"), and idiosyncratic: One contained "cap-a-pie" but omitted "ocean" and "newspaper," another omitted words ending in *-ly* and *-ness* to save printing costs, and all contained lingering English spellings and references.

Harlow Giles Unger's account of Webster at work on his dictionary is the most evocative description of a labor of love since the "Black Coffee" chapter in Stefan Zweig's biography of Balzac.

We see the aging Minuteman pursuing the magisterial Dr. Johnson through word thickets, sniping at "the last vestige of British rule in America." We follow him around the room as he places himself at one end of a long table covered with dictionaries in all languages; looks up a word, makes a note, and moves on, circling the table again and again in his endless stroll through comparative philology.

We look on, stunned, as he teaches himself to read Chaldaic, Arabic, Hebrew, Persian, Celtic, and Anglo-Saxon so that he can trace the history of each word; and we travel with him to Paris's Bibliotheque du Roi, remembering to keep very still while he pores over the first dictionary published by the Academie Francaise in 1694.

The two-volume work took him 20 years: 70,000 words, definitions, and origins, all researched and written by hand by a 66-year-old scholar working entirely alone—the last lexicographer to do so. As we come to the end with him we can only bow our heads.

Webster achieved the cultural unity he sought. America developed regional accents but we are the only major country in history without dialects. Said a newspaper editorial after his death: "Here, five thousand miles change not the sound of a word. Around every fireside, and from every tribune, in every field of labor, and every factory of toil, is heard the same tongue. We owe it to Webster."

He also practiced "compassionate conservatism" without straining for it. His spelling book, used in American schools for more than a century and in some areas until the early 1930's, taught generations of children, native-born and immigrant, to speak in a single voice of Standard American English, erasing their differences and raising their self-esteem in ways no government program can match.

Unfortunately, government strained for compassionate liberalism and now its efforts have virtually erased his. Today, writes Unger, bilingualism and multiculturalism have created:

> a huge new nation within the United States—a nation whose children are growing up semiliterate in both English and their native tongues and who are developing little or no love or allegiance to their new land. As the dissimulative purveyors of multilingualism divide the nation culturally under the banner of individual liberty, they will all but surely divide the nation politically and provoke anarchy, as their predecessors have done throughout history.

Don't miss this stirring book. When it first came to my attention I wondered if the subject of lexicography could hold its own in a post-impeachment, all-Monica-all-the-time atmosphere, but Unger's memorable final assessment says it all: "Webster's life was not about a dictionary. It was about creating a new nation—the *United* States of America—and making everyone in America an American."

The American Spectator, April 2000
Book Review

"Helen Dear"

*I'm Wild Again: Snippets From My Life and
a Few Brazen Thoughts* by Helen Gurley Brown
(St. Martin's Press, 287 pages, $24.95)

Twenty-five years ago when I wrote for *Cosmopolitan*, I was lunching with one of the editors when the conversation turned to the enigma that was Helen Gurley Brown.

"I guess we'll have to wait for her autobiography," I said.

The editor shook her head. "Helen will never open up."

She was right. Brown's new book, far from being the tell-all of its advance publicity, is exactly what the subtitle says it is: snippets from a life, some of them taken almost verbatim from her earlier books, which in turn were variations on the theme of her first book, *Sex and the Single Girl*, the 1962 self-help land mine that gave her her start.

What makes her latest venture into print interesting—even, in a grotesque way, inspiring—is how successful she is in wrestling introspection, along with fat and aging, to a standstill.

Helen Marie Gurley was born in Little Rock in 1921, the younger of two daughters of Ira and Cleo Gurley. When she was ten something terrible happened. Any other writer would make a calamity of this magnitude the centerpiece of her childhood and devote a long chapter to it, but Helen settles for a parenthetical—literally—account of her father's death in a freak accident.

(Daddy had died five years before in an elevator accident in the

Arkansas State Capitol Building, had run for the elevator, jumped
on just as the doors were closing—you could do that then—life got
snuffed out.)

Unless she's a psychopath this has to have been a devastating
trauma, but the only aspect of it she discusses is the financial crisis
that ensued when her widowed mother had spent all the insurance
money. She says nothing about her reaction to her father's death,
nothing about her feelings—or lack thereof—for him, and nothing
about the man himself. He was a member of the State legislature; was
he planning a political career?

She doesn't even say whether the manner of his death left her with
any feelings about elevators. Is she leery of them? What goes through
her mind when she gets on one? Something? Anything? Or did she
block out the whole incident and transfer her unresolved feelings for
her father to the entire male sex? She has spent her adult life pleasing
them in bed and out, and built a career around telling other women to
do the same. Is her whole *Cosmo* stance an attempt to make up to her
father for what happened to him? It's food for thought, but Helen
Gurley Brown, dieter par excellence, won't touch it.

Tragedy struck again when Helen's sister, Mary, got polio. Mother
moved them to Los Angeles, where Helen graduated from high school
and business school and embarked on a secretarial career (130 wpm
shorthand) and what would eventually become a storied sex life.

She lost her virginity at 20, having no need to lose it earlier, she
explains, because "I could be brought to orgasm by kissing." At 24
she was kept for a year by her boss, a rich 43-year-old real estate
developer; "not a beauty, but not a mongoose . . . I could handle it."
Her object was to get enough money from him to take care of her sister, who was now permanently confined to a wheelchair, but she
admits she did not know how to handle him. He pulled strings to get
her an apartment during the WWII housing shortage but she ended up
paying the rent from her salary. When he happened to find $750 cash
in a file drawer he gave it to her, but no jewels or stocks. Like most
kept women she was home alone a lot. "Television hadn't arrived. I
read." What did she read? She doesn't say.

Her stint as a professional mistress lasted about a year. Her next lover was a vast improvement—"he was bow-wow in bed"—then came former heavyweight boxing champ Jack Dempsey, whom she met when the ad agency she worked for hired him to endorse Bulldog Beer. Then 62, Dempsey would visit her for bed sport, yell "Straighten me out, darling" at the climactic moment, then be taken home by his driver who was waiting outside. She can be excused for not being introspective about this interlude; not even the Bröntes could come up with a deeper meaning.

By age 37 she knew enough about men to get David Brown to marry her. He said "Why can't we go on as we are?" and she said "Don't call me again unless it's to tell me you're ready to get married." She stuck to her guns and it worked. David, then an executive with Darryl Zanuck, became her Pygmalion. It was he who came up with the idea for *Sex and the Single Girl*, urged her to write it, used his contacts to get it published, and then came up with an even better idea as he watched her knock herself out writing personal replies to the tons of fan mail she received.

The fan-mail story is Helen at her nicest. Somewhere in her makeup is a well-mannered Southern girl who knows that a lady always sends notes. As editor-in-chief of *Cosmo* she did wonders for her writers' morale with warm little messages, always with an inverted salutation ("Florence Dear"), saying how much she appreciated our latest effort.

It would be just like her to take it upon herself to answer every single fan letter. She might still be at it had David not spoken up.

"If you had your own magazine," he said, "you could answer them all at once. "

The rest is history—or should be. But she devotes little more than a page to how she breathed life into Hearst's dying magazine and turned it, for better or worse, into a greater influence on women's liberation than all of feminism's tomes put together. It would be fascinating to read a detailed account of her first year at the helm. Even more fascinating would be hearing her version of some of the great *Cosmo* legends, such as the "Breast Article" (how to fondle them, how to kiss them, etc.) that was leaked to the press by a treacherous staffer.

But instead we get a stitch-by-stitch account of her cosmetic surgeries. She's had three face lifts; the first at age 60, the second at 67, and the third in 1995 at the age of 73, when she also had her bosom augmented from the A cup nature gave her to the B she regards as her ideal size. She offers no explanation for why she waited so long, or why she even bothered at such an advanced age, except to say that fashions were bosom-revealing that year.

A year or so later she was diagnosed with breast cancer, but denies—twice—that it had anything to do with the "massive doses of estrogen" (two 1. 25 milligram tablets a day) she had taken "for the past thirty years." A little while later she says it again: "I also don't dwell on the possibility of my having given *myself* cancer with the heavy dosage of Premarin for thirty-three years. Occasionally a doctor suggested taking less but nobody slugged me."

In other words, she started gobbling estrogen at 44. Why? Was she trying to ward off the menopause entirely and menstruate forever? She doesn't say.

Nor does she explain why, at 75, she sprang for a lumpectomy instead of a mastectomy, saying only, "Whew! I get to keep most of my breast." Keep it, please God, for *what?* We never find out because she would rather explain that Crisco shortening, which she used as an emollient after surgery, also helps nails grow strong. Now she carries a tub of it everywhere she goes, prompting David to observe that it's like "being married to an apple pie."

Her other surgery was a hysterectomy that she almost undid when she insisted on doing her regular daily exercises in defiance of the doctor's warning that she could burst her sutures. The exercises are described in a prose style that manages to be both giddy and numbing at the same time; whenever she finds herself somewhere unamenable to a full work-out, such as an airplane, she goes in the lavatory and exercises by sitting down on and getting up off the toilet, over and over again. Her life's ambition is to have a "concave tummy," which still eludes her even though she weighs only 99 pounds.

Most of the book consists of the "brazen thoughts" of the subtitle, fragmented observations in no particular order, whatever pops into her head:

—"Good drivers are good in bed."

—How to Tell What *Size* He Is: Check out "the vertical indentation in a man's ear that dips down into the fleshy part of the lobe." In the best-endowed men it's so long it looks like Italy.

—Another firm statement (she had one in her first book) about the total absence of lesbianism in her life.

—Rewriting the Lord's Prayer to make it jibe with her definition of temptation. ("Don't scoop all the petit fours off the plate at a tony restaurant into your purse and, if scooped, don't eat them all at once when you get home. Try to make yourself throw them in the john.")

Her favorite word is "pippypoo," whose definition ranges from shallow and superficial, to silly fun and frivolity, to decorative and cute. (I already knew this from her editorial notes on one of my articles, which contained the cryptic observation: "Well, we never get anything pippypoo from Florence, she's always so warpy-and-woofy.")

Her disquisition on the dangers of gossip contains the worst writing in the book:

> We had a nice lunch one day, chatted like old friends, but when I couldn't get another friend to return my phone calls, finally reached her, and asked about the blackout, she said Diane had told her I had said she, Maudie, the non-phone-call returner, never left her house these days but stayed in bed smoking pot. I'd actually told Diane about her staying in bed but not about the pot because I didn't know about it, that was said by Diane to me but whoever said it, you wouldn't tell the person it was said about them, would you, if it's something they won't like?

Like all skinflints she prefers to think of herself as "thrifty." She buys one bottle of spring water for $2.98, then refills the bottle with tap water and serves it to guests. She takes New York buses at senior-citizen rates, even after chic theater parties, and makes David ride them too, happily reminding him how much they saved on cabs. She once jumped out of a cab taking her the long way around the San Antonio airport rather than pay the $8 on the meter, and ended up walking down the freeway. Is it any wonder she recommends semen as a facial mask? It's free.

She won't come right out and admit it, but it's obvious that she hates children. Once she even screamed "shut up!" at a crying baby on a plane, mortifying the *Cosmo* editors traveling with her. The other time she lost it in public also happened on a plane, when they ran out of the baked salmon she had ordered and the stewardess brought her "fat sausage and runny eggs." Exploding, "I can't eat this s--t!" she upended the plate and dumped it in the aisle.

She doesn't connect these two episodes of air rage, but the reader does: Babies and fat sausages both ruin the figure.

The American Spectator, September 2000
Book Review

"Uncle Cleve"

*An Honest President: The Life and Presidencies of
Grover Cleveland* by H. Paul Jeffers
(William Morrow, 385 pages, $27)

B
ill Clinton usually identifies with FDR and JFK, but a time
came when his narcissism inexplicably receded in favor of a
president most Americans knew nothing about. In late 1997
a newsmagazine reported that he had become fascinated with Grover
Cleveland, seeing in him an underappreciated reformer ahead of his
times and something of a "soul mate." Two months later, these murky
ruminations fell into place when Monica Lewinsky fell out of the
Oval Office closet and the ever-helpful media plucked Grover
Cleveland from the dust bin of history and made him a household
name. Over and over we were told that during the campaign of 1884,
Republicans leaked the story that Democrat Cleveland had fathered
an illegitimate child. What the media did not dwell on was how he
handled it. When the scandal broke, Cleveland, unlike his self-
appointed soul mate, turned to his campaign manager and spoke six
unparsed words: "Whatever you do, tell the truth."

Stephen Grover Cleveland was born in 1837 in Caldwell, New
Jersey, the fifth of nine children of a Presbyterian minister. When his
father died, 16-year-old Steve, as he was then called, left school and
went to work to help support his mother and sisters. After a stint of
teaching, he was about to go to Ohio and try his luck in Cleveland,
named for his ancestor who founded it, when an uncle in Buffalo

invited him to move there and read law. He became a Buffalo institution: a lawyer who refused to defend anyone he knew to be guilty, a sheriff who put an end to public hangings, and an incorruptible mayor who forced his city council to renegotiate a street-cleaning contract when he discovered they had made a kick-back deal with the highest bidder. His reputation for probity with public money would soon get him elected governor of New York.

In his off hours he was known as "Big Steve" for the 300 pounds he carried on his medium-height frame, acquired in Buffalo's German restaurants and beer parlors. He showed no interest in getting married, but in 1871 at the age of 34, he took up with a young widow, Maria Crofts Halpin, who also "entertained" several of his friends, among them his married law partner, Oscar Folsom.

In 1874, Maria gave birth to a son and named him Oscar Folsom Cleveland. She told Cleveland he was the father and he offered to pay child support, but when she began drinking and neglecting him, a judge committed her to a mental asylum and put the boy in an orphanage. Cleveland reimbursed the orphanage for his expenses until the child's adoption by a prominent western New York family. When Maria was released from the asylum, Cleveland gave her the money to start a business and she disappeared from his life, eventually remarrying.

In 1875 at the height of the imbroglio, Oscar Folsom was thrown from his carriage and killed. Cleveland served as his executor and looked after his widow and 10-year-old daughter, Frances. Around this time he announced without explanation that he wished to be called by his middle name—his symbolic way, perhaps, of banishing Big Steve.

The scandal remained dormant while he was governor (he won by the largest majority in New York history), and so, apparently, did Big Steve. The Albany paper described his lonely routine as "works and eats, eats and works, works and eats." As governor, his efforts to restructure city administrations to root out bossism earned him the hatred of Tammany Hall and the attention of the national Democratic Party. "We love him for the enemies he has made," said his supporters at the 1884 convention. Reform was in the air and Cleveland emerged as the John McCain of the Gilded Age, nominated on the third ballot to run against GOP Sen. James G. Blaine, "continental liar from the state of Maine."

When the Maria Halpin story broke, Charles A. Dana, the pro-Blaine editor of the *New York Sun*, called him "a coarse debauchee who would bring his harlots with him to Washington and hire lodgings for them convenient to the White House," but his up-front admission of paternity won most voters to the view expressed by another newspaper editor, who said he "preferred Cleveland's private unchastity to Blaine's public corruption."

Next came the charge that he had shirked military duty in the Civil War. Yes, said Cleveland, it was true. The draft law permitted the hiring of substitutes and he had hired one because he was the sole support of his mother and sisters.

As the campaign drew to a close, still another editor, Joseph Pulitzer, wrote: "There are four reasons to vote for Cleveland. 1.) He is an honest man, 2.) He is an honest man, 3.) He is an honest man, 4.) He is an honest man."

Cleveland's victory put a Democrat in the White House for the first time since the election of James Buchanan in 1856. He was also the first bachelor since Buchanan, but that would soon change. In 1886, amid rumors that he planned to marry the widow of his old friend and law partner, Oscar Folsom, the 49-year-old President announced his engagement to her 21-year-old daughter, Frances, whom he called "Frank." She called him "Uncle Cleve."

They were married in the White House—another first—with John Philip Sousa conducting the Marine Band. A stunning brunette, Frances instantly won the hearts of press and public; even one of Cleveland's arch-enemies was moved to say, "I detest him so much I don't even think his wife is beautiful." Despite her youth, Frances brought a polished aplomb to her first-lady duties, especially receiving lines, which she actually appeared to enjoy.

Honesty puzzles the flexible majority of men and Cleveland's was no exception. A firm believer in the gold standard, he used his first State of the Union message to condemn the free coinage of silver and the practice of redeeming silver certificates in gold, predicting that it would drain gold from the Treasury to overseas banks, cause gold hoarding, and wipe out savings.

He called for the suspension of "free silver," but as a strict Constitutional constructionist he refused to use pressure and patronage to win on the issue. Congress had the money power and he had the veto power, he explained, and "I believe the most important benefit that I can confer upon my country by my Presidency is to insist upon the entire independence of the executive and legislative branches." The absence of presidential cajolery and arm-twisting enabled Western silver interests to prevail and left gold-standard congressmen pondering what, to their way of thinking, was a lack of leadership.

Next he gored a sacred cow. The House and Senate voted to award a pension to every disabled Civil War veteran with at least three months of service. Cleveland vetoed it, arguing that the bill was so loosely worded that it covered men who had not seen combat or even reached the front, and might be used for present disabilities unrelated to the war.

"It is sad, but nevertheless true," he said in his veto message, "that in the matter of procuring pensions there exists a widespread disregard for truth and good faith. . . . [T]he race after the pensions offered in this bill would not only stimulate the weakness and pretended incapacity for labor, but put further premium on dishonesty and mendacity."

Public and press largely agreed, but the GAR (Grand Army of the Republic, forerunner of today's American Legion) savaged him. When it was learned that he planned to return captured Confederate battle flags to Southern states, the rancor mounted, causing his advisors to question whether he should go ahead with his already scheduled appearance at the GAR's convention. Like Bill Clinton at the Vietnam Memorial, if he went he would be booed; if he canceled he would be called a coward.

Clinton went and was booed, but Cleveland canceled for a reason that his "soul mate" could never understand: "I might, if I alone were concerned, submit to the insult to which it is quite openly asserted I would be helplessly subjected if present; but I should bear with me there the people's highest office, the dignity of which I must protect."

He achieved another first with his 1888 re-election bid, winning the popular vote but losing the Electoral College to the gnomish Benjamin Harrison, whose main achievements were the Sherman Silver Purchase Act and the overthrow of Hawaii's Queen Liliuokalani. Neither event captured the public's attention as much as the birth in 1891 of the first Cleveland baby, Ruth, who was immortalized by a candy bar that most Americans think was named for a baseball player.

Their second daughter, Esther, became the first baby to be born in the White House when her father became the first president to win a non-consecutive second term in 1892. He promptly withdrew Harrison's Hawaiian annexation treaty, which was still in committee, saying, "The United States cannot be properly put in the position of countenancing a wrong after its commission any more than of consenting to it in advance."

He won repeal of the Sherman Silver Purchase Act, but it was too late. Foreign and domestic demands for conversions of silver for gold had reduced the Treasury's gold reserves to a record low. The combination of the gold crisis and high tariffs brought on the Panic of 1893.

Amid bank failures, farm foreclosures, and railroad receiverships came Cleveland's greatest crisis, the Pullman Strike led by railway-union organizer Eugene Debs. As it spread, the Illinois Central was paralyzed, Chicago was edged toward anarchy, and post-office operations ground to a halt. To Cleveland the strict constructionist, the threat to the mails reduced the matter to a simple question: "Did the people elect Eugene Debs or Grover Cleveland president?" Without consulting Illinois Governor John Peter Altgeld, he sent in federal troops and placed Chicago under martial law.

It was the first time since the Civil War that soldiers were ordered into action against American citizens, but Cleveland had one more first to go: "Coxey's Army," the rag-tag band of dispossessed silverites who made up the first march on Washington.

In 1896 the Democrats repudiated Cleveland and the gold standard and nominated silverite William Jennings Bryan. Grover and Frances bought a house in Princeton, where the ex-president spent the remaining 12 years of his life serving as a university trustee, writing articles for magazines, and compiling a volume of sketches on hunting and fishing. The Princeton years were more notable in another way: Frances had two more babies, both boys, the last born when Big Steve was 66.

An Honest President provides a thorough overview of Grover Cleveland's public life, but readers who enjoy "psychohistory" may find it disappointing. In fairness to the author, it could hardly be otherwise. Psychohistory requires a certain degree of torment, but Cleveland was as simple and hearty as the big German meals he enjoyed in Buffalo's restaurants. Though not placid in the sluggish sense, he had a rare gift of contentment.

It deserted him only when he had to cope, not once but twice, with the unique problem of being an ex-president:

> After the long exercise of power [he wrote], the ordinary affairs of life seem petty and commonplace. An ex-President practicing law or going into business is like a locomotive hauling a delivery wagon. He has lost his sense of proportion. The concerns of other people and even his own affairs seem too small to be worth bothering about.

This is as honest a statement as we are likely to find of what lies uneasily in the minds of those who know Bill Clinton.

The American Spectator, March 2001
Book Review

"Hyperethereal Holmes"

Law Without Values: The Life, Work, and Legacy
of Justice Holmes by Albert W. Alschuler
(University of Chicago Press, 325 pages, $30)

O liver Wendell Holmes, Jr. is the only U.S. Supreme Court justice to be the subject of a best-selling novel, a hit Broadway play, and a movie, but this frantic little book does everything it can to bork him into oblivion, and blames him for every crisis in contemporary American life from the politics of resentment to the spread of obesity.

The best way to sort all this out, to the extent that an author like Albert W. Alschuler can ever be sorted out, is to begin at the beginning and examine what would today be called the post-Civil War Stress Syndrome that Holmes experienced first-hand and the nation as a whole subsequently experienced as a cultural and philosophical sea change.

The America into which Holmes was born in 1841 based its judicial system on natural law: intrinsic or divinely inspired moral absolutes that were simply "there," such as the "inalienable" rights to life and liberty. The young Holmes shared this philosophy and laid his idealism on the line, joining the Abolitionist movement and leaving Harvard in 1861 to serve as a lieutenant in the 20th Massachusetts.

He was seriously wounded in the chest at Ball's Bluff, took a bullet in the neck at Antietam, and another in the heel at Chancellorsville. That he also suffered from battle fatigue is evident in his letters from the front. Their morbid thoughts and macabre descriptions might have signaled a nervous breakdown in another kind of young man, but instead he came home full of a Nietzschean conviction that war, heroism, and danger make life worth living, and that everything hangs on the struggle for power.

It led to the formation of a point of view that he held for the rest of his life and never hesitated to express in his disarming way: "I come devilish near to believing that might makes right."

The war had made him contemptuous of idealistic causes like Abolition, but his new Nietzschean outlook drew him inexorably to an ethos that found favor in late nineteenth-century America: Social Darwinism. Applying the theory of the survival of the fittest to industry, commerce, and social problems was catnip to a rapacious Gilded Age. It gave the buccaneers of capitalism a rationale for exploitation, and gradually replaced natural law with a judicial system of "utilitarian pragmatism"—the law of "what works" when competing groups vie for power and dominance in an increasingly complex modern society.

The author believes that the law has been on a downward path ever since, and blames Holmes for leading it there. America's most influential jurist from his appointment to the Supreme Court by Theodore Roosevelt in 1902 to his retirement in 1932, Holmes promulgated a "brutal worldview," was indifferent to the welfare of others, sneered at all progressive movements except eugenics, and was a nihilist and existentialist who held human life meaningless.

Holmes is not for the fainthearted. He believed that mankind was of no cosmic importance, and that it would not much matter "if the whole ant heap were kerosened."

Defining a right as "what a given crowd will fight for," he confessed: "[I] place no stock in abstract rights and equally fail to respect the passion for equality." An unabashed elitist, he "loathed the thick-fingered clowns we call the people."

Welfare moved him not: "As to the right of citizens to support and education, I don't see it. I see no right in my neighbor to share my bread."

To a humanitarian incensed over the practice of "treating people like things," Holmes replied: "If a man lives in society, he is liable to find himself so treated."

In racial matters he extended the separate but equal doctrine, ruling that Alabama could require a private college to segregate because it operated as a corporation at the pleasure of the state. In general, he held that because the white South was the dominant de facto power in the community, it could subordinate blacks if it wished, and there was nothing the federal courts could or should do about it.

His decisions on bilingual education and women in the workplace would cause cardiac arrest today. In a flurry of isolationism after World War I, several states banned the teaching of *all* foreign languages. The Supreme Court declared the laws unconstitutional, but Holmes dissented on the grounds that the laws were "a reasonable and even necessary method of encouraging a common tongue."

Do employers who impose lighter work standards on women violate the Equal Protection clause? No, said Holmes: "The Fourteenth Amendment does not interfere by creating a fictitious equality where there is a real difference."

Holmes's most famous cases produced phrases that have entered the language. Rosita Schwimmer was a pacifist alien who applied for citizenship, but said she would refuse to swear to defend the Constitution. Since this oath was the crux of the naturalization ceremony, the Supreme Court denied her citizenship. Holmes dissented in the name of "freedom for the thought we hate," but later, in private, he left no doubt that he hated the thought: "What damn fools people are who believe things. . . . All isms seem to me silly—but this hyperethereal respect for human life seems perhaps the silliest of all."

He ruled that socialist Eugene Debs had no right of free speech under the 1917 Espionage Act. Debs had publicly condemned the World War I draft but claimed he was speaking against war in general, not this particular war. Holmes ruled that if the speech was intended to obstruct recruiting, and if that would be the probable effect, then it was not protected speech. When Debs was sentenced to ten years,

Holmes opined that isms fare best when tested in the "marketplace of ideas." Later he confided his private thoughts on free speech to a friend: "Little as I believe in it as a theory, I hope I would die for it."

His best-known statement, used with stunning dramatic effect in the movie *Judgment at Nuremburg*, comes from the 1929 case of Carrie Buck, "a feeble-minded white woman," who was the daughter of a feeble-minded woman and the mother of a feeble-minded child. Buck, an inmate in a Virginia institution, was sterilized without her knowledge before being released.

In his opinion, Holmes spoke of the dangers of "being swamped with incompetence" and said it was "better for all the world if, instead of waiting to execute degenerate offspring for crime, or to let them starve for their imbecility, society can prevent those who are manifestly unfit from continuing their kind." Then came his memorable wrap-up: "Three generations of imbeciles are enough."

Afterwards he wrote Harold Laski: "I felt that I was getting near the first principle of real reform."

How did an unrelenting Darwinist and eugenicist come to be revered as the Grand Old Man of the law? The author devotes his best chapter to answering this question. First, early twentieth-century America admired Darwinian principles, especially the celebration of power, and while eugenics per se never caught on, the progressive movement in general did: Holmes's America was as committed to trading up as ours is to dumbing down.

Not to be discounted is the fact that he looked like a Grand Old Man of the law. Six-foot-three with a regal bearing and a snow-white walrus mustache, he filled the need for a philosopher king during the Harding-Coolidge era and liberals responded accordingly.

Holmes, who never met a sycophant he didn't like, was engulfed by Harold Laski, Max Lerner, Walter Lippmann, Benjamin Cardozo, John Dewey, Francis Biddle, and the undisputed leader of the pack, Felix Frankfurter, who laid on flattery with a trowel, calling Holmes a "tender, wise, and beautiful being," and said that to discuss his legal opinions "is to string pearls."

For whatever reasons of their own (psychology is not the author's chief concern), this entourage convinced themselves that Holmes was a civil libertarian and New Dealer who had revitalized the American judicial system, led a revolt against legal formalism and deductive reasoning, and made the law a living instrument of progress and pragmatism able to meet the needs of a changing society.

To the contrary, Alschuler argues that the revolt Holmes led was actually against natural law and objective standards of right and wrong, and now we are paying the price in the malaise, alienation, narcissism, and cultural collapse we see all around us.

Alschuler may sound like a conservative but his grammar gives him away. Whenever he needs a collective pronoun he uses neither the traditional and now sexist masculine singular, nor the prevalent "he or she" of standard political correctness, but the new usage favored by absolute paragons of sensitivity, the feminine singular: "In the end, a person can do no more than assert her own personal, existential belief."

Like the heavy-handed kid in the commercial who likes a little salad on his dressing, Alschuler, a professor of law at the University of Chicago, likes a little book on his footnotes. His text is only 194 pages long; the rest of this 325-page volume is taken up by footnotes—actually end notes—that require constant backing and forthing and lead to sprained thumbs.

Lawyers will cite anything that moves, but Alschuler cites things that would stand perfectly still if only he would let them. In the text he tells us Holmes was the subject of a best-selling novel, a hit Broadway play, and a movie. Instead of giving the titles then and there where they logically belong, he hits the brakes and finishes his thought in the notes (*Yankee from Olympus* by Catherine Drinker Bowen, and *The Magnificent Yankee* by Emmet Lavery, made into a movie of the same name starring Louis Calhern as Holmes).

What really makes this book exhausting is the author's unflagging enmity toward Holmes. One suspects that it is not so much a difference in legal philosophy that bothers Alschuler, but a quintessentially American discomfort with complicated personalities. Our ideal is a simplistic poltroon who fits the tag, "What you see is what you get." Enigmas like Oliver Wendell Holmes need not apply.

The American Spectator, April 2001
Book Review

"Roaring and Wailing"

*Killer Woman Blues: Why Americans Can't Think
Straight About Gender & Power* by Benjamin DeMott
(Houghton Mifflin, 235 pages, $26)

W hen Henry James fretted about "a certain vague moral dinginess" in the emancipated American woman, he meant the inadequately chaperoned expatriate adventuress with bad judgment in letters of introduction, but baby has come a long way since then. If you doubt it, see Demi Moore in *G.I. Jane* yelling "Suck my dick!"

Welcome to the "kickbutt culture," Benjamin DeMott's apt name for the sex-role reversal that has turned women into men and men into guests on "Men Who Are Beaten Up by Their Wives and Girlfriends." The Killer Woman emerged onto the national scene in the Nineties and she is not to be trifled with. Scorning feminism's original goal of mere equality for the higher calling of proving her machismo, she has invaded the locker room, the truckstop, and the playing fields of Wall Street with blood in her eye.

Killer Women come in all types. On the wholesome end of the scale is Brandi Chastain, the soccer player who tore off her shirt after scoring the winning goal, who was praised by one media maven for "meeting the androgynous ideal of women as men who can have babies: muscular, irreverent, aggressive."

On the perverse end of the scale we have New York celebrity-about-town Bijou Phillips, who threw a woman friend to the floor of a nightclub and raped her with a dildo, afterward saying, "So I raped you—deal with it."

In between—if there is such a place—is power publisher Judith Regan, who was overheard advising a male underling, "You can't tell me what to do; I've got the biggest cock in this whole building." Regan is just one of many women in the book who lay claim to this organ, as well as the other two that go with it; evidently the girlish urge to make up a set is still strong, but no longer limited to bridal silver. Often, they don't even have to make the claim themselves; others do it for them: Geraldo said flat-chested Christiane Amanpour had "big ones," and Sharon Stone was proud as punch when a producer called her by the plural of her surname.

Those who aren't ready for outright hermaphrodism can remain technically female and still imitate men by indulging in "in-your-face sexual bravura," like Erica Jong and the Killer Ladies Who Lunch, who expounded to a reporter in lascivious detail just what they would be willing to do to service Bill Clinton, and how, and why.

Killer Womanhood is not a preserve of the elite, but is promoted wherever "Sitcom America" turns for guidance. The dairy industry's milk-mustache ads hint that a healthy diet can erase sexual differences. Commercials feature females, including a little girl, shilling products in gravelly truck-driver voices. Shows about lady cops kickboxing men into insensibility and warrior queens chucking spears are all over the tube. Mass-market women's magazines have articles on "Testosterone Isn't Just a Guy Thing Anymore" and "How To Feel Him Up in the Elevator," and interviews of offbeat amazons such as the six-foot-three, 200-pound professional wrestler who calls herself "an empowered woman who kicks guys in the nuts for a living."

For those who prefer to read books, a collection of essays by women fantasizing about being a man for 24 hours is called *Dick for a Day: What Would You Do If You Had One?* One of the contributors is the matey Australian feminist Germaine Greer, author of *The Female Eunuch*.

Self-help? Try *The Princessa: Machiavelli for Women* by Helen Rubin, whose idea of a role model is Lady Macbeth.

Crime novels? Patricia Cornwell's feature a female medical

examiner who coolly performs hideous autopsies while her male morgue assistants gag and pass out.

Anti-intellectual intellectuals? Camille Paglia, whom DeMott calls the "socker scholar," extols the superiority of hardhat, red-blooded masculinity and thinks wife-beating is great because a lot of "hot sex" goes with it.

The ultimate Killer Woman, in DeMott's view, is none other than the frail-looking English professor, Joyce Carol Oates, whose novel *Zombie* (1995) describes frightful atrocities with an "iron imperviousness to horror" and "a seemingly exuberant embrace of barbarity." Equally shocking to him is *In the Cut* (1995) by Susannah Moore, about a woman who welcomes torture, not out of female masochism, but to prove that she can take it just like a man.

What, pray, is going on with women? The author nails part of the answer when he cites "the power still exerted, despite women's advance, by stereotypical masculinity." This accurate assessment offers ambrosial food for thought, but unfortunately, DeMott loses conservative readers by blaming everything on capitalism.

His thesis is that Killer Woman is a "stand-in for the corporate ethos . . . a whole new line of defense—a new savior—for the country's profit-maddened."

It came about, he says, like this: By admitting ambitious, aggressive women into its ranks and allowing them to achieve executive power and status, Corporate America engineered a convenient makeover for itself. Women are reputed to be the gentle sex, the "nice" people; if there were enough of them in high-profile positions, the thinking went, long-held images of "ruthless" corporations would fade from the public mind.

Everything depended on the willingness of the female of the species to be deadlier than the male, but that was made easy by a feminism that had whetted their appetites before running out of answers. Deprived of positive images of sexual equality, women relished the chance to kick butt and crack nuts and make like Michael "Greed Is Good" Douglas. Which should surprise no one, says DeMott, because toughness as virtue and flexibility as vice have been embedded in American culture since Teddy Roosevelt raged at "mollycoddles":

Toughness is the majority will, the *national* voice of gender shift. And toughness has been voted in. . . . Toughness indicts sentimental liberalism. . . . Toughness erases after-school programs, developmental workshops, school-based group activities, slashes day care centers, youth jobs programs . . . ends city funding for soup kitchens and teenagers' sports leagues, cuts the Board of Education's capital budget in half. . . . Toughness is a conviction among the powerful that the answer to the bottom sector's so-called needs is intimidation—an end to coddling and pampering.

DeMott calls this "the politics of pitilessness" and maintains that Killer Woman is behind it all, doing such a good job of imitating men that white-supremacist groups are now actively seeking to recruit female members. At this point the book gives off a distinctly primeval smell of fear, as if a male-devouring succubus had just flown over it, and DeMott's readiness to blame women for the failure of midnight basketball is exposed as nothing more than a progressive liberal version of the age-old game of blaming women.

The book disappoints in other ways. DeMott, an emeritus professor of humanities at Amherst, is a lively writer when he is relating the often hilarious fruits of his research into the cultural scene, but when it comes time to interpret them, he all too often slips into the drone of the faculty lounge:

But the central thrust of her work lies elsewhere, in the critique of standard-brand, off-the-rack, gender-frozen attitudes toward cognition—perspectives she views, correctly, as overattached to either-or simplifications, overcommitted to binary oppositions (subjective/objective, impressionistic/logical, hard/soft, intuitive/rational) that split the world of thought into pointlessly rank-ordered, noncommunicating sectors.

Turgid passages like this abound, as do undigestible chunks of quoted dialog from novels, movies, and TV shows, as well as an unintentionally funny tribute to manhood guru Robert "Iron John" Bly. DeMott has a knack for well-turned phrases ("the devitalization of the instinct for decency") and clever coinage ("tough-guy feminism"), but he repeats himself incessantly, adding to the tangle with signposting ("it bears repeating," "putting the point differently"). Given a good pruning and tightening, *Killer Woman Blues* would make an excellent lead article for *Harper's*, where some of his other work has appeared.

The American Spectator, June 2001
Book Review

"Swords, Sandals, and Fun"

The Ancient World in the Cinema, by Jon Solomon
(Yale University Press, 368 pp., cloth: $40.00; paper: $22.50)

This book may sound like a doctoral dissertation but it does-n't read like one. Jon Solomon, a classics professor at the University of Arizona, is not one of those pedantic nitpick-ers who is put off his popcorn by an incorrectly belted tunic or a XVI-dynasty headdress on an XV-dynasty mummy. Leaving such details to those he calls "Ph.D.'d scholars," he goes on an erudite romp through 400 "sword-and-sandal" movies, examining such wide-ranging topics as when historical accuracy is important and when it is disastrous, why moviemakers are forced to "de-Greek" Greek tragedies, and what Roman empress's name became the mod-ern Italian word for "chesty."

Many people today dismiss ancient history as "ancient history," but it was all the rage a hundred years ago when movies began. Late 19th-century culture was awash in antiquity, from serious works such as *The Last Days of Pompeii* by Edward Bulwer-Lytton, *Salammbo* by Gustave Flaubert, and Oscar Wilde's controversial play, *Salome*, to popular reading fare such as *Quo Vadis?*, Civil War General Lew Wallace's *Ben-Hur*, and a short story that threw the entire country into a state of unbearable suspense, "The Lady or the Tiger?" by Frank Stanton.

It was also a time of high standards in education, when "Latin through Cicero," the old five-year course, was a high school staple. Religious belief was so widespread that even uneducated people knew the Bible inside out, and best of all, there was no multiculturalism to worry about. Greece and Rome were universally acknowledged as the wellspring of a universally revered Western civilization, so it's no wonder that early moviemakers focused their cameras on the Mediterranean.

The first big Cleopatra movie in 1908 starred stage great Maurice Costello as Antony. The most famous of the early Cleopatras was a nice Jewish girl from Brooklyn named Theodosia Goodman, who as Theda Bara inspired the observation, "One costume cost $1,000 but Theda wore only ten cents' worth." The discovery of King Tut's tomb in 1924 during the heyday of silent movies secured what was to be Hollywood's longest-lasting marriage. From that day forward the sword-and-sandals genre, as well as its biblical division, tits-and-sand, would never leave the screen.

Biblical movies present the biggest challenge because audiences already know the stories and have visualized the scenes in their imaginations. Of the two halves of the Bible, the Old Testament is the harder to film, says Solomon, because the main character is invisible and the miracles "often involve the disruption of the whole planet."

The New Testament eliminates both of these challenges but creates its own special tension between divinity and humanity. Moreover, it is a tension that need not wait for the movie's release before it makes itself felt. When Cecil B. DeMille directed *King of Kings* in 1927, he made H. B. Warner, the actor who portrayed Christ, eat and sleep alone for the duration of the filming, only to find that the enforced solitude activated Warner's old drinking problem.

The author's watchword for all religious movies is "Render unto cinema what belongs to cinema." Imbuing the Christ character with divine ethereality leads to "the type of cheap piety at which many people in a crowded theater are apt to laugh. . . . Clothing a serene, emotionless actor in white robes and crucifying him amid the gentle tears of women" may yield spiritual satisfaction, "but without the banter of the dice-throwing Roman soldiers the scene will not work. Too much bland reverence yields a dramatic void."

In matters of historical authenticity the author comes down on the side of common sense. Although historians know that crucifixion victims had to carry only the horizontal beam of their crosses, changing such familiar iconography can cause shock and uneasiness in some viewers. "In fact, some viewers would no doubt claim that the film was inauthentic." On the other hand, he objects to the "DaVinci syndrome" in the seating arrangements at the Last Supper. The painter needed all the figures to face out, but movie characters cannot converse if they are all seated on the same side of the table.

The 1961 *King of Kings* with Jeffrey Hunter as Christ inspired one critic to dub it "I Was a Teenage Jesus," but Solomon praises it for its fidelity to *The Histories of Josephus*. What he objects to is the trial scene showing Christ being represented by a Roman lawyer, which "undermines the meaning and purpose of the Passion." He also takes exception to Robert Ryan as John the Baptist, who seems more like "a pious preacher from Ohio" than a man crying in the wilderness.

Some of his other *bêtes noires* include the casting of Lot in *Sodom and Gomorrah*: "When this powerful, physical Hebrew is portrayed by the well-mannered, thin-framed, Oxfordian Stewart Granger, the effect is likelier to inspire laughter than awe."

Solomon and Sheba is worth seeing because "No one ever played Oriental despots and kings like Yul Brynner," but he chews the scenery over the ending, which has Sheba converting to Judaism. Equally ridiculous is Rita Hayworth's *Salome*, who does the Dance of the Seven Veils to *save* John the Baptist from beheading. When authenticity is ignored to this extent, "the costumes begin to look silly."

At the same time, however, "Historical authenticity cannot be allowed to interfere with dramatic necessity or with the traditional understanding of certain biblical events." It's a fine line but Solomon dons his location-scout hat and draws it: Utah with its towering buttes makes a better Judea than the actual but less imposing site: "If Giotto could paint imaginary and inauthentic scenery for his New Testament paintings, why shouldn't moviemakers do the same?"

Solomon believes that authenticity can also be served in small ways that impart the flavor of antiquity, such as the use of aphorisms. The aphorism was to the ancient world what the one-liner or the wisecrack are to modern-day America; screenwriter George St. George coined several originals for *The 300 Spartans*, e.g., "Who can understand the ways of the gods. They create lovely girls and then turn them into wives."

The conflict between reverence and authenticity takes a secular turn in the filming of classical Greek tragedies. Here the reverence centers on two time-honored conventions of the form: the deus ex machina and the chorus.

In the first, having a god suddenly appear on-stage to sort out everyone's problems would destroy all efforts at realism. In the second, it is impossible to render the chorus in its original form without distracting the audience. As its name implies, the Greek chorus did what all choruses do: sang and danced. Transforming them into robed and bearded elders speaking in unison is like filming *Top Hat* without the dancing and having Fred Astaire recite the lyrics to "I'm Putting on my Top Hat."

Combine these problems with the inherent qualities of Greek tragedy—the perfectly constructed plots, the austere settings, the unthinkable events unfolding alongside the prohibition of on-stage violence—and nothing resembling a movie can emerge. "For some inexplicable reason," writes Solomon, "once all the authentic color and costumes are added to a Greek play on film, the psychological horror behind the murders and the matricide tend to lose some of their primordial impact."

The solution? "Remove the Greekness." The result? Eugene O'Neill's *Mourning Becomes Electra*, wherein Agamemnon becomes Ezra Mannon, a Civil War hero returning home to be murdered in New England, with commentary supplied by a chorus of taciturn Yankees. The author prefers the modern-dress *Phaedra* (1962) with Melina Mercouri and Tony Perkins. They make "improbable lovers; she looks more apt to devour him in one bite. Nonetheless, Perkins brings to his awkward role the bizarre intellect and psychological introspection characteristic of his many early roles."

The Ancient World in the Cinema was originally published in 1978 but Solomon has updated this edition to include his analysis of this year's Oscar-winning *Gladiator*, set in the second-century reigns of Marcus Aurelius and Commodus.

He didn't like it and takes issue with its "21st-century bias," specifically its trendy emphasis on family values.

Maximus is offered the throne of the empire but prefers to return home to his wife and son. Lucilla might also take the throne, but her main concern is for her son Lucius Veras. Commodus suggests that he would have been a better human if his father had loved him, and Marcus Aurelius admits that his son's faults are the failure of a neglectful father.

This overindulgence in touchy-feely sentiments distorts history. The actual Lucilla was so ambitious that she was exiled and then executed, and Marcus Aurelius took Commodus with him on campaigns and entrusted him with important tasks, while Maximus, an invented character, is completely out of chronological sync. He is patterned on Cincinnatus, the 5th-century B.C. farmer-turned-general who was twice offered the dictatorship of Rome but turned it down to return to farming. It was his farm, not his wife and children, that Cincinnatus missed; his firm rejection of power in favor of the simple life of the soil is what made him a paragon of virtue to latter-day republican idealists like the Founding Fathers, who would not have understood or respected the modern politician's showy emotional need to "spend more time with my family." To portray the character of Maximus in this way, says Solomon, superimposes modern sensitivity and Roman Republican virtues onto the Roman Empire of the second century A.D.

He much prefers an earlier movie set in the same period, *The Fall of the Roman Empire*, which contains "one of the most atmospheric sets ever used in an historical movie . . . the icy winter fortress in the barbarized European province (modern Austria) gives us the lonely sense of exile to the ends of civilization."

Unfortunately, *The Fall of the Roman Empire* (1964) was caught in the undertow of the moral and financial debacle of Liz Taylor's *Cleopatra* (1963), which gave sword-and-sandal movies a bad name.

The moviegoing public was veni-ed, vidi-ed, and vici-ed out, but the genre was kept alive for the next decade by Italian producers.

Drawn to their own heritage, and with plenty of Mediterranean scenery for the asking, they had first made their mark in 1957 with the low-budget *Hercules* starring Steve Reeves. It cost $120,000 to make and earned $18 million, so with no competition from the big-wigs in the post-*Cleopatra* hiatus, they filled the gap with Muscleman Movies.

Solomon's tongue-in-cheek description of the typical entry is hilarious. The hero must engage in a wrestling match to show off his Mr. Universe build. He must have a fight with "a virgin-devouring or Hell-guarding beast," and a fight in an inn to provide him with an eight-foot solid oak table to use as a shield, or to throw at his dozen or so opponents, at least one of whom he will pick up and throw at the rest. He also throws paving stones, trees, columns, wine tuns, and vats of oil on fallen torches.

His nemesis is "a pointy-bearded tyrant with a pointy-breasted mistress." He himself has "a charmingly innocent and chesty girl-friend with a name like Andromeda, Iole, or Fulvia, who is adept at virtuously bathing his wounds (generally only flesh wounds on the shoulder). She is usually blond, even if she is Egyptian, Greek, or Armenian. Her counterpart, the evil mistress of the pointy-bearded tyrant, has dark hair, a lizard's eyes, the charm of a snake, and the hots for the hero."

The hero always has a loyal companion who is either almost as manly and meaty as himself, or else a wimpy beta male who can't throw doors but is adept at poking enemies in the behind with his dagger. He also looks after the innocent, chesty girlfriend while the hero is away on one of his escapades. The companion always fails at this task and the girl is captured by the pointy-bearded tyrant's sol-diers, but fortunately she has "a pipsqueaky little brother who bites his way to freedom and runs to tell the hero that she is about to be ravaged by the pointy beard."

To free her, the hero must perform a feat dreamed up by the pointy-bearded tyrant. Known as "The Test," it might be a chariot race, a wrestling match with some large, semihuman brute, a gladiatorial fight with a giant (one character must have a shaved head and it's usually the giant gladiator), or a battle with lions, gorillas, or crocodiles. The hero throws them all off ramparts and balconies, or breaks their necks in a full nelson with his 19-inch biceps. Now there's no one left except the pointy-bearded tyrant, who more often than not is dispatched by falling, or more likely, being thrown, into his own crocodile pit.

The dialogue consists of the ever-present "by the Gods!" dubbing that is always out of sync, and jarring translations of ancient-sounding maxims ("He who eats alone, chokes alone"). The script writers pay no attention to historical accuracy, or even historical sanity. "Any age, any place that already boasted of a hero or desperately needed one was fair game for Italian filmmakers." Hercules goes everywhere (*Hercules in New York*) and knows everybody—Samson, Ulysses, Druids, Mongols, and even Incans (*Hercules Against the Sons of the Sun*).

To lend their efforts a modicum of class, Italian producers always hired a well-known English-speaking actor, either someone distinguished, such as Orson Welles (Saul in *David and Goliath*), or Robert Morley (Potiphar in *Joseph and His Brethren*), or else a once-famous American movie star whose career was in decline: Cornel Wilde in *Constantine and the Cross*; Alan Ladd in *Duel of Champions*; Virginia Mayo in *Revolt of the Mercenaries*.

Bad as Muscleman Movies are, Solomon finds some good things to say about them. Greek myths are "flexible, dynamic tales changed and adjusted by every storyteller, songster, and poet," so low-budget producers are merely doing what has been done through the ages. In any case, "whether one laughs at it or laughs with it, it can be entertaining, [and] this is what movies are for, sometimes."

Jon Solomon is that rarity in academe, a down-to-earth intellectual who is secure enough in his own erudition to offer refreshing respect where it is due, and to criticize without sounding obnoxious. I can't remember when I've enjoyed a book as much as this one. There isn't a single supercilious sneer in it.